CHANGE

FOR THE BETTER

Praise for the book

'The best possible compendium on Cognitive Analytic Therapy, presented clearly and thoughtfully in this latest edition.'

Susie Orbach, Psychotherapist

'Elizabeth McCormick has the unusual ability to transform psychotherapeutic concepts into a language that enables clients to draw on these models for their own use. This book should be recommended to anyone wishing to understand and work through their suffering and to gain greater clarity and emotional resilience.'

Jane Ryan, Director of Confer

'This is that rare thing – a wise, compassionate and above all practical book, grounded in years of good psychotherapy practice. Imbued with the understanding that we are selves in relation to others, it is straightforward without being simplistic. It delivers what it promises, whether for self-help, a supportive resource in therapy or as a readable introduction to therapeutic change.'

Glenys Parry, Emeritus Professor University of Sheffield

Praise for the prior edition

'An unusual self-help book with real depth'

Sue Gerhardt, author of *Why Love Matters: How Affection Shapes a Baby's Brain*

'This is a good book made better. It retains the clear writing and useful exercises of earlier editions but manages to invite an even more comprehensive exploration of the self'

Dr Anthony Ryle, pioneer of CAT at Guy's and St Thomas' hospitals

'This is a really welcome guide to modern therapy – blending traditional psychological wisdom with a practical cognitive programme that anyone can follow'

Philip Hodson, psychotherapist and broadcaster

Elizabeth Wilde McCormick

CHANGE
FOR THE BETTER

Personal development through practical psychotherapy

fifth edition

SAGE

Los Angeles | London | New Delhi
Singapore | Washington DC | Melbourne

Los Angeles | London | New Delhi
Singapore | Washington DC | Melbourne

SAGE Publications Ltd
1 Oliver's Yard
55 City Road
London EC1Y 1SP

SAGE Publications Inc.
2455 Teller Road
Thousand Oaks, California 91320

SAGE Publications India Pvt Ltd
B 1/I 1 Mohan Cooperative Industrial Area
Mathura Road
New Delhi 110 044

SAGE Publications Asia-Pacific Pte Ltd
3 Church Street
#10-04 Samsung Hub
Singapore 049483

Editor: Susannah Trefgarne
Editorial assistant: Charlotte Meredith
Production editor: Rachel Burrows
Copyeditor: Elaine Leek
Proofreader: Clare Weaver
Marketing manager: Camille Richmond
Cover design: Sheila Tong
Typeset by: C&M Digitals (P) Ltd, Chennai, India
Printed in the UK

Library of Congress Control Number: 2017930351

British Library Cataloguing in Publication data

A catalogue record for this book is available from the British Library

ISBN 978-1-5264-1171-6
ISBN 978-1-5264-1172-3 (pbk)

At SAGE we take sustainability seriously. Most of our products are printed in the UK using FSC papers and boards. When we print overseas we ensure sustainable papers are used as measured by the PREPS grading system. We undertake an annual audit to monitor our sustainability.

Dr Anthony Ryle 1927–2016, in gratitude

Contents

About the author

Elizabeth Wilde McCormick has been in practice as a psychotherapist for over thirty-five years in both private and NHS settings. She is also a teacher, trainer and writer. Her background is in social psychiatry, humanistic and transpersonal psychology, sensorimotor psychotherapy and Cognitive Analytic Therapy. She has had an interest for many years in the interface between psychotherapy and mindfulness. She is a founder member and a Trustee of the Association for Cognitive Analytic Therapy.

Also by Elizabeth Wilde McCormick:

The Heart Attack Recovery Book 1984, 1989 (OPTIMA)

Surviving Breakdown 1988, 1990, 1997 (Vermillion)

Healing the Heart 1994 (OPTIMA)

Living on the Edge 1997, 2007 (SAGE)

Transpersonal Psychotherapy: Theory and Practice (with Nigel Wellings) 2000 (SAGE)

Your Heart and You (with Dr Leisa Freeman) 2002 (Piatkus Books)

Nothing to Lose: Psychotherapy, Buddhism and Living Life (with Nigel Wellings) 2004 (Continuum), 2012 (Woodyard Publications)

The Pale Green Room, a novel 2011 (Woodyard Publications)

Foreword to the fifth edition

Dr Jason Hepple

It is a great pleasure to be asked to write the Foreword to this fifth edition of *Change for the Better*. Liz McCormick has successfully created a style and approach to her writing that is accessible to both those seeking a guide to self-help for emotional and relational problems and those interested in learning more about psychotherapy and counselling. The fact that this is the fifth edition is testimony to the popularity and approachability of her work. This edition has been re-worked, based on feedback from readers, in order to condense, illustrate and further clarify some of the ideas and techniques; it has succeeded in all of these aims.

Liz has the ability to talk to the reader with respect, compassion and curiosity. Even when tackling topics like abuse, neglect and emotional trauma, Liz gives the reader permission to take things at their own pace, look after themselves during the process and retain a sense of hope that things can really change for the better; even if this may be a gradual process with occasional ups and downs along the way.

Change for the Better relies on a relational understanding of emotional problems that comes from the psychotherapy known as CAT (Cognitive Analytic Therapy), which was originated by Dr Anthony Ryle, who sadly died on 29 September 2016 in his ninetieth year. CAT was always designed to be user-friendly, and central to the model is a collaborative, non-judgemental, doing-with relationship between client and therapist. There are no secret theories in CAT and Liz has illustrated this through her clear explanations of the different tools that can be used in CAT and by her moving illustrations of how people's problems can be reformulated, mapped out and exited from.

CAT recognises that things that happen to us at earlier stages of our life can leave us with scars and unhelpful ways of trying to survive the world and the way we have learned to expect it to be for us.

This recognition of the resonance of the past in the way we relate to others is central to Liz's approach, with the use of narrative tools like traps, dilemmas and snags, and the use of life stories and time lines to see how we have got to where we are. This understanding gives weight to the studies and personal accounts of people who have experienced different forms of abuse and neglect earlier in their lives or as children. An approach that does justice to the past goes beyond self-help to manage the symptoms *caused* by the past but offers recognition, understanding and the possibility of transformation through compassion for oneself and others.

The relational idea that is central to CAT and to the way Liz explains things in *Change for the Better* is not immediately obvious to people when we look around us at the conflicts in the world today. So many times we see the claim that one side is 'right' or 'true' and the other 'wrong' and 'deceitful'. It is all so black and white. Good against evil; us against them. A relational understanding gives us the awareness that what we chose to do has roots and that our actions cause a reaction in others. In many ways both sides can feel in exactly the same position – angry, defensive, critical, crushed. This is the idea of the reciprocal role – the central tenet of CAT theory. When we can see where we are in relation to others we can chose to stand back, take a breath, observe, reflect and make choices about how to proceed without making the whole problem worse. This is the essence of *Change for the Better*.

Throughout the book Liz maintains an empathic and compassionate stance in relation to her reader that is grounded in her decades of experience of being with people who have emotional problems and trauma, and also from the strength she derives from her own mindfulness practice. In addition to understandings from CAT therapy, Liz integrates accessible techniques from mindfulness approaches that make a valuable addition to the range of things that can be learned from this book.

Change for the Better is a self-help book that I could recommend to anyone and is also the best introduction to CAT and relational understanding of emotional problems and conflict that I know of.

Dr Jason Hepple MA (Oxon), FRCPsych,
UKCP registered
Consultant Psychiatrist in Psychological Therapies
Somerset Partnership NHS Foundation Trust
Chair of the Association for Cognitive
Analytic Therapy (ACAT)
Co-editor *CAT and Later Life: New Perspectives on
Old Age* (Brunner–Routledge, 2004)

Acknowledgements

This book is based on the model of time-limited therapy created by Dr Anthony Ryle at Guy's and St Thomas's Hospitals called Cognitive Analytic Therapy, CAT for short. Since 1984 CAT has blossomed, and this method of focused therapy is now taught and used in different settings within the British National Health Service and also in Finland, Spain, Ireland, Greece, Italy, Poland, Australia, India, New Zealand and Hong Kong.

The first edition of this book was published in 1990, the second in 1997, a third in 2008, a fourth edition celebrated the book's 21st birthday – and this fifth edition is written in the year of the sad death of Dr Anthony Ryle, and in celebration of him.

Dr Ryle has been intimately involved with all editions and encouraged their development. His skill was to sift through complex theoretical ideas and research, and keep in mind their relationship to the human being. At the core of CAT is the emphasis on what constitutes a truly relational, dialogic connection with people; to not pathologise human struggle with life or social ills, but to name accurately why things have been as they are and to encourage change where possible.

This fifth edition is a simplified version of the fourth. Several of the chapters have been rewritten. The exercises have been edited and improved. A section on trauma and complex trauma has been added to Part Five. There is a more integrated approach to the use of relational mapping, the healthy self and healthy island, and the practice of mindfulness.

Many colleagues have contributed to the formation and continual growth of this book. Sage sought feedback from a wide psychological readership about its use in different settings, for which I am very grateful, and which has been addressed.

Grateful thanks go to Annalee Curran, Shakir Ansari, Deirdre Haslam, Jackie Baker, Jason Hepple, Steve Potter, Dr Julia Clark, Liz Fawkes, Mark Dunn, Steven White, and the late Norma Maple and Angela Wilton. Thanks also to Alison Jenaway, Stephen White, Susan Mitzman, Michelle Hamill, Robert Watson and Claire Tanner.

I would also like to acknowledge my many teachers of the practice of mindfulness: Ven Thich Nhat Hanh, Vietnamese Zen Buddhist; Tibetan Buddhist nun and author Pema Chodron; Buddhist psychologist Dale Asrael; Becca Crane at the North Wales Centre for Mindfulness, Bangor; my friends and colleagues Nigel Wellings and Philippa Vick.

A special thank-you goes to all the patients who agreed to have their life stories, charts, letters and diagrams used for publication. All names and some details have been changed to protect their identities. Their examples show us how difficulties can be faced and how lives can be changed.

Change for the Better has had a curious journey since its first publication by Unwin Hyman in 1990. For over twenty-seven years it has survived the vagaries of publishing and, as well as appealing to readers looking for a book on how to change, found its way into many different training settings: universities, specialist NHS services, day centres, career counselling services, psychotherapy training and GP practices; groups seeking conflict resolution. It has also been offered to patients on waiting lists. It takes complex ideas born out of research and practice in psychotherapy and simplifies them for general reading.

The author and publisher would like to acknowledge and thank the following for permission to quote material from: *Why Love Matters* by Gerhardt, S. (2004), Routledge, p.217; 'Kindness' from *Words Under the Words: Selected Poems* by Shihab Nye, N. (1995) and reprinted with the permission of Far Corner Books, Portland, Oregon; *The Mindful Path to Self-Compassion* by Germer, C. (2009), Guilford Press, p.78 and reprinted with the permission of The Guilford Press; the website www.mindfulselfcompassion.org by Germer, C.; *Speech Genres and Other Late Essays* by Bakhtin, M.M. (1986), translated by McGee, V.W., edited by Emerson, C. and Holquist, M., by permission of the University of Texas Press; *Treating Type A Behavior and Your Heart* by Friedman, M. and Ulman, D. (1984), Knopf, p.38; and 'The autonomic arousal model', reproduced from Ogden, P. and Minton, K. (2000), 'One Method for Processing Trauma', *Traumatology*, VI (3) 1–20, by kind permission of the Pat Ogden and the Sensorimotor Psychotherapy Institute®, Broomfield, CO.

For more information on all aspects of Cognitive Analytic Therapy as it is taught, researched and practiced in the UK please visit: www.acat.me.uk
And for Italy, Ireland, Finland, France, Greece, Poland, Spain, Hong Kong, India, Australia, New Zealand please visit: internationalcat.org

List of resources available on the companion website

Visit **https://study.sagepub.com/counselling** to find additional student and practitioner resources.

When you see this icon ⟹ in the book, visit the website to download the resource. You'll find a range of learning exercises and resources to aid learning, and to support and enhance your professional practice.

Resources include:

1. **The Psychotherapy File** – an aid to understanding ourselves better (extended version) – a diary to track moods and behaviour in relation to traps, dilemmas, snags and difficult states
2. **Personality Structure Questionnaire (PSQ)** – a questionnaire to obtain an account of an individual's personality

3. **Identifying your states** – a guide to identify ways of being and feeling
4. **Detailed descriptions of your states** – a questionnaire analysing each state selected from 'Identifying your state'
5. **Mindfulness exercises and meditations** (extended version) – exercises for mindful relaxation
6. **Personal Rating Chart** – chart for recognising symptoms and patterns of behaviour
7. **Critique of CBT and CAT by Dr Anthony Ryle** – critical analysis of the therapeutic effectiveness of CBT and CAT
8. **Dave's complete case study** – using the CAT approach to help a person in prison
9. **Kayleigh's complete case study** – using the CAT approach to help a person with long-term illness
10. **Linda's complete case study** – using the CAT approach to help a person with anorexia and depression
11. **Sheila's complete case study** – using the CAT approach to help a person with long-term physical illness and depression
12. **Further reading**

Introduction

Understanding leads to change

This book takes the reader on a journey through the steps of a Cognitive Analytic Therapy (CAT). Alongside these clearly defined steps are suggestions for the practice of mindfulness, which brings spaciousness, and kindness, for the process of self-reflection and change.

The book can be read individually, or as part of a therapy or in co-counselling.

Cognitive Analytic Therapy was founded in the early 1980s by Dr Anthony Ryle at Guy's and St Thomas's hospitals in London. It is a highly relational therapy that sees human beings as evolving as social beings in a web of relationship with others. It offers a safe structure for revising old habits and patterns that are no longer useful. Its scaffolding allows many other approaches to psychological work to be embraced, and by a wide range of mental health professionals. It was with this in mind that Dr Ryle first began integrating already well-researched psychological theories into one active and focused therapy, for time-limited interventions.

Mindfulness is a learned process of paying particular attention, moment by moment, to our immediate experience, just as it is, and kindly, without judgement. The understanding and application of mindfulness has been growing in Western countries over the last ten years and been found to be highly effective in helping people find a safe spaciousness within which to reconsider their lives.

The strength and success of working within the structure of Cognitive Analytic Therapy is that UNDERSTANDING LEADS TO CHANGE. The levels of understanding are as follows:

[1] Understanding the many different learned dances of relating and the myriad invitations to the dance allows us to choose whether or not to join the dance.
[2] Understanding patterns of learned responses and behaviour in terms of Traps, Dilemmas and Snags allows us to recognise and make maps of our habitual procedures.

[3] Understanding and mapping self states and unstable states of mind allows us to have more control over them and to know when we have lost our observer position.

[4] Writing our own life story, known in CAT as reformulation, from the point of view of being inside it, allows us to engage with both the hand we have been dealt, and how we have dealt with that hand.

[5] Making manageable goals for change along these lines:

- noticing
- reflecting
- trying something new

gives us a step-by-step approach to change. And these steps foster hope, that we can change what we have learned that is no longer of use to us.

[6] Getting off the symptom hook frees us from feeling a victim to a label or diagnosis and allows us to engage more fully with who we are, just as we are.

[7] The revision of learned survival patterns allows us to create space for the human being we naturally are.

This book provides suggestions for developing a **kindly observer self** to support the process of a growing self-awareness, for checking out habitual patterns of thinking, responding and patterns in relationship both to others and to oneself.

It will provide active and creative ways of making useful maps of our interactions using the reader's own language.

It will provide suggestions for how to be with difficult feelings that arise when we stop running away, or avoiding, so that we may learn to care more for what has been neglected.

Through the stories of people who have generously contributed to this book we can see how to make realistic goals for change and to find helpful ways to hold on to change.

The limits of self-help

It is important to say that not all difficulties and symptoms are the reflection of problems in living. Some are the effects of bodily processes and may need medical treatment. Many common symptoms, such as undue fatigue, headaches, indigestion or appetite changes, are most frequently the result of emotional stress, but can, in some instances, be caused by physical illness. If there is any doubt about the nature of such symptoms then medical advice should be sought. Someone whose depression is severe, who suffers from marked physical or mental lethargy, or whose sleep is broken regularly in the small hours with gloomy wakefulness thereafter, should seek medical or psychiatric advice. More generally, if the mental distress is severe or prolonged, and is associated with experiences of the mind not working normally, it would be appropriate and kind to oneself to seek professional help.

Equally important is to continue recognising our own Zone of Proximal Development, or ZPD, a term developed by Lev Zygotsky (1896–1934) to describe the difference between what we can learn on our own, and what we can learn with help. Our individual ZPD will change as we start to make either internal or external changes and reflecting upon this gives us an idea of what can be manageable for us at any one period of time.

Other problems are due to causes that are not primarily emotional, psychological or medical; they are social and political. The American writer Henry David Thoreau, in *Walden* ([1854] 1988), observed that 'the mass of men live lives of quiet desperation'. While much of this desperation may be rooted in the personal domain of marriage, family and career, and might be eased by the methods discussed in this book, to be poor, unemployed, prematurely retired; to be exiled or a refugee, wrongly imprisoned, discriminated against, badly housed; to have to work at intrinsically boring tasks under the arbitrary control of others, are also potent causes of desperation. The impact of these factors is, of course, upon the feelings of individuals, and CAT's relational and dialogic model is helpful to describe the interaction between groups and leader, countries and those in power. The appropriate action may be political and beyond the scope of this book but CAT's dialogic model has value for many settings and is illustrated in articles on the Association for Cognitive Analytic Therapy (ACAT) website, in the new *International Journal of Cognitive Analytic Therapy and Relational Mental Health* and in *Reformulation*.

PART ONE

Change Is Possible

Why change? What is it that changes? How to begin the process of change

The new information that science has offered in recent decades makes it clear that something can be done to alleviate many social and mental health problems.

Sue Gerhardt, *Why Love Matters* (2004: 217)

ONE Change is possible

Serenity is not freedom from the storm but peace within the storm. What lies behind us and what lies before us are tiny matters compared to what lies within us.

Ralph Waldo Emerson

How many times in a day do we think about change? How often when things go wrong do we wish it were different, that perhaps *we* were different? And how often do these wishes remain just wishes?

We might feel inside that something is wrong; we feel unhappy, lost, hopeless. Or, things go wrong outside: we don't fit in, our jobs perish, partners leave, or we can't rid ourselves of habits or thoughts that make us feel bad. So we try to make changes – a new look, job, partner, house – and for a while things are different. But then the same patterns arise and our hope of change fades. We might feel stuck or jinxed, and anger and helplessness begin to well up.

This book is about change. It sets out well-researched methods of identifying what we can *usefully* revise about learned patterns of behaviour, and suggests manageable ways to change them; and to hold onto those changes. It will provide methods for individual self-examination, for self-monitoring habitual patterns, for making personal maps to illustrate the kind of relational and thinking webs we weave that ensnare us. And it offers creative ways for changing the patterns that have become unhelpful.

- We *can* learn to become better observers of ourselves. And these observers can be kind rather than critical.
- We *can* identify the learned behaviour patterns of thinking and relating, based on our earlier need to survive, that have become unhelpful and which are redundant.
- We *can* then clear space for the potential of a kindly observer and healthy island within and practise different ways of expressing ourselves.

And we do this actively by:

[1] Using the Psychotherapy File (see p. 273) to identify our problems, which in CAT are called traps, dilemmas and snags; and the thinking, feeling and relationship dance that accompanies them.

[2] Finding creative ways to name the patterns of responses and behaviour we take for granted when they occur in daily life, and writing them down.

[3] Making maps to keep close by so we can look at where we are in the pattern sequence day by day.

[4] Making realistic goals for challenging and changing the sequences.

[5] Writing our individual life story, and link what has happened to us with the traps, dilemmas, snags and unstable states that have become our everyday reality.

[6] Finding resources to support this process of awakening and the shifts in perception that come with change as well as helpful ways to hold on to change.

[7] As we begin to clear the ground of unhelpful patterns we feel more 'real', because for the first time, we have more space and energy. This space and energy helps us to nourish a healthy island within.

When we change problematic patterns, we change our lives.

We don't, however, change the fundamental core of our being, the individual seed of the self with which we were born. We all have our own unique character, gifts and tendencies, as well as our genetic patterning. In early life this potential self is a bit like a seed planted into the garden of the family. Using this image, it's easy to see that the seed's growth and development is bound up with the nature of the soil and its environment. We cannot isolate ourselves from our context within social culture, language, family, our own biology and history. And as people travel more widely, the culture in which we were brought up may have given us messages that conflict with the environment we end up in. All of us must find ways of dealing with these early experiences in order to survive. When life challenges us through difficult feelings or habits, or when things have gone wrong, we confront aspects of ourselves we had previously taken for granted. We all carry a part of us that is compromised or wounded in some way. How we carry this wound makes the difference between a passive attitude of 'I am a depressive, no one can help me' and the active 'There is a part of me that is depressed and I will address it and take care of it'. Once we engage with ourselves in this way we are more open to enjoy and use our inner world of imagination, dream and insight, and to accept ourselves, just as we are.

If we follow the idea of newborn humans being like seeds planted into the garden of life, we can imagine that each seed has to develop a 'survival self' in order to manage what might be the less-than-ideal conditions. Few seeds are given the ideal soil and some find themselves on stony ground. Developing a survival self, with coping tactics for adapting to a difficult, hostile or just strange environment, is always necessary, and a mark of the human capacity for adaptation. Human beings are extremely creative!

Understanding and contrasting the difference in energy and flexibility between our learned patterns for survival, with possibly restricted ways of living and relating, and the potential of a healthy self that is able to reflect, observe and transcend identification with suffering, is at the heart of psychotherapeutic work.

Throughout this book we will be looking at some of the ways in which we have become accustomed to think and feel about ourselves and other people, and how this affects our relationship with ourselves and others. We now know from neuroscience that because of our brain's neuroplasticity, it is possible to learn new ways of responding and behaving that in time surpass the old. Once we start using strengths developed by actively thinking and reflecting, we often stimulate other changes. We find we have more inside us than we thought. We may find that the numerous threads running through our life carry more meaning, are even a gift. We begin to feel there is more in life than being on automatic, which many of us are reduced to when things are not going well.

Each of us can take up the challenge of looking at ourselves afresh: to see what things we can change and to accept those we cannot, and to know the difference. Setting aside time to ponder on what we can change, and actively working to achieve those changes, means that we free ourselves from the restrictions of the past, and that our changes are changes for the better.

This book seeks to spotlight *how* we live with what we feel and *how* we have adjusted, and what changes, if any, are needed. I would also like to add that I have met many people who seem to carry an overwhelming sense of pain and suffering for reasons that are unclear. Not everything has a linear cause. We can only bear witness to the suffering we experience in ourselves or in others, and honour its reality as it lives within the individual, and not seek to concretise or rationalise its source.

Why change?

There are really only two certainties in life. One is death, that one day we will die, and the second is that 'everything changes'. But it is these two certainties that we often run away from, seeking escape or comfort in trying to control pleasure and pain. It's usually when we suffer that we wonder what we can do to bring about change. Everyone seeks change for different reasons – to feel less anxious, to overcome debilitating problems like depression or phobia, to feel more in control of life, to stop making destructive relationships. Or perhaps we seek change because we feel sad or bad, unhappy or empty; because things keep on going wrong. Learning to draft a 'road map' of our development as a person and finding exits to those knotty attitudes that need adjustment means that we take charge. Many people speak today of feeling caught up in social and work systems that are demanding, dehumanising, even punishing. Learning who we are and claiming freedom to be who we are is not simply a short-term solution to problems, it is one of our remaining enduring freedoms. This book might be a first step toward that goal.

Are there things better left unchanged?

The myth of Pandora's Box and the old superstition it 'doesn't do to meddle with things you don't understand' suggests that whatever we have locked away will wreak havoc once made conscious. Then there are the old adages 'Let sleeping dogs lie' and 'Better the devil you know than the devil you don't'. These are powerful messages that would stop us searching and ultimately using our power of choice. They encourage avoidance and ensure that we are limited by fear. But if we don't find out what our 'devils' are, they have a habit of being projected, seen as if they were in other people who become the very devils we fear; they pop up in relationships, in dreams and they bind us into traps and dilemmas. The 'shadow' in Jungian psychology refers to all that is not in the light, often all that we fear and dislike. Accepting this shadow as a valid part of being whole (there is no sun without shadow; no day without night) means we are willing to see it for what it is. We have it rather than it having us.

Through the exploration of our learned patterns we are often rewarded by the gift of insight. Insight – that feeling of 'ah, that's how it was' – is a leavening process through which we begin to trust that there is inside us something that understands what is going on. Just knowing rationally is not enough; we need to open up our other senses – sensing, intuiting, imagining; and then checking it out against what we have learned.

In her moving book *My Father's House*, Sylvia Fraser (1989) describes how for her first forty years she split herself in two – the self that had a secret and the self that lived in the world. The secret self that had been split off leaked out via dreams, impulsive behaviour, irrational revulsions, in rages, incredible sadness and feelings of emptiness.

What is it that changes?

Human beings are not fixed, although patterns of thinking can feel very rigid and dominating. Subtle shifts in our perceptions, feelings and our thinking go on all the time simply because of ordinary living in a web of relationships. The call to homeostasis (balance) and to feel whole is strong and, as understood in Jungian psychology, is always inviting us to 'individuate', to become who we really are.

Two things can change. One is our attitude. We can breathe life into our experience by observing thoughtfully the hand we have been dealt, accepting that we have done the best we could with what we had at the time, without judging or getting depressed. Acceptance is a start, and it's never too late to begin. Every day is an opportunity to witness afresh what happens inside and outside of ourselves and to develop a kindness toward all that has happened.

The other is standing back enough to make conscious revision of the unhelpful patterns we have got used to inhabiting. In reading this book you are entering a new dance of relating: listening in relation to being listened to, and heard. Over time you might find that you become more accepting and kindly to yourself and to others in relation to feeling accepted and loved.

Old patterns that are redundant can be sloughed off like a snake's skin. We can free a space so that our natural self may start to breathe. But we cannot grow if we are living out of old ideas that need revision, that contribute to our feeling stuck. We cannot take in good things, however much they are offered, if inside we believe we are not entitled to receive them. We cannot relax or let go if we fear being persecuted or abused. And we cannot be assertive if we believe we will lose affection. In order to change and grow we must challenge the presumptions that limit our choices of how to be.

The dance of relating, with ourselves and others

Major studies of neurobiology suggest that our brains are embodied social organs, and that the neural pathways dominating our nervous system develop in accordance with our relationships with others.

Neuroscientists describe how from birth our infant brains are finely tuned for social engagement so that every sense of 'me' evolves from communications, through signs, words or sensations with others (Schore, 2003; Porges, 2005). During infancy and childhood our brains are tuned to be fantastically responsive and adaptive, and the wiring of our brains gets fired in relation to others. Professor of neurology and musicologist C. Trevarthen (1993) speaks about the music of preverbal contact between the infant and other, of how the baby will respond to the communicative sounds of the parent and then wait in anticipation of the continuing response, the baby altering its sounds as the parent alters theirs. The baby's tiny nervous system and brain is finely tuned in responsiveness, like a whole orchestra at concert pitch, waiting for the mutual chords to be struck, the dance of the conjoined music to begin. Professor of psychiatry and director of the Mindsight Institute Dr Daniel Seigel has researched extensively into how effective therapy stimulates neuronal activity and growth toward a more integrated state of being (Seigel, 2010a, 2010b).

Our patterns of relating are founded upon the ways in which we are intimately bound up from the time of our conception with an 'other'. Our brain wiring and nervous systems develop in reciprocal relationship with 'others'; which dances are helpful and which are more problematic. Our model of 'other' may be built from a mother or series of mothers or fathers, by siblings or caregivers, and later in life by friends, partners, pets, employers or even the government. We carry different aspects of this learned 'other' inside us and learn to anticipate their responses. This lays down patterns for relating, both to other people, to the outside world and to ourselves. The strength of CAT is in its use of descriptions to name and map the different dances of relating we have learned.

If, as an infant, we get fed when hungry, warmed when cold, held when anxious, we learn that our non-verbal signals are effective, that we are understood and the appropriate response is given. *Imitation plus exchange is the basis of communication.* We learn that it is safe to be close to another, and this is how we begin to experience our value, to feel that we are worthwhile and lovable, and to love others. This secure attachment, and our anticipation of it, gives us the space and freedom to express ourselves in a natural way as we grow into maturity. We learn that it is OK to be ourselves, to be different, to be separate, to go our own way, all within appropriate limits.

Most of us experience 'other' as a mixture of good, bad and indifferent, sometimes there and sometimes not. Whoever is 'other' will have responses and actions based upon their own patterns and expectations. Because of our adaptability we learn to respond to what our caregivers want of us and upon whom we are dependent. If our acceptance by 'other' is conditional upon our being always good, we may develop compliance, always wanting to please others, a placation trap might result. We may develop a rebellious style, refusing any kind of relationship because of its demands. We may develop a form of anxiety over 'other', fearing their disapproval, or abandonment, and become clingy and needy in relationships, which may last into later life.

If we experience 'other' as unsafe – perhaps as 'not there', as constantly changing, as unpredictable or neglectful – our natural anxiety rises. Our tiny autonomic nervous systems become flooded with adrenalin and cortisol that has no means of release. Our 'fight or flight' mechanism is not yet mature. We may 'freeze' and become flat, avoiding contact for fear of more anxiety; or, we may become hypervigilant, always on the lookout for something unpredictable or difficult. These patterns protect a young nervous system from more unmanageable fear and are to be welcomed and valued. However, the anticipation of responses from 'other' as being in a certain way governs our inner dialogue – the way we think about ourselves inside and what we allow outside, and continues into outside relationships. These patterns will continue in a variety of ways – some more problematic than others – until they are recognised and revised, and alleviated or replaced with other, more helpful, ways of relating.

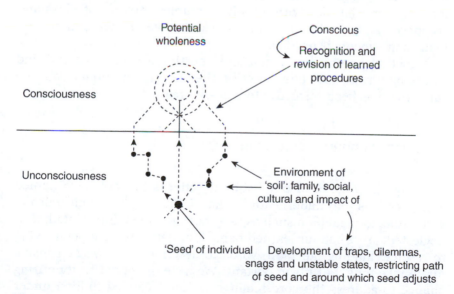

Figure 1.1   Seed and soil diagram of reciprocal role of seed in relation to soil

Problems in relationships occur when, in anticipation of 'other' being conditional or abandoning or rejecting, the individual sees even the slightest difference in attunement as extreme and reacts accordingly, as if it were a foregone conclusion. Because we are so helpless in infancy we make all kinds of arrangements not to be abandoned.

Understanding the fundamental building blocks of our engagement in the dance of relationships, the resulting emotional response and behaviour is the cornerstone of this book, and throughout the different chapters we will be returning to this in many different presentations.

Getting off the symptom hook

We need to get off the symptom hook and understand what patterns contribute to our symptoms. When we start to take our problems seriously and want to change our life, the most important first step is one *away* from the symptom we suffer – whether this is related to depression, relationship failure, dissociation, eating problems or addiction. This book invites you to look underneath your symptoms, diagnosis or questions about treatment. There is no specific list of symptoms but many symptoms and problems are referred to and included in the index. Symptoms can be seen as the 'tip of the iceberg', for what lies within us is a complex mixture of ideas and responses, and it is that rich inner world that we can get to know and make adjustments if needed.

A good beginning is to reach underneath our symptoms and find words or images that best describe the chronic emotional pain we carry that has been formed into a no-go area.

Chronically endured core pain

We may know some of our habitual patterns but not have named what feelings lie underneath. What CAT names as chronically endured emotional pain such as fear, hurt, crushed, humiliated, lost, neglected, are what our learned behaviour patterns have been trying to resolve. Finding our own words to describe what we feel inside might take time, but it's important. We have the opportunity during change to address the core feelings we have carried hidden under habitual behaviours for years. In this next section we look at some descriptions of emotional pain that have become beliefs and the lens through which life is experienced. As you read, see if you can find your own words, and identify the relational dances you are invited into that maintain emotional suffering. These relational dances are described in CAT as reciprocal role procedures. They contain both the emotional pain-inducing and pain-maintaining experience – for example, criticising in relation to criticised; bullying in relation to bullied (see Part Two).

'Whatever I do, it's never good enough'

It's as if, however hard we strive, we never get the approval or the love we long for. We may overwork or become addicted to work or give up and fall into depression. We may become a perfectionist and achieve a great deal. But whatever the fruits of our striving in the outside world, we are unable to feel good inside, and we are snagged by this core feeling of limitation and judgement. We may end up exhausted and martyred, suffer burn-out, or even suicidal urges.

A learned dance of *anxiously striving* in relation to *conditional and demanding* maintains the core pain feeling of rejection and worthlessness.

'Everything has to be difficult, whatever I do'

This is a 'yes ... but' snag. It's also a depressed way of thinking and being where no matter what improvements are made we cannot allow them in. The core pain feelings are connected to emptiness. The inner dialogue is between a restricting pessimist in relation to a restricted and defeated small self.

'No one ever helps me. I have to do everything myself. If I didn't, nothing would happen'

This struggle grows out of an early environment where it was hard or impossible to ask for help and we were expected to do most things for ourselves. The harassed single mother or too busy parent may reward their child for self-sufficiency. In families where parents were ill or absent for long periods, or when children have been moved from one foster home to another, the art of self-sufficiency may be the only means of survival. As a child it is very hard to bear the helplessness or inadequacy of a parent as well as our own. We may develop the fierce independence of a brittle coper, masking the unmet emotional need of our own helplessness, fear and loneliness. *This core pain may be maintained by the internal dialogue between our neglecting internal bully in relationship with our needy child self.*

In some of us this assumption is so well developed we have no concept of being allowed our own needs and feelings. We survive by our independence, 'gutting it' through many of life's crises without apparent difficulty. Problems arise when loneliness or exhaustion become severe. We may develop a cynicism and bitterness in our belief that we are the only people who do anything, and become exacting, demanding company. The fear of letting go enough to allow someone to help us or be close makes us cold companions.

Try the following exercise:

Exercise: 'No one ever helps me ...'

Monitor the number of times you find yourself doing things automatically with a resigned, sinking heart, feeling put upon and all alone, secretly grumpy and resentful. You might find yourself thinking: 'Why is it always just up to me?' Do this for a week. At the end of the week look and see how much this happens in your everyday life. Start questioning it. Need it be so, every time?

Experiment with putting off tasks for as long as you can bear and note the feelings that come up.

Note how much the presumption that things will not get done unless you do them actually heightens your anxiety.

Talk about what you feel to someone. Explain how difficult it is for you to leave things to others, but how you would like to do this more.

Can you identify the inner dialogue that might go something like 'exacting/demanding to inadequate and worthless'?

'I always pick the bad ones'

We may notice patterns of feeling excited and carried away by meeting exciting others, and having exciting experiences of which we have high hopes and often getting lost in the excitement. We project our ideal into the other person and become enthralled, secretly hoping they will offer all the comfort, love, nurture and satisfaction we have never had. In doing so we become passive, vulnerable to being victim. Sooner or later the rosy spectacles come off and the person, ideology or group become just ordinary or worse, and we feel terribly let down, even abused by the loss of the projection of all our hopes. We end up feeling angry, humiliated, beaten, frustrated. We can get cynical and bitter, fearing that all experiences are the same.

The dance of relating is of a *neglected self* in relation to the *fantasy of perfect care*. We may also notice that throughout the day we have a number of different extreme feelings and no idea how we got from one intense feeling to another.

Notice these patterns in yourself. In Part Seven, 'Making the Change', we will be looking more specifically at how to nourish the neglected part of ourselves.

'Only if I am allowed to have what I want on my own terms can I feel I exist'

The core pain feeling associated with this is terror of annihilation, as if our only hope for staying alive, or sane, is to make sure we have control over every interaction. As a consequence, people experience us as rigid and over-controlling, and if we do not have things on our own terms we experience depression and its associated sense of annihilation.

The work with change is to find a way of stabilising the emptiness inside so that we can relinquish control in very small steps. At the end of this book there are exercises for befriending fear so that we can take more risks in varying our interactions. In Chapter 13 we see Alistair's diagram of the void and how he took these steps for himself.

'When I have something nice it is bound to be taken away from me'

The core pain here is unbearable loss. We may have experienced the actual loss of someone precious early in life. Perhaps we carry an irrational guilt about something for which we were not responsible which makes us unconsciously sabotage anything good. It's as if, because of our loss, we have vowed never to let anything become important to us again. We might feel as if we are living 'on hold', lonely, unable to get close or be happy, and our core pain may present itself as phobia, isolation or chronic anxiety. There are exercises designed to work through this in Part Seven.

You will see from these examples how important it is to get beneath our symptoms or problems to reveal the underlying patterns. The symptoms or problems that entrap us and the core emotional pain are maintained by the internalisation of our early dance of relating. We absorb these learned patterns of interaction which then influence both how we relate and anticipate relating with others and also the conversations we have within ourselves.

How to begin the process of change

In this section we look at different ways to begin to reflect on change. As you read, imagine yourself on a journey of exploration about yourself and the mysterious inner world that accompanies your every day. Use a notebook or tape recorder as you start to make connections with what goes on inside you.

Drawing the life line

As we reflect upon the entrenched old beliefs and core pain we carry we start to see the patterns of thinking around them, so it's useful to look back and get a sense of when these patterns started. Take a clean piece of paper, or a new page in your notebook, and spend a few moments feeling into what kind of original seed your own being might have had: any image you like. Work with what arises. Then see that seed planted into the soil of your original garden. Notice which words, images or qualities arise for this environment. Draw a line emerging from the seed and begin to mark the transitions or changes that altered the natural direction of the seed. Most of us have had to bend away from our natural growth in order to accommodate our environment and this is all part of who we are. In making your own drawing, look at transitions formed by going to school, births and deaths, house moves, and take your life line through infancy and childhood into adolescence and adulthood. See what arises and what you notice. Write down words or find pictures or images to describe these lines of your life. Notice anything you had to do to compensate for failures in your environment. Remember that the small person inside us does what he or she can at the time with what they know or do not know. We can learn to develop compassion for ourselves, for the self that made the journey so far. If you like, you can experiment with making a dotted line to illustrate how you would have liked things to have been. What we are looking for in all the exercises in this book is greater awareness, not blame, and awareness can be developed, through understanding and with the practice of mindful attention. Have a look at Darpana's life line (Figure 1.2) as an example.

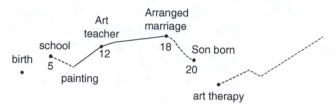

Figure 1.2   Life line from Darpana illustrating two episodes of feeling invisible: birth to 5 years, and at 20 to 25 years during post-natal depression

When I see someone for the first time as a therapist I usually hear a phrase that tells me something about the story of survival and begin to sense the feeling of the reciprocal roles that have been learned. This often arises from what occurs in the space between us. For example, I might start to feel invited to rescue a 'helpless victim' survival self; I might start to feel as if my open questions are being experienced as critical or powerful and the other person feels put down or judged; or, I might feel small and inadequate in the face of experiencing the other's powerful need to control or blind me with their own science. This is all good! It's all information, letting me know the nature and feeling of the survival pattern.

Take a few moments now, to experiment with this:

Exercise

Imagine sitting with someone you know well. See them in the chair in front of you. Without struggling, see if you can find words that describe the invitation from the other – that you are 'nice', or 'clever' or 'in charge' or that you are just happy as yourself. Find words that might describe the dance of relationship between you.

Traps, dilemmas, snags and unstable states of mind

Survival patterns tend to decree that *only* certain ways of behaving are valid, thus presenting us with a very limited range of options and choices about how to express ourselves. In this book, we describe these limited options as traps, dilemmas or snags, and as difficult or unstable states of mind.

A **trap** occurs when we carry on with our adaptive behaviour beyond its sell-by date. Rather than protect us when we are vulnerable, it actually leaves us feeling worse. For example, if the habit of pleasing and smiling even when we are hurt seems to save us from others' anger or rejection, it tends to lead us to feel used and worthless. We feel angry and resentful underneath but have not developed the skills to stand up for ourselves and we feel defeated, stuck in the trap of placation.

When we have bargained with ourselves in a black-and-white way, either 'I'm this', or 'I'm that' – or we think, 'If I do this ... then I am this ...', we end up living at one end of a **dilemma**. For example: 'If I'm not living on a knife edge of having to strive constantly to be perfect, I will make a terrible mess.' Dilemmas can also form an 'if ... then ...' quality: 'If I get close to other people *then* I will have to give in to them.' Either I try to look down on other people, or I feel they look down on me.

And a **snag** occurs *internally* when we unconsciously create a pattern of self-sabotage. We are just about to take up a new job or relationship, for example, when something goes wrong and prevents us from being happy or successful. Or, *externally* when we fear the response of others to our success, as if this would hurt or deprive others.

Sometimes the way we experience ourselves keeps shifting and it is difficult for us to be consistent. It's as if in our early life we have had to keep on the move from contact with 'other' in order to avoid feeling overwhelmed. These **unstable states of mind** may include intense or uncontrollable emotions, being unreasonably angry with others, blanking off or feeling unreal. They may include experiences of dissociation or depersonalisation. **Depersonalisation** means feeling detached from one's body; it's familiar in phobic anxiety and panic attack. **Dissociation** means that we cut off and dissociate from whatever is going on in the moment; it develops as a way of dealing with unbearable pain or terror.

We may have compartmentalised aspects of experience that have, in the past, become unbearable. When something in current time triggers an unbearable feeling we cut off, usually without being aware this is what we are doing.

Fear, stress and self-regulation

Skirting around no-go areas and living 'as if' we had only a limited range of options keeps us linked, through fear, to the past. Many of us carry a lot of fear in our bodies. We might not know it as fear, it might just be that sometimes we blank off and other times we feel highly on alert. When the chemistry of fear is dominant we may find that our sensory experience overwhelms us and stops us being able to reflect or take stock of what is happening. This is called stress. Learning to really listen kindly and gently to our bodies and what they are trying to tell us is an important step in the creation of a reparative inner dialogue with ourselves. It takes courage and some skills, which you will be learning throughout this book.

The diagram in Figure 1.3 helps us identify when we are in hyper- or hypoarousal – when our responses are dominated by the body reflexes of flight/fight or freeze.

Spend a few moments considering where you might be on the diagram right now. Make a copy for yourself and carry it around with you. Whenever you feel you are out of the 'window of tolerance' stop and try one of the self-regulation exercises you can find described on the companion website to this book. Whenever you can, just try to notice the triggers to getting stressed and write them down.

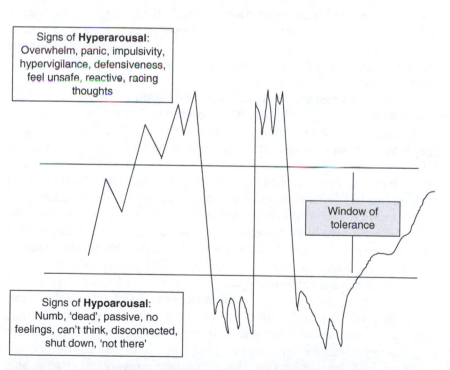

Figure 1.3   The autonomic arousal model. (Reproduced from Ogden and Minton (2000) *Traumatology,* **6 (3), 1–20, by kind permission of Dr J. Fisher, Center for Integrative Healing, Boston, USA, and Dr Pat Ogden, Sensorimotor Institute, Boulder, Colorado.)**

Finding ways to recognise when our stress response inhibits self-reflection, and learning how to stay within the 'window of tolerance' is a first step to taking control of our stress responses and to change. In regulating stress we are freer to think clearly about ourselves and others.

Our internal core pain will be unique to us. It is based upon what, for us, was both the nature of, and our response to, the people, atmosphere and events of our early life. Many people carry a strong sense of 'past', contained within the stories and myths of their families, tribes or cultures. This may affect their lives deeply, and may require acknowledgement rather than psychological analysis. The task of the focused psychotherapeutic approach outlined in this book is to offer the tools for revision, adjustment, healing or forgiveness only *where they are needed*.

The need to tell our own story

We are all embedded in our own story. And we are not the story! But stories are important, the fabric of everyday events into which our own individual pearl is sown. They shape the context in which we find ourselves, we cannot escape our story, but we can make it work for us.

Stories have been an invaluable form of communication since time began. Long before psychology, the storyteller was often experienced as the one who 'knew things'. Stories honour experience, giving it shape as well as containment. The continuum of past, present and future widens the way we collect our ordinary life together. Stories, even about the most horrible and painful of situations, help to bring a dignity to our individual lives when it is *our* story: this is what happened to *me*; *I* felt this, *I* did this, *I* went there and it was as if ...

In CAT the retelling of the life story is one of the foundations for shared communication. It pays particular attention to the learned patterns of coping and survival, and is called **reformulation**. This reframes our personal journey and places us as a hero or heroine of that journey. In a CAT therapy this process is a shared collaboration between therapist and patient. It offers a witnessing process that helps us to feel understood and respected, and provides us with an opportunity to understand and respect ourselves. In the therapeutic story we find descriptions for the adaptation we want to change and we add intention for change and hope for the future. As we look at the patterns in our own life story we may find associations with themes from well-established stories: 'Sleeping Beauty', 'Bluebeard', 'Hansel and Gretel'. The recognition, as well as wisdom, in these ancient stories can help us to feel not so alone. Others have come this way and their patterns of suffering have been woven into story and fairy tale.

The stories that will be shared within the pages of this book are all from real life, woven with threads that illustrate each person's struggle to live a life and have the courage to change. I thank again all those people who have given permission for their stories to be included here so that their themes can inspire us to look at our own lives afresh.

Developing an 'observer self'

We can prepare for and assist the process of change by developing new, non-judgemental 'awareness and observation muscles'.

We can train ourselves to:

- notice
- reflect
- revise
- try something new
- accept our every effort, whatever outcome, including our forgetfulness!
- learn kindness to ourselves and others

Psychotherapy nourishes flexible mind muscles, and fosters self-observation and self-reflection. Some of the changes we make concern shifts in thinking, perception and attitude. What may take longer is becoming more aware of what non-verbal stories are carried by our bodies. We may know 'about' our lump in the throat, pain in the heart, ache in the back, but we may not have asked 'if you could speak, what would you say?' In Chapter 14 there are suggestions for exercises to help support our explorations.

We might also want to consider practising each day a few moments of:

- awareness of our breathing and body sensations
- awareness of our feelings and emotions
- awareness of thoughts and what follows from thoughts

Preparation for your own therapy

This book might be a useful way to find out what patterns contribute to difficulties and may help in the decision to invest in personal therapy.

There is no substitute for the journey of therapy with another human being. The therapeutic relationship is a gift well worth giving to yourself, an investment in your emotional future.

This book can also be seen as a helpful companion whilst undergoing a personal therapy. It may also be an accompaniment to understanding the process of someone close to you who is in therapy.

 The first task is to complete the Psychotherapy File, which you will find in Appendix 1, with an extended version available on the companion website to this book. This helps to distil the issues you are currently struggling with and the patterns of behaviour to which you have become accustomed. Keep a journal for thoughts or ideas, responses from completing the exercises in each chapter. Allocate special time for yourself in a way that you may not be used to, even five minutes may be new. Mark out time in your diary, or set aside particular days which you devote to self-reflection and keeping an eye on your aims for change. In each section there are instructions on how to proceed, and examples from people who have already travelled along this path.

Notebook, pencil, colours and loose paper

We have already discussed keeping a notebook, small enough to fit into your pocket so you can jot down thoughts and reactions as you go through each day. It's useful to record dreams too, and ideas and fantasies. A larger notebook is useful for any drawings, cartoons, or doodles, open letters to people who come up for you in the course of this programme, your life story, your target problems and aims, and anything else that intrigues you. Keep your notes and thoughts as *you* would want to, not for others.

Creating a safe space

Find a place to sit where you feel warm and comfortable. Close your eyes if you are OK with this. Invite into your awareness a time when you felt safe and loved, however fleeting this experience. If there are no times, find a place you know, or one you imagine, that is safe. Notice the atmosphere, the colours or shapes, the people. Notice how this feels in your body, place your hand where you most connect with a feeling of safety and know that you can return to it at any time.

It is useful to keep the image of the safe place close to you. A photograph or magazine cutting posted by your fridge or bathroom mirror can help remind you. If at any time you realise you are becoming disorganised in your thinking, overly distracted or ruminative, in the way described on page 20, return to the feeling of the safe place. When you have restored regular breathing and the 'window of tolerance' (Figure 1.3), note down what seemed to be the triggers. Knowing your 'triggers' helps you to anticipate or prepare throughout your day.

Once we have made maps that outline the way our survival self has had to operate we need techniques for managing the feelings we are going to allow to emerge for the first time. At first this might mean simply naming them: 'afraid' or 'angry' which allows recognition, and gives a small space from feeling engulfed. We can also ask: what does this feeling most need right now?

The early five minutes

It is a very good idea when beginning a programme of self-examination to start each day with a few minutes' silence. For the first few weeks don't try to 'do' anything with this time, just quietly reflect; on how you feel, how your body feels, and simply notice thoughts and stream-of-consciousness impressions. Writing down these early morning experiences helps us to validate them. Most of us give very little time, if any, to pondering on how we feel emotionally or physically, and when we have problems we tend either to shut down and go onto automatic, or feel flooded with uncontrollable feelings. This early five minutes will be a kind of anchor, a chance to be in silent communion with yourself. And, as you write your own story and goals for change, each day will feel different.

Self-monitoring

One of the most useful methods of keeping aware of what is happening inside is through self-monitoring. You might like to start by monitoring the number of times you think negatively or unkindly about yourself. Keep a note of the time of day, what is happening, what you are thinking, who you are with.

You can also monitor feeling depressed or any physical symptoms and panic or phobic attacks. Monitoring helps us connect feeling or symptoms with beliefs. Monitoring the occasions when certain traps and dilemmas operate in your life can offer a space for insight and control, where we choose to think and behave differently.

Co-counselling

If you decide to share the process of reading this book with a friend, set aside a certain time each week to meet in the privacy of one of your homes, and treat the time as you would a counselling session with a professional. Keep to your own individual reflective time in between, for recording the process. Take turns at being counsellor and client and go through the findings from the Psychotherapy File with each other. You will enter a collaborative dialogic process, each helping with the process of identifying attitudes, thinking and problem areas, and in answering the questionnaires. Part Six, 'Gathering Information', is laid out in such a way that the 'counsellor' may read out questions and allow the 'client' time for reflection. Helping each other in writing the life story can be enlivening.

Learning mindfulness and compassion

A basic definition of mindfulness is 'moment by moment awareness'. This awareness helps us to stay present, with whatever is arising, so that we may experience it fully. Developing the capacity for mindfulness helps us in the journey of exploring our inner worlds. It helps us to see things clearly and also to develop calm. Buddhist nun Pema Chodron describes how the investigative aspect of mindfulness helps to begin to melt the frozen ice in oneself in order that we discover our potential for a more fluid nature.

On retreat at Arnhem in Holland in June 2006, Zen Buddhist Thich Nhat Hanh said:

> The practice of mindfulness is to remain in the present moment without trying to change or avoid it. It has the quality of attention that notices without choosing, a sun that shines on everything equally. The energy of mindfulness carries the energy of concentration and establishes us in the here and now. It allows us to touch the island within. Only when mindfulness is established can we know what is happening in the present moment.

Practising mindfulness can help us gain insight, and also wisdom. In Appendix 2 there are some suggestions for practical exercises and meditations, and there are more on the companion website to this book.

The CAT structure offers a container for naming and changing the problematic patterns that have had a hold on our lives. Just as important is to value the things we *have* done that we can feel good about, and in doing so we nourish our healthy island. To have survived a childhood of loss or abuse and be making our way in the world, working at what we can, trying again and again to make a relationship, is brave. Observe your own braveness, and wonder at your resilience!

Survival procedures and irrational guilt often prevent us from choosing joy or happiness. Several people I have met have said that they could envy a dying person, because they no longer had to struggle at life, they could just let go. It is a sad thought that we have to wait to live until we are about to die.

Maybe we all need permission to be happy in the present moment. Traditional Mindfulness meditation is taught with an emphasis on **Maitri** – a Sanskrit word meaning 'unconditional friendliness' or 'loving kindness to oneself'. During conflict, distraction or difficulty, remembering to practise Maitri helps a hardened attitude to be more flexible. This is rather alien to Westerners, who regularly suffer from low self-esteem, self-criticism and self-dislike which are less known in countries where a contemplative way of life is predominant. The Tibetan people who fled to Northern India, North America and Europe after the invasion of China, with all the problems of being refugees from their own land, do not suffer low self-esteem.

The formal practice of Maitri, called Karuna or loving kindness compassion, begins with practising loving kindness first toward ourselves, then to those closest to us, then someone neutral, then someone we have difficulty with, and then all people, plants and animals. (For a loving kindness meditation, see Appendix 2.) The concept is that we need to learn to love and accept ourselves in our humanity before we are able to love others.

In my practice as a psychotherapist I describe Maitri and invite people to practise with it. In Chapter 11 Susannah shares her journey of therapy, where she used Maitri to help her challenge a reciprocal role that dominated her relationships where she felt merged and lost.

Sometimes just saying 'yes' to life and choosing a joyful attitude makes a difference: to walk in the street and see what is happening rather than what is not; to greet a person and recognise what is in their hearts rather than defending against what might hurt us. And the poets have been there before us. Their words can help:

Kindness

Before you know kindness as the deepest thing inside,

you must know sorrow as the other deepest thing.

You must wake up with sorrow.

You must speak to it till your voice

catches the thread of all sorrows

and you see the size of the cloth.

Then it is only kindness that makes sense any more,

only kindness that ties your shoes

and sends you out into the day to mail letters and purchase bread,

only kindness that raises its head

from the crowd of the world to say

It is I you have been looking for,

and then goes with you everywhere

like a shadow or a friend.

PART TWO

The Building Blocks of Who We Are

Feelings, emotions and relationships: with ourselves and others

We belong and grow in a continually changing web of relationship, with others and the outside world.

Dr Tony Ryle in conversation with the author July 2011

TWO Understanding the dance of relating

Feelings and emotions

Like the seed in relation to the soil we are planted in, we grow within the garden of our early environment of family, our social and cultural structure and in response to its demands and prejudices. We learn to recognise, name and express or contain feelings and emotions through our daily life with caretakers. Feelings and emotions tend to get defined for us from these early reciprocal relationships, from the relational patterns our early caregivers learned. We may have been told we were 'naughty', or a nuisance because we were crying or frowning when in fact what we were feeling was something else, frightened perhaps, or confused. Drawing the life line (Chapter 1) sometimes helps us to see this long chain of family behaviour and attitude as we place our early caregivers in context. People brought up by parents traumatised by life events such as war might have experienced them as cold and rejecting in relation to their feeling shut out. We know now that trauma can result in our emotional life being frozen, and expression of feelings silenced. Whilst this understanding does not alter our experience, it helps us to feel that what we received was not to do with us personally, and to feel less guilty and responsible in relation to feeling bad or worthless.

The way in which what is considered 'emotional' in families is important. Many people with eating disorders, for example, have had their emotional needs responded to with food and not recognised as having individual and separate meanings. When we are afraid or feel threatened as a child we experience the feeling as a sensation in the body. If our fears are responded to with understanding and support we learn to recognise the body sensation as being connected to fear and we are able to find words for our feeling and sensation and thus express ourselves appropriately. In giving words to our sensations and feelings we learn both to define our experience and in doing so to make a slight space around it, allowing us to develop self-soothing and self-care, and to be able to befriend our fears. These skills are of huge importance throughout a life that will inevitably bring unexpected, fearful and demanding experiences. If our fear is met with a rejecting, belittling and dismissing response our fear learns no words but remains as an unmet body sensation, and we do not learn emotional literacy. We will therefore need to seek different ways to address this non-verbal body experience. We might find reparation through a nurturing relationship that encourages us to care for our fear. Or, more problematic, we might have to seek soothing or relief through avoidance or withdrawal, through substances or behaviours that compound our problems rather than meet them. So if what is in fact our hurt or pain or fear gets expressed as angry rebellion or acting out, this invites anger from others, and compounds our problem.

As we identify how our feelings have been interpreted and the reciprocal roles around them, we start to understand the difference between feeling and emotion.

Feelings remind us we are alive as human beings and are responding to the outside world! They are in essence quite simple things that communicate through our body's experiences such as happiness, joy, wellbeing or anger, sadness, fear or jealousy. When not entangled in thoughts, feelings can rise and fall like waves in the ocean throughout our daily life. By practising awareness we can watch this process and allow its natural rhythm without any interpretation from our thinking mind.

Every one of us has a feeling nature. Feeling is an important function in terms of our sensing, valuing and sensitively judging situations. What can be more difficult, though, is experiencing feeling without being 'emotional'.

Emotions are more complex and denser in quality. They are a combination of our feelings, our thoughts and body sensations that have been, in early life, defined for us by our environment. They are the result of feelings becoming attached to ideas from our past experiences recorded in inner dialogue about what is possible and allowed and what is not. When feelings are identified as emotions they create distortions in thinking and acting.

Examples of how this might be active in inner dialogue are:

'If I show angry feelings he/she will hit me. Being angry is dangerous.'

'If I expose need they will laugh. I'm not allowed needs.'

For many of us, feeling and emotion get blurred together and develop in the course of relationships that provide definitions. Being seen as 'emotional', or having our emotions interpreted as 'just drama', is often a cultural judgement on any emotion that is seen as excessive. What constitutes reasonable emotional expression in one culture is unacceptable in others. One example is in expressing grief after bereavement. In Eastern countries wailing, rocking, being dressed in black and supported for a year are a widow's rights and offer a rite of passage; in Western countries we are encouraged to 'get over it and move on', as if the expression of feeling and emotion had no value or purpose.

Feeling angry, hateful or resentful and responding to anger and rage from others is one of the most charged areas within families. The late Anthony Ryle said:

> A very large percentage of depressed and somatic symptoms are located in the inability to express anger in a useful way. [in conversation with the author]

Often our feelings grow into emotions that get generalised as moods and moods accompany particular reciprocal roles. For example: 'low mood' might be associated with a reciprocal role of *withholding* in relation to *anxiously waiting*.

Out of our emotions come our actions

Emotions tend to be dominated by our inner dialogue around what we tell ourselves inside about what we can tolerate and what not. Once our emotional response is dominant it is much more difficult to express ourselves clearly to others. *Either:* We may just shut down and go silent with everything swirling around inside. *Or:* We may swing from one emotional state to another, feeling out of control.

We may have a particular way of controlling responses that seems to conceal our forbidden feelings but may elicit them in others, such as in passive aggression. We feel angry but anger is forbidden so we sulk, withdraw, eat to excess, and others are furious, frustrated and angry.

Learning about our internalised dialogue with all the parts of us is an important step to self-awareness and to choosing how to change.

The dance of relating: Reciprocal roles and core emotional pain

Everything we experience about being a person happens within the context of our relationship with an 'other'. The British child psychologist

D.W. Winnicott (1979) said 'there's no such thing as a baby', meaning that the baby does not grow alone, but with 'others' who care for the baby in various ways. We come to know ourselves, and slowly become conscious, through the signs, images and communications toward us and in response to us from others, and the meaning these communications inspire. The reciprocal nature of relating is learned first via our bodies through touch, holding, sound, smell and atmosphere. Each one of these experiences is accompanied by expressions of feeling and a 'language' of gestures, rhythms and sounds. We have an inbuilt ability to identify with the 'other'. For example, newborn infants stick their tongues out in response to someone sticking out theirs. We have mirror neurons that have been discovered to be the biological basis for empathy, for being with and feeling with another human being. For most of us, mirror neurons and other implicit knowing continue to help us become attuned with ourselves and others throughout our lives.

Our early experience in reciprocation with our all-powerful carers invites a number of what are defined in CAT as 'roles'. Each role is complex and describes how we see, respond and interpret, how we feel and attribute meaning to, and how we act with others and in internal dialogue with ourselves. As we are always in dialogue with an 'other' in both anticipation and relationship, these interactions form a dance and are called, in CAT, Reciprocal Role Procedures.

As we saw earlier, the experience of being held safely creates an internalised capacity to both *hold* and *be held* with the resulting healthy island feelings of secure, happy, loved. An experience of being left or neglected leads to an internalised *abandoning* part of the self in relation to an *abandoned* self with feelings of being 'dropped' or feeling unwanted and bad. And these early experiences are anticipated in relation to both ourselves – I to me – and others – self to other.

Feeling held when helpless, and fed when hungry and crying offers a reciprocal dance between *caring* and being *cared for*, and the resulting feeling is contentment and safety. In our growing brains the growth of the frontal lobes that govern thinking and reflecting is assured, and we are free from the chemicals of fear.

Conversely, feeling hungry and being deprived of food creates a reciprocal experience of *needy and helpless* in relation to *controlling and withholding*, and the feelings, not yet understood, but held in the tissues of the body, are of anxiety and rage. The sense of potential healthy self is restricted.

The epidemiology of the mental and physical health of children and adolescents the world over reflects: the genomes they inherit (and the modifications those genes undergo in utero); the pregnancies that led to their births, whether their mothers survive those pregnancies, and whether their births were welcome; the parents, the neighbors, and the neighborhoods they 'inherit' along with their genomes; when and where they live (by cohort, by country, and by province); the air they breathe; the water they drink; what and how much they eat; the schools they attend (and by whom they are taught what and for how long); the energy they expend; the family status in the social order; the friends they have; and last but not least, the amount and kind of medical and psychiatric care they receive. (Eisenberg and Belfer, 2009: 26–35)

All of us carry a repertoire of reciprocal patterns learned from early care relating to care and dependency; control and submission; demand and striving. These patterns are internalised automatically and serve to maintain the self in the social world. They become our automatic pilot. Once named and reflected upon adjustments may be made to the more problematic roles, and new, healthier, reciprocal roles can be created.

Deficiencies of early care such as excesses of control and demand or a critical, judging and conditional acceptance may lead us to suffer from psychological problems. Major inconsistencies or unpredictable responses such as violent acting out or traumatic separations and abandonments that are not explained or understood leave us out of dialogue, feeling lost, confused and bewildered.

Parent and child reciprocal roles

The analogy of the seed in relation to the soil gives us a context for the evolution of our reciprocal role relationships. As well as environmental influences we must also consider the individual nature that is uniquely ours – **it isn't just what happens to us, it's what we make of what happens to us and how we act.** We are not looking to blame an early life seen as fixed and irredeemable. We are looking at that rich mixture of what happened, how we met our experiences, and at what now needs to be revised and changed.

So, in the earth of the early environment we learn a relational dance, a three-way pattern of relating to the world, others and ourselves:

- One pattern is connected to the way we feel towards others and our reaction to them.
- The second pattern anticipates the way we have learned that the other person is going to react towards us.
- The third pattern is the way we relate to ourselves inside.

For example, if my early experience has been with a mother who was perhaps absent for a lot of the time – either because of illness or depression or because of having to go to work, or simply because I didn't feel close to her – my core pain may be around abandonment or rejection and part of me will feel like an abandoned or rejected child. I will also carry an abandoning or rejecting other and act in a rejecting or abandoning way toward others, or toward myself, unable to accept my own or others' efforts as good. My internal dialogue will reflect themes of feeling rejected by a rejecting other. I may talk in a rejecting way to myself; telling myself off or not caring for my needs. The inner dialogue may be mild and occasional, and it can become repetitive and ruminative, giving rise to anxiety or feeling obsessed with anticipating rejection.

Sometimes our early reaction to quite small problems with parents, or small instances of absence or neglect, can be quite extreme, and until those reactions are modified and looked at afresh they live on to inform the way we relate to others in quite a profound way. We all suffer from our attempted solutions to our core emotional pain.

Sometimes our more problematic reciprocal roles are compensated for or accompanied by reciprocal role procedures derived from good experiences such as kindness or positive examples of care, however small, from others. We may also benefit from a rich imaginative life that supports us through fantasy and dreams that are meaningfully different from the environment we endure, and we are able to make this work for us. There are some people who survive the most neglectful and abusive of backgrounds who have been able to create a healthy island from which a healthy self beams in openness and grace in spite of it. There is no clear reason for this except for the hypothesis that within their natural being is the means to transform suffering and create meaning and inner strength. Or, this potential for a healthy self, which is in all of us, has been nourished by one good experience of a loving attitude.

Re-enactment of early life parent/child roles

What we learn from early experiences becomes a sort of hidden 'rule book' laying down patterns of relating which form the steps of the dance we take in relationships, with ourselves and with others. We can play *either* role, inviting others to play the reciprocal role. It is important to grasp that we learn *both* roles (the *judged* and the *judging* role, for example). Thus our *core wound* is maintained by both the damaged and the damaging aspects we learned early on.

Look through Table 2.1 and notice how you respond to each section. There may be thoughts, feelings, body sensations. Follow your response, in order to discover your own dance repertoire of reciprocal roles. Using the words or images that come to you, write down your own connection with patterns of reciprocal roles. Remember that we manage ourselves emotionally as we were managed and cared for and what we have known becomes part of us.

These old patterns give us a clue about the structures of learned relationship patterns that we can revise. As you record the relationship patterns you have got used to, you will be finding descriptions of the ways in which you look after yourself, how you expect to be responded to by others and how you relate to others.

Exercise

Using your developing new voice, the voice you are internalising in this book, write down the areas in your life that work well and, where you can, assess the following patterns. For example:

The care you experienced	What you felt	Some good experiences
GOOD ENOUGH		
Not 'too good'	Lovable	Responsive ↔ held
Not 'too bad'	Sense of self	Trusting ↔ trusted
Loving	Secure	Loving ↔ loved
Caring	Cared for	Healthy

Choose words to describe your healthy self.

It is important for each of us to find our own actual words to describe our experiences. We are not looking to find 'literal' answers. For example, it is quite possible for us to recognise feeling punished when we have been criticised as if we have been beaten physically. If the word 'punished' best describes our core pain then it's important to understand the three-way process that lives on in our relating. Our *internalised punished child self* expects others to behave in a *punishing* way towards us. We may unconsciously choose others who behave in a punishing way, thus maintaining the core pain *punishing/punished* and coping devices such as being cowed or pleasing. Our *internalised punishing adult self* may continue to behave in a punishing way, creating demanding timetables or being overcritical, beating up on the *internalised child self* and maintaining a feeling of punishment. Or, we may behave in a punishing way towards others, particularly those who appear 'punishable', and remind us of our own cowed or wounded self. Quite often our coping mode only works partially for us and is accompanied by depression or other symptoms. Sometimes we evoke a punishing response that seems to confirm the original pattern and deepens our depression or other psychological or physical symptoms.

Another example is of the childhood experience of abandonment. This might invite an *internalised abandoned child*, whose experience was either of actual abandonment or of a parent or caregiver who felt remote, depressed or preoccupied. And then there would be the *internalised abandoning adult*, who continually abandons their 'child self' by not attending to needs, or who chooses an *abandoning 'other'* in relationships, which keeps the core wound in search of healing.

As we grasp how these patterns of relating continue, in our present everyday life, we may expect all three 'roles' to be enacted at different times, or within the same relationship. The child 'role' still feels fresh and sore, but it is maintained, within us, by the adult 'role'. Thus the two 'roles' are reciprocal, they go together and need to be understood in this way. It is important when embracing change to look at both ends and not just strive to heal the wounded child. We also need to modify the adult reciprocal role; to recognise when we are picking on, punishing or rejecting toward ourselves or others and find other ways of being.

Table 2.1 Patterns of care that can dominate our relationships until we revise them

The way we experienced care	What we felt	Attempted solution (survival pattern)	Reciprocal role (with self and others)
ABSENT Rejecting Abandoning	rejected abandoned	placating parental child	rejecting ↔ rejected abandoning ↔ abandoned
CONDITIONAL Judging Belittling Demanding Blaming	judged humiliated crushed blamed	striving striving hypervigilance hypervigilance	judging ↔ judged admiring ↔ rubbished exacting ↔ crushed blaming ↔ blamed
TOO TIGHT Overcontrolling Fused dependency Flattening	restricted merged flattened	rebellion flight into fantasy giving in	controlling ↔ controlled merging ↔ merged flattening ↔ flattened
TOO LOOSE Anxious Not there Abandoning	anxious fragile abandoned	avoidance anxious striving 'nowhere world'	abandoning ↔ abandoned conditional/disapproving distancing ↔ distanced

The way we experienced care	What we felt	Attempted solution (survival pattern)	Reciprocal role (with self and others)
TOO BUSY Overlooking Depriving Silencing	overlooked deprived silenced	excessive striving searching 'not there'	overlooking ↔ overlooked depriving ↔ deprived silencing ↔ silenced
ENVIOUS Envious Hated Picking	envied hated picked on	magical guilt self-sabotage self-harm	harming ↔ harmed hating ↔ hated picking ↔ picked on
NEGLECTING Neglecting Physical neglect Emotional neglect Mental neglect Attacking	neglected hurt hurt/angry fragmented attacked	can't take care mood swings feel in bits unstable states develop 'false' self	neglecting ↔ neglected switching states unstable states unstable states attacking ↔ attacked
ABUSIVE Abusing	abused	bully/victim	abusing ↔ abused fantasy of perfect care
VIOLENT Abusing states	hurt/ abused	split into fragments unexpressed rage	fragmented hitting out ↔ hitting self

When we are able to see that the way we feel is maintained by the tension between both roles we can learn to choose healthier ways to relate.

When early experiences offer no relief from painful or unbearable anxiety and fear, and we have no way of processing this, the different feelings may get split off into different parts inside us. Sometimes there is no connection between the parts and we find ourselves in emotional states with no idea how we got there. In Part Five we will be describing the more unstable states of mind and looking at how to create a continuing observer within oneself.

Exercise: Inner dialogue of relationship

Self to self

Rest your attention on the general flavour of your close relationships, starting with the relationship you have via inner dialogue with yourself. Take your time. Notice how you think about and speak to yourself inside. You may find you have imaginary conversations, with real-life or fictional

(Continued)

(Continued)

others, and that there are themes to these. Themes might include trying to be heroic, or happy, or pleasing someone; conversations may be being critical, judging, or encouraging, hopeful or longing toward an imaginary other.

Self to other

Notice how you anticipate how others will behave toward you, especially in close relationships. Notice how this anticipation manifests in the tension in your body, in your thoughts. You may anticipate and hope for special words only to be met with words that do not meet your hopes and expectations and you end up feeling disappointed or dashed. You may anticipate harshness, criticism and hold yourself back or even make yourself vulnerable to what is expected. Notice all your reactions when with others.

As you explore your own reciprocal roles and notice the core pain of the child-derived role such as punished, criticised, bullied, forgotten, think about what you would feel if you saw a child being treated as you were.

THREE Problems and dilemmas within relationships

Relationships challenge all the ways in which we feel about and experience ourselves. It is through flesh and blood human relationships that we enter into the drama of the dance of relating and are invited into the reciprocal roles we have learned. Difficulties in relationships arise when the more powerful not-yet-understood emotions that may be linked to our early life survival patterns are activated, which bring up the more fragile and less-known aspects of ourselves.

All relationships, when our attachment needs are pressed, return us to the world of childhood where we strive to maintain control over what feels like helplessness and powerlessness. We are brought into our vulnerability, our smallness, alongside our need for closeness and intimacy. Often it isn't until we have been in a relationship for some time, or have perhaps had a series of similar relationships, that we realise there are meaningful patterns at work. Because we learn to be a person with an 'other', the patterns of inter-being are the foundation from which we seek attachment to others. So we are naturally drawn towards people with whom we engage in ways similar to those we learned with significant others in our early life. When this is balanced by mutual sharing and respect, these patterns can be mediated, even changed. But when we realise we are repeating the more negative reciprocal roles, such as being *controlling* and in relation to feeling *restricted*, or being *judging* in relation to feeling *crushed*, we find ourselves caught up in potentially destructive patterns. Once again we become the child who felt humiliated or rejected, hurt or abandoned, lost, furious, uncared-for and needy.

Our core wound is pressed over and over again by our experience in relationships. We may avoid involvement with others and keep relationships superficial, limiting contact to people at work, or only talking on the telephone, in order to cope with fear of closeness but pay the price in loneliness and isolation. We may rush from one relationship into another hoping to heal the pain inside us. We may long to find 'perfect care' only to feel crushed and disappointed over and over again.

Revision of patterns allows us to develop enough awareness to choose not to join the invitation to an unhelpful dance. We then have space to develop less rigid or dominating patterns. We can create new reciprocal roles that are helpful and healthy. Reciprocal roles such as: *listening* in relation to *listened to*, *caring* in relation to *cared for*; *loving/nurturing* in relation to *loved/nurtured*. By reading this book you are developing an observer self who is witnessing all you have been through, and thus creating *respectfully witnessing* in relation to *respected and witnessed*.

In this chapter we look at the more complicated difficulties that arise from our relationships with other people, which press our core wound against which we defend ourselves in the old learned way. In order to understand this we need to identify the patterns we learned in childhood.

Learning to recognise the 'shadow'

What was done to us we do to others and to ourselves. Sometimes one way of coping with painful emotional early experiences is to cut off from pain and try to live in a controlled but restricted way. We try to protect the hurt and fragile child in us by looking after it in others, or by hitting out at it in others. It is very hard to acknowledge this in ourselves, because in acknowledging that we have taken on the parental role in our relationships we are admitting that we are behaving like the people who once damaged or hurt us. If we understand that our choices were limited by our need to be in reciprocation to others we can invite revision and embrace change. It's usually harder to acknowledge the more negative aspects of our relational dances which may mean facing our critical side, the side that secretly enjoys humiliating others, that likes to be possessive, demanding, cruel, taunting or over-controlling.

When these aspects remain unconscious they cause more trouble than if we face them. If we have experienced humiliation when young we will do anything to avoid it – for example, by living life 'above reproach' or 'beyond criticism'. But the fear will remain, unconsciously. Because we have put it down so firmly in ourselves it's likely we will do the same when we meet it in others. We may get into a relationship with someone we have idealised and admired and wanted to live up to and please. All might be lovely at first, and then we find that they are no longer 'special' and we feel disillusioned and disappointed and leave, looking for another ideal. And so the pattern continues.

We may find parts of ourselves that do not emerge until we are in a relationship. For example, the successful, ambitious young woman, whose hard work and effort have come from being a striving but neglected child, becomes once again the young, frightened little girl. From behind the admired, glossy, confident mask to which the partner was initially attracted steps a small person craving assurance and wanting to please, whom he or she does not know or understand.

Dilemmas relating to our relationships with others

If–then and either–or dilemmas restrict other possibilities in relationships. All of us feel vulnerable when we are in a dependent position, which is part of attachment. If we have had an early experience (our very first dependency) which was 'good enough', we do not fear or avoid dependency. When relationships are going well, there is give and take on both sides and a feeling of equality.

See if any of the following dilemmas relate to you.

If I care about someone, I have to give in to them or they have to give in to me

When we care about someone and feel we have to give in to them it tends to be because we want their approval or affection so much that we will do what they want, as in the placation trap (see Part Three). We do not feel free to be ourselves, and are ruled by others' demands. Our 'giving in' is to be based upon self-protection, with the learned assumption that if we do not give in to those we care about something bad will happen. Our sense of self feels under threat.

This learned dilemma could arise from an experience of conditional caring in early life, or from *dominating/powerful* in relation to *powerless/needy*.

The other part of this dilemma is the opposite – if the child in us was over-protected or given in to, we may expect our strong feelings to be reciprocated, and our every demand met.

If I depend on someone, I have to give in to them or they have to give in to me

This is a deeper version of the first dilemma and is connected to what we have learned about dependency and independence. If we do allow ourselves to depend on someone, it feels as if they are in control and we have to give in to them. We feel powerless and helpless, which can express itself in passivity and sometimes a feeling of emptiness, coupled with feeling afraid of being at the mercy of another, feeling as helpless and needy as when we were small. If we establish a relationship with a strong caring other, it feels as if we can be dependent with nothing to fear. But this may be challenged when we do have to grow up and stand alone. We may accept this and grow within this care, and if the other person is flexible we can indeed overcome a fear of dependency and allow some interdependence.

However, if we recognise that we feel resentful and cross at having to give in when feeling dependent, and we are expecting others to give in to us, we have to realise that we are using our neediness as if it were our only 'strength'; that, were it not for our need keeping someone with us, they would not stay. There might be a fantasy that 'growing up' means others leave us. Sometimes this is related to the actual experience of a mother who found it very difficult to let go of her mothering role and wanted her children to remain as her 'babies'. If we believe that this dependency is our only power or strength we will undermine our ability to grow up and move away independently.

Questionnaire: Caring and depending on someone

How many of these statements apply to you?

If I care for someone, I feel:

- ☐ eager to be seen in the best light
- ☐ I must give in to them so that they might care for me
- ☐ I withdraw and become passive and helpless
- ☐ I must control my fear and anxiety and learn all about the other person and please them
- ☐ I expect others to care equally about me; and to look after me, meet my needs and demands

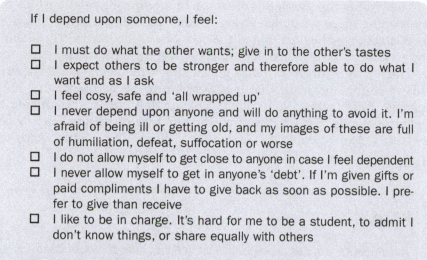

If I depend upon someone, I feel:

☐ I must do what the other wants; give in to the other's tastes
☐ I expect others to be stronger and therefore able to do what I want and as I ask
☐ I feel cosy, safe and 'all wrapped up'
☐ I never depend upon anyone and will do anything to avoid it. I'm afraid of being ill or getting old, and my images of these are full of humiliation, defeat, suffocation or worse
☐ I do not allow myself to get close to anyone in case I feel dependent
☐ I never allow myself to get in anyone's 'debt'. If I'm given gifts or paid compliments I have to give back as soon as possible. I prefer to give than receive
☐ I like to be in charge. It's hard for me to be a student, to admit I don't know things, or share equally with others

If you answered 'yes' to any of the above, ask yourself: what gets in the way of your allowing yourself to be in a dependent position? Is it connected to an unresolved memory of being let down, hurt, or suffocated?

Spend some time pondering on what you discover from this questionnaire. Look at the number of times you have shied away from any kind of dependent position. Write about this in your notebook, and let the images or memories stay with you as you read on through Part Six, 'Gathering Information'.

I'm either involved and hurt, or not involved and in charge, but lonely

This dilemma can operate whether we are in a relationship or not. Our vulnerability is towards feeling hurt and we associate involvement with hurt. Because we anticipate hurt, we may be highly sensitive to words, nuances, actions and hidden meanings that support this belief. To cope with hurt we have learned to withdraw, either literally or inside ourselves, and this remains our position, keeping the dilemma intact. Others may not realise how we feel, because we don't communicate it directly; all they may know is that we are hard to get close to. This may be because we are so brittle and scratchy when we come up against our fear, or because we depart moodily to nurse the fear on our own, or we may fear our own capacity to hurt or destroy if we get close.

Many of us cope with this dilemma by not having relationships or by keeping those we do have very limited and superficial. This gives us control over the hurt, but at the cost of our loneliness. Those daring to enter relationships may find them a torment because of fear and difficulty with trust. It may take a long time before we overcome this dilemma and learn that it is possible to be with someone and manage hurt feelings helpfully. Unfortunately when this dilemma operates it's as if we are waiting for our fear of getting hurt to be activated. Many people do feel lonely, either within relationships or nursing their hurts alone.

PAUL

One of Paul's ways of coping with hurt feelings was to bottle them up. His social isolation was also a coping strategy. He had been very close to his mother, who had died when he was six and he was then passed around the family. He promised himself he would not get close, and therefore hurt, again. On falling in love at the age of forty, however, he risked expressing his deeper feelings and therefore became vulnerable to opening the old wound of hurt. He became depressed when the initial intensity and closeness of the relationship began to wane, and he had overheard remarks from the children of his new love that he had taken personally. Before this time he had kept in his 'lonely but in charge' position. His therapeutic work involved working through much of the unrecognised mourning for the loss of his mother, and to understand and feel for the lonely boy who had only had encyclopaedias for company.

He monitored all the occasions when he felt slighted or got at by others, the times when he fled to his own room after feeling excluded or misunderstood. He recognised *needing to be 'special six'* in order to feel safe in relation to *perfect but unobtainable*. ['Special six' related to the years he had his mother, which he saw as special.] He saw that his hurt was that of his much earlier young self and could be triggered by the smallest nuance, and that what felt heartless by others was just ordinary banter and exchange.

Exercise

It is important when pondering on this dilemma to realise that the part of you that feels hurt corresponds to when you were a child. It is he or she who needs your care. When you feel hurt by someone, spend time examining what happened. What was actually said, and what was it that confirmed your worst fears? Write it down. Try to describe the tone, feeling, image of what happened and its effect on you. Notice your eye level when you are pondering this. Are you looking up, or down?

With others I'm either safely wrapped up in bliss or I'm in combat. In combat, I'm either a bully or a victim

This double dilemma refers to our need to return to the safety or hiding of a womb-like environment when we get close to others. We're either enclosed in the relationship in a 'garden of Eden' type bliss, or we react aggressively to others, always ready for a fight and adopting either the victim or bullying role.

In this dilemma there is no comfortable breathing space in between, where we can experience a mutual interdependence. It's as if we have found it hard to learn a model of being with someone which allows for the ebb and flow of energy and difference. We may find that we lurch from one extreme to another: feeling the dependency of being all wrapped up one minute, only to swing into combative mode the next. We may have the 'wrapped-up' relationship with one person and be in combat in all our other relationships.

The dilemma often arises because of our longing for 'perfect care' and fusion with another. This may be the result of an over-close or 'tight' relationship with an early carer, or conversely, because we have had deprived early beginnings, where it was left to our imagination to provide an ideal model of care. Our relationship dances are between *idealised 'perfect'* in relation to *neglected/forgotten*.

It can be hard to accept that our idealisation is the very thing that stops us having satisfactory relationships. Whilst the longing for another who can meet our every need can feel good in fantasy, it puts others and us under huge pressure and dooms our inner child self to disappointment. The fact that no one other mortal person can meet the needs of our deprived inner child can make us depressed. But out of this sense of despair we may begin to find the seeds of giving and receiving care from others that eventually becomes 'good enough'.

If we can see that our 'combat' style is an attempt to gain independence from the fantasy of being all wrapped up, we can build on this, finding more robust and realistic ways of relating.

Exercise

Write a story about 'perfect care' or 'perfect revenge'. Make it as dramatic as you wish. Read it aloud to someone you trust. Allow yourself to experience the feelings or longing behind the words, to identify the 'core pain' of the person in the story, and inside you, who wishes to relate to others.

Write another story about how you might care for the child inside whose feelings you have identified in the first story. Use everyday people and objects that have had some reality for you, or invite characters from your imagination who might serve the needs of the child today.

Either I look down on people or they look down on me

How much do we know of a haughty self, who feels compelled to compete when speaking, who secretly looks down on others? How well do we know the self that feels looked down upon, laughed at, both by ourselves and, we fear, by others? Much of this dilemma stems from a time when we felt treated contemptuously by admired elders and at an impressionable time. We learned to believe that we were contemptible, even a joke, not to be taken seriously.

We often are not aware we have this sense of inferiority. We just know that we feel hollow, living behind a mask, which no one sees behind. We may feel unreal and our life meaningless, and that unless we are constantly striving to overcome our inferiority by either being 'above' others, we remain in the pits. We may even give up and not try, preferring to live in the shadows with the false belief that we are all the things we despise and that others will look down on us, whatever we do. Many compulsive workers – men or women – who become addicted to their work do so because they are trying to manage this false belief. They fear that if they are not sustained by the admiration of others whom they admire, they will be exposed and then will have to feel contemptuous or suffer feeling contemptible. In their studies of post-heart-attack patients, *Treating Type A Behavior and Your Heart*, Meyer Friedman and Diane Ulmer make the following observation:

> Type A behaviour is above all a continual struggle, an unremitting attempt to accomplish or achieve more and more things or participate in more and more events in less and less time, frequently in the face of opposition – real or imagined – from other persons. The Type A personality is dominated by covert insecurity of status or hyper aggressiveness, or both. (1984: 31)

We may not know that what we fear is contempt, and we will not know that at times we appear contemptuous. It is usually when our outer adaptation – which takes up most of our time – fails, when we fall into the contemptuous place we most fear, that we start to question ourselves.

Questionnaire: Either I look down on people or they look down on me

Can you recognise this statement to be true?

☐ Others I relate to have to be special and see me as special. If they fail, then they are objects of contempt. If I fail, then I become contemptible.

In which of the following ways can you recognise your own contemptuousness?

☐ I have to keep 'one ahead' of others, which makes me competitive. I am constantly striving to win.

☐ I am judgemental of others whom I see as weak and pathetic. I ignore them, or bait them by teasing and provocation over matters on which I know they cannot cope. Or I sneer, am sarcastic.

☐ I enjoy others' discomfort when I have 'found them out' or tricked them into falling into their own mess.

☐ I am secretly envious of others' success but cannot bear this feeling, so I repress it and am only aware of it if I appear 'less than' at any time.

How do you use your contemptuousness?

☐ I am aware I am envious and competitive, and I use it to get me going, to make sure I keep up and ultimately overcome those in whose company I was made to feel small.

☐ I am revengeful to those whom I feel have put me down. I fantasise about situations in which I am the victor over someone who has treated me with contempt.

☐ When things go wrong I swing from being contemptuous, angry and bitter towards others, to feeling contemptible and alone, self-destructive and suicidal.

Which of the following is an indication that you feel others look down on you?

☐ I often make jokes about myself, putting myself down.

☐ I try to rise above these feelings by being very intellectual and clever.

(Continued)

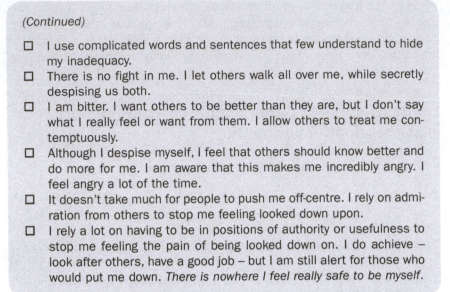

(Continued)

☐   I use complicated words and sentences that few understand to hide my inadequacy.
☐   There is no fight in me. I let others walk all over me, while secretly despising us both.
☐   I am bitter. I want others to be better than they are, but I don't say what I really feel or want from them. I allow others to treat me contemptuously.
☐   Although I despise myself, I feel that others should know better and do more for me. I am aware that this makes me incredibly angry. I feel angry a lot of the time.
☐   It doesn't take much for people to push me off-centre. I rely on admiration from others to stop me feeling looked down upon.
☐   I rely a lot on having to be in positions of authority or usefulness to stop me feeling the pain of being looked down on. I do achieve – look after others, have a good job – but I am still alert for those who would put me down. *There is nowhere I feel really safe to be myself.*

What we have to cope with in this dilemma is the feeling that we are contemptible, and the fear that we will be forced to feel this again as we once did. The way in which we lessen the gap between feeling we have to look down on others and their looking down on us is to submit ourselves to the pain of that despised place. In that place we do indeed get in touch with many of the feelings that arose during our experiences of humiliation as a child. But when we experience them during a programme of self-discovery or therapy we bring to the damaged place another awareness of ourselves: that we are more than the child we once were, even though the feelings we suffer may seem overwhelming.

In Figure 3.1 we see how this dilemma operates. If we are not living in the top section (admired and admiring) then we inhabit the bottom (contemptuous or contemptible). When we experience 'the fall' from the idealised heights of success, we so fear being humiliated ('beyond the pale') that we turn our fear into a contemptuousness towards others.

Healing by mourning the loss of idealisation to become 'real' and 'good enough'

As we become conscious of this dilemma we begin to dilute its power and 'splitting' nature by recognition, and by bearing the 'ordinary'

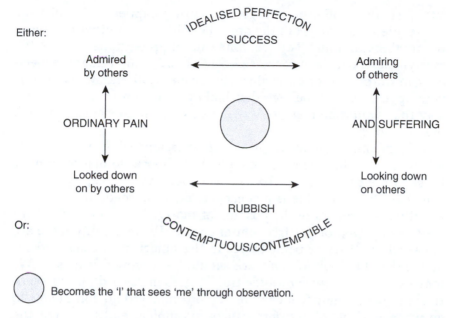

Figure 3.1   **Looking down on others or looking down on me. The aim for change is learning to tolerate ordinary everyday pain and suffering**

pain and suffering of our core pain. This then gives more space for the 'healthy island'. Here, ordinary pain and suffering, loss and disillusionment will be experienced as we grieve for the loss of 'idealisation'. Healing can take place, often through being in a relationship with another person where we take the risk of being an ordinary mortal, suffering ordinary pain. It is through daring this that we start to experience a sense of healthy self.

Either I'm a brute or I'm a martyr

This dilemma relates to how we cope with our angry and aggressive feelings. If we express angry feelings we feel like a brute, or we imagine that our anger is brutish. Conversely, we feel angry but don't say anything. We take on the martyr role, with all the internal resentment and hostility this evokes. There is no middle place for assertion or appropriately angry responses, and at both ends of the dilemma each position blames the other. The martyr says, 'I'm not going to get myself involved in anything that's unpleasant or brutish, I am better than that'; while the brute will say, 'It's no good sitting back and letting oneself be slaughtered, let's just steamroller on and get something happening.' Each pole of the dilemma brings out the opposite, either in another person or within the individual. For everyone caught up with the myth of the martyr there will be a repressed brutish side, emerging unexpectedly in outbursts, often against defenceless others. Many people who appear brutish believe that if they were not to act in such a way they would be martyred by others or to some cause in which they do not believe.

This dilemma stems from the unconscious choices we made when very small. If someone consciously chooses to martyr him- or herself for a cause they believe in, as people with a deeply religious conviction may do, this is a conscious decision made from choice. But if we are caught in the position of martyr in our everyday lives we feel deprived of our freedom of choice. We feel guilty if we are not serving others or being slaves to the object of our martyrdom, and we tend to look for ways we should be serving this master. We may expect to receive gratitude from others in reward for our sacrifice. But others may feel enslaved by our martyrdom and unable to go along with it. Martyrdom can be tyrannical and bring out the brute in the best of us! Martyrs can easily become depressed victims, inviting the oppressor in others and thus actualising and extending the period of martyrdom still further. If and when the martyr's hidden anger emerges, it can be quite devastating to others, because it is so unexpected.

JOE

Joe experienced his mother as a martyr to his macho brutish father. He had a good bond with his mother and was devastated when she died of a heart attack when he was only eleven. He came into therapy because he was very depressed and phobic about death. Unable to go out to look for a job, obsessed with death and the after-life, he had become reclusive. In asking him to monitor the feelings prior to his panic attacks, we discovered that they arose in situations where he feared he might have to be assertive to someone: a man in the shop, on the end of the phone, when out running with his dog. He was terrified of getting into a situation where he would 'boil over in rage like an exploding volcano'.

We could see that Joe related more to his mother's way of relating than his father's. But the week before his mother died, his father had thrown a lamp at her in a fit of temper. Joe unconsciously associated his father's anger with a murderousness that had led to his mother's death. He had never put this together before, but he saw that he had blocked off any assertiveness, frightened that it might turn into anger and aggression. When he could see how this dilemma had ruled his life he was able to learn to be properly assertive, to choose his own way of being angry appropriately. Then he could begin to go back into the world less afraid, free to express himself when he needed to.

Questionnaire: Either I'm a brute or a martyr

How would you answer the following questions?

If I am a martyr, is it because:

☐ I believe it is the only way I can receive gratitude and thanks from others?
☐ I don't see any other way to be?
☐ for me it is a form of love?
☐ I can't bear anger or conflict?

Name the martyrs in your family, or in your experience – from literature, the Bible, films, stories. Do you identify with any? Do you fear being identified as a martyr, and so adopt a brutish role?

In what way do I express my hidden 'brutishness':

☐ against myself?
☐ in fantasy?
☐ in sudden outbursts of temper directed against others?

If I am a 'brute', is it because:

☐ it's the only way I can keep on top and avoid victimisation?
☐ I enjoy the power and letting others live out the martyr role?
☐ I feel so much hatred?

Brutes also have feelings. What are they?

The male/female dilemma: as a woman I have to do what others want; as a man I can't have any feelings

All men and women are influenced by their cultural, familial and political attitudes to gender, but also by their male and female genes and endocrines. All influence how we behave. In many cultures both men's and women's roles are changing and all relationships, whether hetero-sexual or same sex, are being challenged and redefined by religious, cultural or political norms. Children in many cultures are learning a variety of relational roles as they are brought up by one parent or a series of different carers. In demanding economic times, the conflict between work and home life and expected roles is often excruciating for both sexes. Men and women have both 'masculine' and 'feminine' qualities – but what's most important is to not fall into stereotypes!

ALICE

Alice, a successful architect with two children, is aware of the tension in roles in her own life:

At work my role is very clearly defined and I am respected. I say my piece and it is heard and acted upon. I experience myself as being free and powerful in a creative sense. It is stimulating and exciting and I love the work I'm doing and the feeling of expansiveness and generosity it gives me. But when at home something else seems to take over. I fear being seen as 'boss' as if it's a threat to the safety of my relationship. I give in to my partner's wishes. I don't say what I really think and believe in. I feel that were I to be more assertive he would see me as strident and demanding. He says: 'I'm not one of your office minions … you can't behave like you do in the office here.' I don't feel I can answer because I feel he's right, that somehow I've got to be accommodating in my private life to make up for 'getting away with it' – success – elsewhere. The awful silly guilt. I know I'm resentful. I often get headaches at the weekends and feel unbearably tired when I get home. I associate that with my confusion, not knowing what to do, and a general weariness and lack of clarity about the whole thing.

Some women sacrifice their own views when they marry or enter a relationship, and upon having children. For some it is a relief not to fight or struggle any more, but be content with the age-old passive role of serving home, husband and children. And, indeed, within this role there are many modes of expression. But to give up one's own voice because of a fear of not being feminine causes only confusion and struggle, with resentment and anger building up inside.

Thanks to feminism, these old myths are under revision, but women tend to slip back into them when things get difficult or they try out new ways of expressing themselves that are misunderstood.

Nevertheless, in this transition of male and female expression lies the hope for a way of being a woman that brings into the light the most positive qualities of the feminine principle:

- Receptive, rather than passive.
- Empowering, rather than selflessly giving to others.
- Flexible, adaptable, yielding and creative, rather than submissive with 'no mind of her own'.
- Centred in body and emotions and unafraid of each, rather than overemotional, flighty, frivolous, self-conscious.
- Attractive, sensual, rather than seductive, posing.
- Nurturing, rather than manipulatively feeding and devouring.
- Containing, rather than possessive.
- Holding close and letting go appropriately, rather than over controlling.

As a man, I have to be a 'proper' man, which means not expressing anything to do with feelings

This dilemma remains unrevised if men find both work and relationships that avoid the need to get into anything of a feeling nature. If a woman needs to define being feminine as not being assertive or having independent views, the men with whom she is involved will look to her to contain the feeling side of the relationship. Many men appear to avoid having anything to do with feelings, until something happens that hits them personally on that level – their partner leaves them, they get ill and become dependent on others, they fall in love, or they lose someone they never realised was important to them.

With the change in the role of women in society, relationships between men and women are having to adapt radically, and men are finding that they must deal with their feeling side earlier than in previous generations. For many men who have been brought up in a traditionally 'macho' environment, there is little or no developed language for expressing feeling or emotion. The myth seems to be that a man must be in the outside world where his rational, focused side is uppermost, and that the convoluted, diffuse world of the emotions would only impede progress and draw a dangerous veil over the masculine purpose. When men cut off their feeling side because they are afraid of being overpowered by it, they tend to become brittle and lonely, appear unfeeling and strident. They are unable to relate to others in a meaningful way and can become depressed.

The old myths about men and masculinity persist: tough, macho, in charge and command-driven, strict, controlled, focused, unyielding, unable to compromise. Any show of softness is seen as a weakness. Although a man may have strong feeling instincts and a strong feminine side, he may have been discouraged from using or expressing this aspect of himself because of the powerful taboos that exist against it. There are a hundred little injunctions – 'boys don't cry', mother's boy, cissy, hiding in a woman's skirts, floppy, spineless, weedy, wet, impotent, foppish – all linking the feminine side with negativity.

Questionnaire: The male/female dilemma

What do you feel are the important qualities of being a woman/being a man? How much do you include expectations like these in your own life?

I expect men to:

☐ be strong
☐ make all the decisions
☐ not be bossed or affected by a woman
☐ not to be fazed or bothered by anything
☐ have the most important role
☐ not give in to any weakness

I expect women to:

☐ have warm feelings
☐ be the peacemaker
☐ care about children and relationships
☐ keep themselves looking nice
☐ never be aggressive or macho

Perhaps there is a middle ground in relating, where men and women can share:

☐ strong ideas
☐ an understanding of each other's 'no-go' areas
☐ strong feelings
☐ decision-making
☐ tears and sadness
☐ assertiveness at all times, and aggression when appropriate
☐ anger when appropriate

We all probably recognise and relate to a wise leader such as Desmond Tutu, Mahatma Gandhi or Barack Obama, who would seem to have combined the (feminine) strength of a feeling heart with hard (masculine) judgement, and when this happens it feels transformative for everyone around. But we can also see that this combination is not without its problems too!

PART THREE

Getting Off the Symptom Hook

Naming the problem

Fear has a story and an emotional display – our fearful mind tells stories about what's not happening.

Mark Epstein and Jack Kornfield in conversation
at the Centre for Ethical Studies, New York,
28/29 September 2012

FOUR   Traps

Certain kinds of thinking and acting result in a 'vicious circle' when, however hard we try, things seem to get worse instead of better. Traps are called traps because they feel like behaviours we cannot escape from! In order to remove ourselves from a trap we need to revise what, in terms of our thinking, ideas or presumptions, keeps us there.

The 'doing what others want' (placation) trap

What begins as a simple way of keeping ourselves safe by pleasing others, particularly early carers who might be hostile or judgemental, becomes a painful cycle. We hope that pleasing others will help us find love and care, so we take on others' beliefs or desires, and never find our own voice. In our eagerness to please we get taken advantage of. Then we feel used and abused, hurt and resentful, especially when we have tried so hard. I often hear people saying, 'I gave him everything he wanted, never argued, never disagreed ... I even changed my way of dressing for him,' or, 'I stopped seeing friends she didn't like, gave up my car/hobby for her, and then she left me for someone else who doesn't listen to a word she says.' When what we really want is respect, care, love, it's bitterly disappointing to find it backfiring in this way. The more we are taken for granted and abused for our attempts to please, the more our uncertainty about ourselves is confirmed.

We need to challenge the learned belief that we have to please others in order keep ourselves safe, and be liked. As long as our energy is taken up with pleasing others, moving into their world to try to make our own safe, we are not developing our real inner selves; we develop only a coping, or survival self.

When we feel let down or ignored because we are in the placation trap, our own actual needs *are* being ignored, which makes us feel resentful and needy. Sometimes these needs burst out in a childlike way. We feel out of control, and because the pressure to please others causes such restriction and tension, we may find that we put things off, that we actually let people down. Or we may hide away, increasing people's anger and displeasure with us, and thus compounding our uncertainty about ourselves.

PAT

Pat recognised being caught in the 'doing what others want' trap. She could not bear to say 'no', or to feel she had let anyone down by being different in opinion or action. To her, failure to comply meant hostility and rejection, which she could not endure. In her self-monitoring diary she wrote:

> Bought new dress. Didn't buy the one I wanted but the one the sales girl insisted looked the best. It was more expensive than I wanted and not the right colour, but somehow I couldn't refuse her. When I got home I just cried, I felt so upset and cross and helpless.

Pat also wrote about incidents with her children when she had given in to them over bedtimes. She swung from shouting at them and feeling bad to giving in to them, and getting into arguments as they tried for more. 'I was giving them what they wanted and they threw it all back in my face.' She recalled similar incidents with her husband and friends, and one friend in particular to whom she had acted as 'agony aunt'. Pat wanted to confide in her about her own problems, but the friend cut her off sharply. When Pat seemed tearful and hurt, the friend suggested impatiently that they meet the following week. Pat duly turned up on time, but the friend arrived one hour late. Pat was boiling up inside with a rage she could not express and which only made her more fearful of losing her friend. She had convinced herself that it was her fault the friend was late, that she must have written down the wrong time, even though she knew this wasn't true. Pat couldn't speak because she was so upset, and the friend became cross and impatient again. As a result Pat felt guilty, alone and cross, but these feelings were hidden in her headache and sore feet.

When later we looked at the pattern of Pat's need to please and at what compelled her to keep doing this, she selected one of the images she'd written down during her monitoring and got into the feel of it. The trigger point for giving in to, and pleasing others seemed to be linked to a compelling and demanding look from others that hooked her in.

In staying with this she was reminded of two important images. One was related to her English teacher, for whom she had written some good essays. This teacher had been very nervous as it was her first job; she looked to Pat when things got difficult in class. The look said: 'don't let me down'. Pat then realised that the look went further back, to her own mother, who had experienced similar feelings of insecurity, and had looked to Pat for help in making her life more comfortable. Pat's adaptation to having to do as others wanted began here. Her most basic fear was that if she did not respond to the eye-call her mother would become cross, upset and withdrawn, and Pat's world would be in chaos. She dreaded her mother's disapproving cold silences, which made her feel isolated and abandoned, and which she interpreted as her fault. The habit of pleasing had served her reasonably well during childhood and adolescence, because her mother responded and things were kept safe. But underneath Pat wasn't developing her own voice or her own ways of being; she was bending and twisting to her mother's.

This learned habit of pleasing wasn't questioned until Pat came into therapy because of her depression, which was largely a response to living in the placation trap. She had married a man who benefited from her pleasing skills. He was resentful when she burst out angrily at the children, or when she tried work of her own that was different (she had recently given this up because she felt so guilty). Then everything was thrown into confusion by Pat's depression.

She saw that her habit of pleasing was rooted in the world of her childhood and carried with it the force and pain of the child's fear. She recognised that if she wanted to grow and be free she had to take risks that she couldn't have taken in childhood, and she chose to risk saying no when she needed to, doing something different from others.

Although Pat's husband felt threatened at first by her being more assertive, he came to recognise that his wife had many more 'real' qualities than he had seen before, and it was a relief when she was not so 'nice' all the time. She stopped being depressed. Pat had some surprises too: people she had previously feared would not like her actually took more notice, and the friend who had let her down said, 'It's good sharing ideas with you now you're no longer a doormat!'

In my experience, people don't want 'doormats' and placators, because they invite the 'bully' in us. To be 'too good' encourages others to behave badly – often in the hope of getting a real response. Also, if people are seen as 'too good', their underlying anger is more fearful because it is hidden.

Pleasing others is a useful and necessary skill in the making of relationships and in human interaction. But when our entire life is lived through it, it becomes a damaging and self-negating trap, perpetuating our worst fears.

Questionnaire: The 'doing what others want' trap

Do you act as if any of the following were true?

I fear not pleasing:

☐ those close to me
☐ people I work for
☐ anyone and everyone

If I don't please them:

☐ they won't like/love me
☐ I'll be rejected/ignored/abandoned/criticised/abused

Pleasing people means:

☐ doing what they want regardless of how I feel
☐ never getting cross or upsetting anyone, whatever they have done to me
☐ squashing what I really feel in case it slips out
☐ feeling dependent upon the goodwill of others to feel alright inside

If the feeling you have to please sometimes makes you feel out of control and increases your uncertainty about what to do to ensure the goodwill of others, do you find yourself:

☐ putting things off because I'm unsure I've got it right and I can't bear to be wrong?
☐ being unable to say 'no', ending up taking on too many tasks, agreeing to inappropriate things, and ultimately letting people down?

If you find that you have answered 'yes' to more than one question in each section of the questionnaire then you are in the placation trap. You may find that your relationship dances are *conditional/disapproving* in relation to *anxious/striving*. Stay with what you have marked in the questionnaire and concentrate on the feelings you have identified. See if you can locate any images or memories that help you understand the origin of these feelings. Make a note of them in your notebook and we will return to them more fully in Chapter 11, 'Writing our life story'.

The 'I'm bound to do things badly' (depressed thinking) trap

We may expect that we will do things badly or fail in some way because we feel we have done so in the past. We may have lost confidence, or never had it, and this can grow until we believe that we are a failure. Thinking about oneself in a depressed way perpetuates the trap of feeling depressed. Although depression can be complex and have an actual physical basis that needs medication, research has shown that recognising and challenging depressed thinking alters depressed mood.

Using self-monitoring, over the next week write down how many times you find yourself thinking in a depressed way: 'I'm not going to be able to do that.' 'Last time I went near that place I couldn't bear it.' 'Oh, not another day.'

To self-monitor depressed mood, make a chart like the one shown in Figure 4.1. Rate each hour, either by using different colours, of from 1 to 10, to indicate the level of your depressed mood. Low scores start at 1 and 10 would signify a highly depressed state. Mark the chart for each hour for one week and see where your lowest and highest points come. This process asks us to be aware of our mood and what we are feeling; it also gives some loose structure to the shape of our day.

	Mon	Tues	Wed	Thur	Fri	Sat	Sun
7 a.m.	10						
8 a.m.	10						
9 a.m.	9						
10 a.m.	9						
11 a.m.	9						
12 noon	7						
1 p.m.	7						
2 p.m.	6						
3 p.m.							
4 p.m.	7						
5 p.m.							
6 p.m.	7						
7 p.m.	4						
8 p.m.	5						
9 p.m.							
10 p.m.	5						

10 = very depressed, down, sad, not coping
7 = depressed but coping
5 = mildly depressed
3 = low, but able to take in other things and look around
1 = not depressed but enjoying the moment

Figure 4.1   Chart for self-monitoring depressed mood

So often when people feel depressed they curl up in a ball and do nothing, presuming that whatever they do will not work. The chart will show you, first, at what times you feel most depressed (you may find it is often in the mornings), and second, that you may not be at number 10 all the time. If you find that you are, then perhaps some professional help should be sought, unless – and this requires honesty and self-observation – it may be that you are angry underneath your depression and don't want this to be relieved until you have been allowed to be angry. We will come back to this in Chapter 5. By monitoring what you are thinking at the times when you feel most low, you will get an indication of where your fears about yourself lie.

There are several ways in which this trap operates, and for everyone who recognises it, it will have different origins.

MALCOLM

Malcolm had become increasingly depressed about himself and life because of his disappointment with other people's failure to recognise the value of his work. On retirement he feared that he would be forgotten. Although on a deeper level his problems were connected to an early dilemma of 'if I'm not seen as special I feel empty and insignificant', which we will look at in Chapter 6, he was also caught in this depressed thinking trap. Every day he contributed to his depressed mood by thoughts such as, 'No one wants me any more.' 'There's no point writing to X because they probably won't reply.'

Malcolm began to see that he was approaching each day with the following attitude: 'I feel doomed before I start, so I jeopardise my own life by not valuing anything I do or say.' One of the ways he got out of this trap was to start to reevaluate his efforts, past and present. As an English teacher, he had many grateful students and many fine examples of his work, which he dismissed. His criteria for acceptance and value were limited by his need to be special, to have public recognition. At first he couldn't see how much he was already valued without this. Malcolm's depressed thinking was accompanied by feelings of hopelessness and pointlessness, and by thoughts of death. Fortunately he was angry enough about feeling so stuck that he was able to use his anger to re-evaluate, and reignite his energy.

We may also be trapped by our negative and depressed thinking in a passive way, which makes us feel victimised.

CLARE

Clare felt very weak after being in hospital for a knee operation. She had been feeling depressed before this because she was unable to continue her work at home or at the consultant engineering company where she had been a valued member of staff for five years. When the ordered world she knew was removed during her hospitalisation and convalescence, she was 'out of role' and became more and more depressed. She told herself, 'I'm useless,' 'No one will want to see me like this.' She feared that her husband would not understand, and she would not be able to make him understand. Eventually, she got to the point where she was almost permanently in tears because of this trap. She and her husband both attended a therapy session, where we drew up a self-monitoring chart to record her depressed mood (as in Figure 4.1). When she realised that she was not depressed all round the clock, but that there were some grey areas, she rallied enough to use the better hours to draw or paint what she was feeling and write down what she wanted to say. At first she dismissed all of what she wanted to say as: 'It's silly, he'll never listen to this ...', but with the help of her husband she was able to make use of the less black periods and free herself from the more depressed times.

When you have monitored your own negative thoughts for a week, spend some time with your findings and try to see if you can identify where these thoughts and ideas stem from, and how much they are self-perpetuating.

Questionnaire: The depressed thinking trap

How much do you exaggerate your fear of doing things badly? Use self-monitoring methods to put together a really accurate picture. Use a chart like the one in Figure 4.1 or monitor the time and place when you expect a negative outcome to:

☐ a thought/idea
☐ what you say
☐ what you do

(Continued)

(Continued)

If you feel you have done something badly, what was your involvement? Were you:

- ☐ doing something you liked?
- ☐ doing something you wanted to do?
- ☐ doing something new?

The social isolation trap

Sometimes we take the view that the trauma resulting from contact with other people just isn't worth it. We feel so anxious that people will find us boring and stupid that we avoid contact. It isn't that we would rather be on our own; it's that we believe that because things don't go well for us socially we have no choice. When we are forced to make contact with others we may find it difficult to know what to say and appear unfriendly and standoffish, and people leave us alone. This is the very opposite of what we really want. We want to be able to relax around others as part of being human! But if we avoid contact we are not developing the relational skills that would help us gain confidence and break the negative cycle of the trap. We can also build our idea of our own incompetence into dramatic proportions. Our sensitivity to other people's reactions to us can also be heightened, as we imagine rejections and criticisms in an exaggerated form. Jeff recalled his own experience of this: 'When I began to speak to a group of people at the party, I felt as if my whole being was lit up in stage lights and everyone was watching my performance.'

PAUL

Paul decided very early on that being involved with people wasn't worth it. As we saw in Part Two, in early life we cut off from feelings when they are unmanageable in order to survive. When Paul was six his mother became ill and died the following year. The rest of his childhood was particularly isolated: his father worked very hard and was absent much of the time. Paul was passed around the family, who were also busy and not welcoming. Paul withdrew into the world of study and encyclopaedias.

When we met, Paul had a successful career as a rational scientist, but his emotional world was very split. He felt he was either the powerful scientist at his computer or the very lonely boy. The social isolation trap maintained this split. He said: 'I'm better off on my own.' Then, at the age of forty, he fell in love and all his deeper feelings of longing, excitement, togetherness, came to the surface. At first things were wonderful, but when the initial wonder and magic was at all threatened he once again became the six-year-old boy who feared abandonment by the woman he loved (originally his mother).

We will return to Paul's story in Chapter 5, but having identified the way in which he kept his split going by his isolation he was prepared to make more effort to be with others. He also risked allowing some of the repressed feelings in his internal world, so different from the carefully controlled world of the scientist.

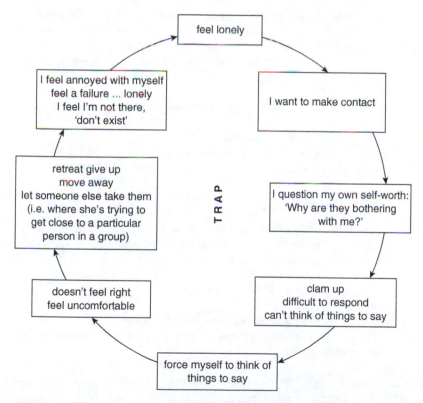

Figure 4.2 Mary saw her problem in this way. The chart helped her to see how she was trapped into being 'better off on her own' as a way of coping

Mary saw her problem in this way too. The chart shown in Figure 4.2 helped her to see how she was trapped into being 'better off on her own' as a way of coping. Mark down in your notebook which statements in the following questionnaire apply to you. We are gathering important information, which we will use when we reconstruct our life story and make our plan for change.

Questionnaire: The social isolation trap

Do any of the following ring true:

☐ I'm not used to being with people and don't know what to say to them when they start talking to me.

I expect people to talk to me because:

☐ I don't feel I'm an outgoing person. (Where does this come from? Who said this? Is it really true? Check it out by asking someone.)
☐ if people don't come to me then it's not worth it
☐ I don't feel I should have to make an effort. Nice things should just happen

I lack confidence with others. I presume I will be:

☐ rejected, that people won't like me
☐ ignored – people will find me boring and stupid because I believe I'm not clever/attractive/rich/don't speak with the right accent

When I do meet people:

☐ I can't look at them, my hands sweat or I can't get my breath
☐ I feel as if my whole body is lit up and that everyone is looking at me, waiting for me to make a mistake

I fear if I open my mouth I will:

☐ say the wrong thing, and people will laugh at me
☐ get in a muddle, panic, perhaps become cross or start swearing, that I will say something awful

What is your image of how you would like to be with others? Describe the qualities you would like to have.

Practice speaking with others in small safe ways.

The avoidance trap

If we avoid things we find difficult, we will discover in the long run that our avoidance only increases our difficulties and our sense of ineffectiveness and lack of control. Perhaps the most powerful example of this is people who suffer from phobic anxiety such as agoraphobia.

Every agoraphobic will have experienced something frightening outside, when they were waiting in a bus queue or a shop, or just walking along a street. Sometimes it can happen in a cinema or other public place. Knees turn to jelly, the pulse increases and it feels as if the heart might jump right out of the body; breathing becomes difficult, there is a feeling of faintness or nausea, buildings and surrounding vistas may become distorted and the overwhelming terror can be momentarily incapacitating. People have said, 'I really thought I was going to die.'

The physical manifestations of anxiety have always startled people with their depth and insistency, and can often easily be confused with real organic illness. The symptoms are identical, but the cause is different. What tends to happen in these instances is that we become frightened to go out again in case the same thing happens. The feelings are so fearful that we become involved in the fear of the fear itself and stay indoors, thus avoiding the situation of the fear. This may give temporary relief, although many sufferers from agoraphobia feel anxious about being alone inside, and only feel safe when everyone is home, safely tucked up in bed. Avoidance of anything fearful may relieve us from the anxiety, but it is at considerable cost to our freedom and may restrict our life severely. Many agoraphobic sufferers do not go out of their houses for years.

A mindfulness-based approach encourages us to explore the feeling of a racing heart and related thoughts in great detail. In his chapter within *Mindfulness and Psychotherapy*, psychologist Christopher Germer writes:

> It is like cutting up a scary film into individual frames and laying the frames on the kitchen table for scrutiny. The film loses its horrifying impact on scrutiny. The process of being aware, moment to moment, dismantles the fear by distinguishing the raw facts of experience from the frightening conclusions we draw shortly after. (Germer et al., 2005: 155]

Some people avoid contact with others for fear of being rejected; others avoid making decisions in case they are the wrong ones; many people avoid telephoning in case they get a difficult response; others avoid their everyday tasks, leaving them for others to do or until they are forced to do them. Most people get into the avoidance trap because they do not believe that they can cope with unforeseen or imagined circumstances. The sense of 'what if ...', followed by the dramatic scenario of rejection, anger, ridicule, or worse, can make us feel incapacitated, and so we avoid the situation.

Our avoidance trap usually leaves us frustrated and alone, feeling bad, with our anxiety untouched. And this can actually be worse than the fear we are trying to avoid.

TERRY

Terry lost both his parents before he was three and was brought up by his grandmother. She felt very protective towards him, and he was never encouraged to go out and experience the world for himself. During his early school life he was often absent due to long periods of hospitalisation to rectify a birth defect, and he missed out on a lot of schooling. When he was asked to give answers in class and found he couldn't reply, he felt embarrassed and 'stupid'. Later, when he wanted to ask a question about something he didn't understand, he avoided it lest he be called 'stupid' again.

Unused to having to deal with confrontation and nastiness, and with no preparation for an outside world that was so very different from life with his grandmother, Terry developed avoidance tactics to cope with potential stress, mistakenly believing that he couldn't handle whatever might be asked of him. The 'avoidance' trap meant that he didn't stay in any one job for long in case he was asked to take on more advanced things that he believed he wouldn't be able to handle. He had avoided making any commitment in terms of his work or future, and was plagued with the idea that he shouldn't have to ask but should just know.

When he was able to face his imagined fears he took the risk of not avoiding things, and experienced all the physical symptoms described previously in relation to agoraphobia. But he did overcome his fears and entered into a training programme for a proper professional career.

Questionnaire: The avoidance trap

- ☐ Do you avoid things because of false beliefs: 'I'm no good at that so I won't try'? (When did this start? Did someone suggest you were no good?)
- ☐ Have you been discouraged by not coming up to certain standards? (Were they your own standards or those of others – important early figures: for example, father, mother, teacher?)

☐ Has there been a period in your life when you felt left behind, when you didn't understand something and were unable to ask or get someone to go over it with you?

☐ Do you put off starting a course, applying for jobs, making contact with people who might help because of fear of failing?

☐ What does failure mean to you? When did you first come across it?

☐ What are the examples of failure from your own life, or the lives of your family and friends?

☐ If you feel you've failed, do you identify your whole self with this failure or can you see it is only one aspect? (What I try for is not what I am.)

Which of these things do you cope with by avoidance?

☐ writing to friends
☐ inviting someone round
☐ applying for promotion
☐ starting a new course
☐ getting angry with someone who has hurt me
☐ trying something new
☐ sorting out sex problems
☐ confronting my partner
☐ mending something that's broken
☐ tidying up

What are your fantasies about what will happen if you don't avoid things?

☐ all be too much, I will become ill
☐ confrontation with things I don't like about myself
☐ fear of getting it wrong, not knowing what to say, how to assert myself
☐ make a mess
☐ be judged

Can you recognise the personal price you are paying by your avoidance?

You will perhaps have recognised some of your deeper fears from this questionnaire. Give yourself time to accept these fears. We do not go to the trouble of adopting avoidance behaviour unless our fears are profound. Write about your fears in your notebook. Knowing and naming what you fear is the first step to overcoming it. Working with your fear will be central to the development of your target problems and aims in Chapter 12.

The low self-esteem trap

Many people suffer from low self-esteem. This means they place little value on themselves or their contribution to life. And in feeling such worthlessness, they become self-effacing, automatically presuming they have nothing to offer. This might manifest itself in an obvious form, such as speaking negatively about themselves, putting themselves down or leaving themselves till last. Or it may take a more subtle form and remain hidden under a brittle, successful exterior or beneath the mask of a 'salt of the earth' coper who always manages. Their low self-esteem may be so well hidden that friends and neighbours are shocked when the person they saw as marvellous and competent takes an overdose, revealing perhaps for the first time just how bad and worthless they feel.

People with low self-esteem find it hard to ask for anything. They have very little sense of 'self' and therefore do not know what they might ask for, or they fear that in asking they will be punished. Feeling worthless tends to derive from having been judged as bad or wanting at some point in our development. We are left feeling that what we express, indeed often who we actually are and what we want, is in some way wrong or not up to scratch. How often have you heard someone say, 'I feel wrong' or 'I feel bad'? And this can be said even by people who have accomplished much, or who are actually well loved. It's as if the self they wake up with in the mornings feels that it has no right to any self-expression or desire, or sometimes even to existence.

What is frequently most difficult about feeling worthless is that the standards we assume we 'should' be achieving are unclear; we are just sure that whatever we do it will never be good enough. Such a negative sense of self-worth means that we feel we cannot get what we want because (a) we don't know what we want, (b) we fear being punished for even mentioning it and (c) anything good we do receive is bound to be taken back or turn sour because, actually, we don't deserve it anyway.

This becomes a trap when we give up trying to express ourselves, at the same time as punishing ourselves for being weak. Such a circular movement in our thinking merely serves to confirm our sense of worthlessness.

SUSAN

Susan came into therapy because she felt unable to make any decisions. As she described it: 'I don't know who to please for the best.' When, after the birth of her second child, a doctor told her that she was suffering from postnatal depression, she thought to herself, 'What does he mean? This is just how I always feel.' She identified feeling worthless, and had often been depressed, sometimes suicidal, claiming the only thing that had stopped her walking out in front of a car was her guilt about how the driver would feel.

She had very few early memories but many images of suffering, and some of these came forward more poignantly after her own children were born. She described her mother as 'hard-faced' and had experienced her as critical, demanding and conditional. Her mother boasted that she had 'never had a dirty nappy' from Susan, but that right from infancy she had been in the habit of 'holding her over a newspaper'. Later on Susan was left out in her pram in all weathers, even snow. Susan learned to survive this early start by expecting nothing from anyone and by fitting in with what other people wanted. She was terrified of feeling cold or hungry, and always wore too much clothing and carried food in her bag.

After the birth of her younger sister, the family's 'golden girl', she became 'mother's little helper' and rather than going to college left school early to contribute to the family.

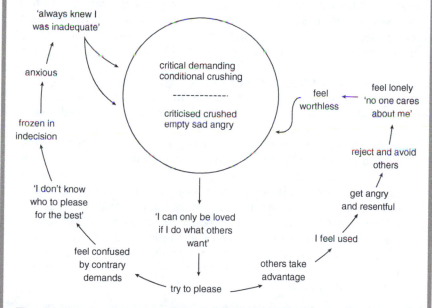

Figure 4.3   Susan's trap diagram showing her reciprocal roles maintained within the trap

Despite these beginnings, Susan had somehow held on to a belief that her life must have meaning. Towards this end she had joined several philosophical, political and religious societies, but the feelings of

(Continued)

(Continued)

worthlessness did not fade, as the groups could provide only outer rather than inner guides.

She expressed her understanding of her particular traps and dilemmas in the following way:

> Feeling unsure of my worth and afraid of rejection, I try to please others by doing what they want. This results either in my being taken for granted and abused, when I feel angry, guilty and start to avoid people, which leads to isolation and confirms my low self-esteem. Or in my feeling confused about whom to please, leading to being frozen in indecision, which makes me feel stupid and worthless.

Susan's dreams variously depicted her as a prisoner in a cage, a dead person underground who hears a voice bidding her to come out, and finally as someone who falls out of a tree but manages to somersault and land on her feet. As she worked with these themes and with the diagram of her trap (see Figure 4.3) she began to find a way out, to find her own feet. Standing firm with others became a part of her that had worth. She found a meaning and direction, which was not dependent on the approval of others. She was at last able to make choices. She wrote:

> I realise now that 'yes' to everything is wrong and 'no' to everything is wrong, and leads to a difficult existence. What I must brave is the disapproval of some people. It's hard, but no harder than the life I lead now.

Susan eventually decided to go to college to study for her O and A levels. About two years after her therapy she wrote the following:

> I am going to do things on my own. Not carry food in my bag and eat it on the bus. I'll wait and buy something in a café. I'll sit at a table on my own and not feel I'm doing something wrong because there isn't anyone with me. When I was young I had an imaginary friend who travelled on buses with me and slept with me at night, who went everywhere I went. Now I feel I've got myself with me and can rely and build on that.

Exercise

Monitor for one week the occasions when your thoughts indicated 'I'm worthless', and make a note of them in your diary. Try to isolate a tone of voice, attitude or look that accompanies you at these times. See if you can give a shape or image to this internal judge. Does it remind you of anything from an earlier time in your life? If your internal judge is a parent, teacher, priest, nun, sibling, friend, write down all the things that person has said to you, and all the messages you have received. Read it out loud. Then ask yourself: 'Is this really true? Do I have to go on living my life according to this judgement, as if there were no court of appeal?'

Spend some time discussing these things with a friend you trust, and begin to value yourself in a new way, concentrating on what you do and feel, rather than on what you do not. Every one of us is worth something. We each deserve the chance to find something of our own truth, and it is this search which can help to both create and maintain our feelings of goodwill towards ourselves.

Exercise: The low self-esteem trap

How do you rate your own value? What words do you use to describe yourself?

If you are struggling in the low self-esteem trap you probably have little sense of yourself at all and are afraid of thinking about yourself. Sometimes it helps to give yourself permission to take time, and as an experiment just to look at your face in the mirror. Practise saying 'Hello, my friend'.

Notice how you think about yourself. Do you think, 'I'm awful', 'I'm ugly', 'I'm nothing', 'I'm bad', 'I'm useless', 'I'll never amount to anything'? Or, 'I'm not going to do any of this, it's useless'? Just notice how much this thinking affects your mood and your sense of yourself.

If you notice that you think in this way, what part of yourself are you referring to? Is it your body, or mind, or feelings? Or does the voice that says 'I'm bad' mean the whole of you? Go back to the mirror again, and be an observer to that face. Experiment with being your own friend, objective, positive. You might notice nice eyes, hair or smile (try smiling into the mirror). Try this exercise each day for a few minutes and see what comes of it.

Do you compare yourself with others? If so, which others? Think how you judge yourself. Is it by comparison with those you presume are superior or better? Are your comparisons fair? For example, Sibyl was always comparing herself with someone heroic she thought might represent the boy that would have made her parents happy and saved their marriage. It was a point she could never win, and her efforts merely reinforced the feelings she had about her own worthlessness.

The question we must ask is how helpful is it to compare ourselves with what we were never intended to be? However you judge yourself, do you always find yourself wanting?

Do you presume that you and what you want are always 'wrong'? Through whose eyes do you view 'wrong'? Experiment with being your own judge.

Can you get help to express the bad feelings you have inside, and recognise where and when they originated? Can you see how much guilt you have assumed for not being what you thought others wanted, or guilt for some failure for which you could not possibly be responsible? Read Chapter 6, 'Snags and self-sabotage', and see if this might throw any light on your experience of the 'I'm worthless' trap.

Have you got so used to feeling worthless that it has become a habit? Sometimes people are afraid to get out of the low self-esteem trap because they feel that more will be demanded of them if they try. I've heard people say, 'If I did it well, people would expect it all the time. This way, at least I can just be unhappy.'

Are you in touch with what you do well? It might be something straightforward like keeping a nice home, being kind to others, writing letters. Ask someone to help you with making a list. When something you do well is recognised, how do you respond?

The fear of hurting others trap

In this trap we believe that if we say what we think or feel, or just express ourselves to others, we will hurt them in some way. So we either avoid self-expression altogether, allowing others to ignore or abuse us, or we find our real feelings bursting out in a display of childish anger that surprises, even alarms, others, thus confirming our original feeling that what we think or express is harmful. And because we believe we will be hurtful, we avoid standing up for ourselves in case we are seen as aggressive.

Sometimes our early feedback emphasised that 'children should be seen and not heard'. Sometimes we have the impression that the way we express ourselves is too demanding, and who we are, what we say, makes people cross. Anger is often a problematic emotion in families. It can be forbidden or punished, or evoke even more furious responses. We may learn that to be angry is bad and dangerous, and bottle it up fearing the 'devil' inside. Sometimes people have felt so oppressed in their early life, either by strict parenting or schooling, that they find it impossible to trust what they feel or need.

Sometimes we are frightened by the kind of thoughts and feelings we have inside, and we have no way of assessing them. We fear that if we let them out they will hurt others, as we have been hurt. This sometimes applies to people who have been abused, either physically or sexually, early in life. They come to mistrust their own instincts and impulses, believing wrongly that it was something in them that made the bad things happen and that they, and what they feel inside, are not to be trusted.

The consequence of being in the 'fear of hurting others' trap is that we fail to assert ourselves with others or stand up for our rights. We don't know what is reasonable, and are so afraid of expressing what we think that we do not develop our own ideas. Sometimes we feel stuck in a kind of childish sulk, weighed down by the unfairness of it all. To cope, we may turn what we believe to be our hurtful ways upon ourselves, inflicting harm by cutting or bruising, drinking or drug taking. In so doing, we avoid contact or blot out the reality of what we feel; making ourselves so isolated that we become depressed and despairing.

Exercise: The fear of hurting others trap

Monitor for one week the number of times you are aware that you fear hurting others when you are with them. Notice the way in which you think about yourself, or anticipate hurting others, and the words or images you use.

When you find yourself alone in a sulk or feeling badly because this fear you have has forced you to withdraw, notice the feelings you have and their nature. Keep a diary of them.

How angry do you feel? What are your ways of coping with anger or expressing it? Have you buried old anger?

How long have you felt like this? Was there a time when you felt that you had hurt someone? Who was this person? What did you either do or say that you feel was harmful to them? How old were you then? What were you feeling at this time? See if you can put words to the feeling. Did you feel angry, shamed, upset, abandoned? What has happened to those feelings now?

Ponder on how you carry your own hurt. What is its nature? How do you express it?

Take a piece of paper and crayons or paints, and draw or paint what you fear coming out of you. Don't censor it as you do with people. Just let the images form. Share them with someone you trust, and see what the images might be telling you about the fear involved in hurt.

Aggression and assertion

Many of us are helped out of the 'fear of hurting others' trap by a reappraisal of aggression and assertion. We may have been taught that to speak our own mind or stand up for ourselves is aggressive, and are put down for this. But aggression is part of our survival and we need to acknowledge its force and power. We can then claim our right to a relationship with it, as well as the right to choose how to express it. Mindless aggression leads to violence and the loss of power that often triggers it. Natural aggression becomes *assertion* when we use it to name or speak out about something important to us, and to stand up for our rights. It becomes our way of 'singing on the boundary', as the birds do in claiming their territory (see also Chapter 7).

FIVE   Dilemmas

Sometimes our choices about how to 'be' are reduced to 'either/or' or 'if ... then'. We choose the pole of the dilemma that is most comfortable for our survival self, usually because what we see as the alternative is much worse. But the result is a sort of psychological lopsidedness.

If we have recognised being in the 'doing what others want' (placation) trap, we might also recognise the dilemma about feelings – either I keep them bottled up, or I risk making a mess. In dilemmas there is no middle way, no grown-up greys!

Read through the following widely held dilemmas and see if any of these apply to you.

The 'perfect or guilty' dilemma

This dilemma is dominated by the need for perfection. In striving to be perfect we are trying to live up to an image of what we have always felt is expected of us. Each one of us will have a different model of what 'perfect' means. It might involve standards of excellence in work, behaviour, morals, lifestyle, accomplishments. Perfection might involve having to climb one mountain after another; it can mean trying never to have a cross thought about anyone.

In this dilemma, if we are not striving for perfection we feel guilty, and the gap left by not striving makes us angry and dissatisfied. Because the dilemma is based on a false choice about how to be, it carries a great weight. It's as if we are slaves to a system that is not fully our own, and we become angry at the imposed restriction. Even the external 'success' that our perfect standards bring about does not relieve us.

Many people live with this dilemma for years, striving for often impossible standards but unaware of internal pressure (see Kayleigh pp. 127–30 and Linda pp. 204–7). However high the external achievement, it brings neither joy nor satisfaction; in fact there is often a sense of feeling trapped, and a nagging sense of meaninglessness.

Perfectionists caught up in this dilemma tend to live on their nerves. In the tension around being perfect they feel depressed and angry; if they don't try to be perfect they feel guilty, depressed and angry. Sometimes an admired and strict authoritarian role model in early life stimulates the creation of this dilemma. 'If a job's worth doing, it's worth doing properly' in its merciless rigidity carries an unconscious message, 'You're nothing if you're not trying to be perfect'. (See Part Seven, 'Making the Change'.)

Another way in which this dilemma can develop is in an environment where the person only feels safe if self-enforced models of perfection are maintained.

MARY

Mary was the youngest daughter of a factory worker. She was beaten and abused by her brother (eight years older) and teased at school for being clever and different. There were no books in her house, but she craved the life she escaped to in the safety of their pages. So she allowed her brother, who found ways to get books, to barter with her for them. She survived this deprived background by holding her feelings inside and never showing them or asking for anything, and by learning to despise the environment which she called 'in the grime'. Her way out of the grime was to work obsessively hard in order to get above those who persecuted her.

Her coping mechanism worked and she is now a successful doctor, but for years she has had to struggle with the depression caused by this dilemma. Her fear was that if she did not try to be perfect she would slide back into the grime, and she had been unable to develop a place that did not involve this slavery to perfection. Slowly she is separating herself from the rigidity of this dilemma – which also cuts her off from other people – and is starting to express not only what she really feels but also how to be content with 'good enough'. She has surprised herself with how philosophical she can be.

Questionnaire: The 'perfect or guilty' dilemma

In which of the following ways do you try to be perfect?

In my home:

☐ I am always cleaning and decorating
☐ everything has to be in its place

With other people I have to be:

☐ polite
☐ interesting/clever
☐ kind and helpful
☐ unselfish

In the way I dress I have to be:

☐ very neat
☐ fashionable
☐ young-looking

I must get everything right by:

☐ knowing what to do in all situations
☐ being always in control

If you don't try to be perfect, how do you feel?

☐ Depressed and empty
☐ Frightened of being left behind
☐ Angry at feeling trapped
☐ Lost without a goal
☐ Frightened of chaos

List in your notebook the number of times you recognise this dilemma. Take time also to notice and record what you really feel. What are the feelings that perfectionism is trying to avoid because they are so painful? The drive can become like a drug-induced 'fix', which, when withheld, causes us to feel small and vulnerable again.

Experiment with allowing yourself to be less than perfect from time to time. Allow the anxious or guilty feelings. Begin to accept and care for them. In Part Six, 'Gathering Information', you will be able to look at the source of this dilemma, and what fears or judgements you have learned to internalise which keep this dilemma going.

The 'perfect control or perfect mess' dilemma

This dilemma is dominated by the need for control of anything seen as 'messy'. This may be to do with the way we express ourselves at work, at home, or in our dress. It may extend to our speech and thoughts, and may be severe enough to involve all kinds of rituals of checking, touching, repetition of words or thoughts, or placing things and ourselves in certain positions at particular times. The need for perfection is linked to our need for control of, and freedom from, feeling guilty or messy. We may not be specifically aware of our fear of mess and its consequences, only dominated by the need to control it inwardly or outwardly, organising things in such a way to make sure we keep safe and in order.

What may have begun as a ritual of protection in early years grows into something more rigid and detached from what it was originally meant to protect. We know from the work of Donald Winnicott (1979) that children grow attached to objects early on – teddy bears, blankets, thumbs, fluff, cotton – and that these objects are important talismen for the dangerous threshold of separation. They represent the safety of the mother, or whoever is the main carer, when that person isn't there. These objects help reduce separation anxiety, until healthy separation has been achieved. When psychological separation from early carers is never truly achieved it's as if crossing into adult-hood or the newness of the outside world is still full of early fears, however grown up we may appear to be on the outside.

When as a child we are confronted by difficult feelings we use objects around us to manage them: teddy is poorly today; the witch in the story is very, very wicked; the dragon in the dream breathes fire and is very cross. If aspects of our early environment become unstable we learn ways to maintain control of our safety and avoid any form of mess or chaos. Our dance of relating tends to express itself as *distancing/controlling* to a fearful *fearful/overwhelming*.

If we learn that 'mess' is bad and in making a mess we contaminate our security, our fears may extend to our emotional or sexual feelings. In order to keep feelings of rejection, abandonment or contamination away, we may develop rituals of control, initially with toys or champions in stories. If the fear remains, the rituals may extend in later life to objects such as floors, surfaces or door handles, as if they carried our mess and have to be repetitively controlled and cleaned. What we are struggling to make safe are unbearable feelings around our separation from what has been held as 'safe'. When we can actively engage in doing something about our fears, such as counting, checking, wiping or cleaning, we have our fear under control. But then, the rest of our life feels hostage to our rituals.

Our need for control may also involve limiting ourselves to certain experiences, and insisting on organisation and order. We may seek to control our anxiety by limiting our lives only to 'comfort zones'. We might manage our anxiety about being attacked or invaded by arming ourselves with weapons, locks and alarms. Today this is becoming epidemic in our world. Whilst it may be an appropriate response to urban and rural violence, the reciprocal role is *persecuting control* in relation to *persecuted/terror* dominated by the terrorist in both political and street life.

The outward expression of control may also tell us something about our struggle with internal invasions of feared violence. Any early influence that restricted our natural growth, that was against us rather than for us, will be internalised and as such will carry on restricting us from inside in later life. We will continue to believe there is something frightening that must be controlled at all costs. We may have experienced these restrictions as frightening episodes of anger or temper, as an overemphatic concentration upon morals, or in the dogmatic insistence on 'right' and 'wrong' behaviour that is characteristic of religious fervour. We may also experience it via the obsessional or repetitive behaviour of those around us.

THEA

Thea was adopted by a couple who had already adopted a boy two years older. She spent her first few months and her first Christmas with her biological mother and was officially adopted when she was nearly two. Her adoptive family emphasised being in control, especially of anger and 'tantrums'. When she was three Thea remembers her grandmother saying, 'Put your anger in the wardrobe'. Her life was very contained, both by her tight family unit and by a strict school where little self-expression was encouraged and any kind of risk-taking severely restricted. At sixteen, on moving to a different school, Thea discovered an aspect of the world that felt 'wicked, naughty, dirty, sexy and very out of control' and which she was ill equipped to handle. Since this time, when she broke down under the strain, she has been bravely learning to cope with this different and difficult aspect of outside life triggering inside feelings, which threatens her safety. One of the ways she copes with strong feelings, especially negative feelings, and with her fear of sex and physical closeness, is to make sure that everything in her house is kept very clean. She may wipe over her doorknobs three or four times when she comes in from work, even though she knows that no one has been there during her absence. She explains:

> If everything is in its place and tidy then I feel I can let myself off the hook and relinquish my obligations. I get cross if people mess up my order. If my bag isn't tidy and I haven't tidied up before I leave the house, then I'm all at sea and things will go wrong.

(Continued)

(Continued)

Thea sees her 'perfect control or perfect mess' dilemma as rooted in her early life's anxieties about being sent away if she were not very good, which meant in her family being neat and controlled, especially with her feelings. This also kept her in a dependent position: 'If people feel I need them they'll stay around more than if they had a free choice.' She feels that if she gave up being dependent people might make decisions over which she would have no control.

Thea is an attractive, very intelligent woman who has done a great deal to separate herself from the early survival modes that helped her get through very difficult beginnings then, but which can sometimes get in the way of her current relationships now. She bravely monitors how she feels when the need to clean is at its most pressing, and these occasions are usually connected with a time of transition or change. She has recently taken the huge step of committing herself to a relationship, where her fears of closeness, of sex and of being out of control of what she most needs are challenged, and she is managing well. She has been able to express many of her hidden feelings about being adopted, and her sense that 'anyone could have picked me up', and the helplessness this puts her in touch with. She is working towards the possibility of freeing herself from the tyranny of 'perfect control' in the future by feeling more loved and 'allowed' as a person.

If you recognise yourself in this dilemma, make a list of all the ways in which you keep in 'perfect control'. You may not be aware of some of the ways immediately, but let your awareness of this problem stay with you and inform you as you go about your everyday activities.

Two of the most frequent ways of keeping in perfect control involve continuous cleaning and checking external situations. A young man came to see me because he had to get up three or four times in the night in order to re-clean his bathroom. When I asked him to describe exactly how he did the cleaning, he began to recite his ritual in great detail. Suddenly, as he was describing how he pulled on 'his pink rubber gloves', he exclaimed, 'I know ... it's all the dirt inside myself I want to clean out, isn't it?' This sudden piece of insight allowed him to work back to the core issue of what he considered the 'dirt inside himself' to be. He was able to release himself from the powerful internal terror of dirt which was manifest by his ritualistic cleanings, and which were threatening his everyday life and work.

Use the questionnaire to identify any issues that apply to you in any way. Write them down in your notebook.

Questionnaire: The 'perfect control or perfect mess' dilemma

How often do you find yourself:

☐ cleaning obsessively (more than is appropriate)?

    ☐ cleaning something before you sit down, eat, go to bed or relax in any way

☐ checking obsessively (more than is appropriate)?

    ☐ gas
    ☐ taps
    ☐ electricity
    ☐ windows
    ☐ valuables (jewellery, money, etc.)
    ☐ things needed for work outside the home or journeys
    ☐ telephone

Record in your notebook how many times you have to check your 'perfect control' rituals. The next time you feel compelled to move into a 'perfect control' mode, spend a few moments allowing your feelings to surface. Do not worry how vague they may seem to be. Do this on as many occasions as you can. When you have a sense of the feelings underneath the 'perfect control' mode, feel into what it is you are trying to achieve through the method of control. Are you:

- keeping things safe (later on ask yourself, what things or feelings)?
- keeping something out?
- bestowing a blessing for safety?
- other?

What do you most fear will happen if you do not check, clean or control in any other way?

- invasion
- contamination
- chaos
- death
- unbearable stress

> **Exercise**
>
> Have you ever seen anyone you know cope with one or more of the above? What is it they do, who do they call upon for help? If you have difficulty in imagining any coping strategies within yourself, is there a voice in you which tells you that you would be unable to cope or unable to enlist help? Whose voice is this? Could you challenge it?
>
> One of the most useful positive thoughts to develop is the idea that, whatever happens, you could find new ways of coping, or asking for help.

The 'greedy or self-punishing' dilemma

This dilemma is related to our basic needs and desires, which have, in some way, been compromised. It's as if we are not fully entitled to anything freely for ourselves; when we approach something we need or desire we feel greedy. To cope, we deny our needs because the pressure of guilt over greed is unbearable and we end up punishing ourselves. Whichever end of the dilemma we inhabit is equally painful, and at its core lies our struggle to cope with early deprivation.

This dilemma finds external expression through problems with eating, sex, gambling, spending money, or any other ritual attached to something important that symbolises having our needs met. The person suffering from bulimia, for example, will allow themselves a certain amount of food. If he or she goes beyond this limit, the solution is to vomit up the residue or take laxatives. Sometimes the self-imposed limit is very small, and the sufferer will feel in danger of becoming fat and being seen as out of control and greedy. Such is the terror that she or he enacts the self-punishing end of the dilemma by getting rid of the food. Someone with a gambling compulsion will be able to have money for only a short time before he or she risks losing it. Some people will allow themselves to spend money on buying things, feel immediately greedy and have to store them away, never to be worn or used. Others may have decided that their needs are simply never going to be met, so they will deny all need or desire or pleasure and 'give themselves away' to anyone, being sexually profligate or exchanging body and sex for money and power.

Sometimes we may feel that the sense of deprivation inside is becoming unbearable and we desperately have to grab what we can in an attempt to fill the place that feels so empty and hurt. We may go on a binge of some sort – eating or spending – or we may compulsively grab at something or someone whom we hope will fill the emptiness. We may get into debt; or try to resist paying for things. (When you feel deprived inside it's hard to give out without resenting it, which usually expresses itself unconsciously, perhaps as hoarding, appearing 'mean', or by attaching an exaggerated anticipation to what other people may or may not give, which always disappoints.) Being torn in this way makes us feel miserable, and the misery may be turned against oneself. When someone in the grip of anorexia nervosa feels longing and hunger of an emotional as well as a physical kind, they feel such terror that punishment through strenuous exercise, or starving for days, soon follows. Other people are compelled to harm themselves by cutting, stabbing or damaging their bodies in some way.

This dilemma carries with it both a social stigma and a religious one, and thus the internal dilemma becomes more absolute as it is judged harshly by the moral tone of society or the Church. Greed can be seen as a sin that deserves punishment. Perfectionism and high achievement are often admired and encouraged. Greed may arise from the perfectionist's desire for bigger and better without reflection on need or appropriateness. It may arise from desperate unmet emotional need. Once basic needs are met – by our recognition, through a relationship with another, or by putting energy into something where our needs are satisfied and we are nourished – then the heat is taken out. Greed becomes recognised as need.

ROSE

Rose started to look at her life closely when she realised that her spending of money had got out of hand. She would see something very beautiful, usually an antique, and couldn't resist buying it. She was very afraid of her husband's anger when he found out, because he said things she didn't want to hear: about her being out of control, greedy, irresponsible, wanting things 'above her status and income'. She knew there was some truth in all of this, but she felt 'carried away by my tastes'.

Rose had been sexually abused, first by her father between the ages of ten and fifteen and then by her uncle from fifteen to eighteen, when she managed to get away to university. She came to see that, largely

(Continued)

(Continued)

because of her secret and forbidden relationship with her father (which her mother refused to believe, and indeed made Rose feel dirty and guilty for revealing), she had linked all of her self-expression, her appetites and her desires and excitement, with guilt, shame and a sense that they were forbidden. She had married a man who helped her 'control' her appetites because he was 'strong, determined, disciplined' and very good at controlling money, which was his specialist field.

For a while she felt safe, that her appetites and tastes were under lock and key. But her instinctual nature and her appetites had to emerge somehow. (Seeds want to grow.) They tended to emerge guiltily, as in some of her compulsive eating bouts, her need to keep lovely 'delicacies' waiting in the fridge and through her compulsion to spend money on lovely things. This all frightened her, and at first served to refuel her old learned and mistaken belief that her appetites and tastes were dangerous and out of control and would lead to disaster.

Rose was a wise professional woman who soon talked things over with her husband, got her own separate bank account, and began working on how her life had been controlled by the 'greedy or self-punishing' dilemma. One of her problems listed on the chart we made was: 'Pleasure, excitement, appetite, forbidden'. The aim was 'To free myself from the effect of past abuses and their grip. To allow a fuller range of feeling'. In the letter she wrote at the end of her therapy she says: 'The short therapy has been a wonderful vehicle for my release, and it showed me some of the ways I can manage the chaos that results from that release.' In allowing herself to get in touch with her instinctual nature she was able to revalue her creative self, which had originally expressed itself through music until it had been put away, like all other instincts, when she became the scientific professional. She was also able to have a much fuller relationship with her husband, no longer assigning him the 'controller' role, and she has recently experienced the 'healing' joy of a second child.

Concentrate on the next questionnaire and become more aware of your needs during your daily experience. As we build a picture of what you would most like to change we will also be building a picture of what you most need and desire in your life – something you may not have thought about. As well as actively changing old attitudes that are now redundant, we are also rebuilding a sense of who we are and the ingredients that our 'seed' self most needs for its growth and development.

Questionnaire: The 'greedy or self-punishing' dilemma

Where do you notice the pull to want more:

☐ with food?
☐ with money?
☐ with possessions?
☐ wanting more contact with others?
☐ with sex?
☐ taking on more than you need or can finish?
☐ in 'hoovering up' experiences: books, others, time, events?

How would you describe the feelings involved?

☐ hungry
☐ needy
☐ desperate
☐ longing
☐ shame
☐ anxious
☐ empty

How do you cope with this dilemma? Do you live only at one end, or swing between the two?

Have you ever talked about it to anyone?

This dilemma involves feelings in our bodies. Take some time to explore this dilemma by noticing where in your body you experience the pull to want more.

Explore some of what you consider to be the basic needs of a human body: include warmth, care, holding, rest, sleep, safety.

The 'busy carer or empty loner' dilemma

Many people find deep fulfilment in looking after others without any problems. This dilemma describes a pattern where **unless** we are looking after others in an expected role of carer, we suffer anxiety. There is the image of someone who faithfully and selflessly devotes all of his or her life to others, but ends up, either in retirement or after the death of the parent or relative, feeling lonely, unsure who they are or what to do, and fearful of feeling out of control.

This dilemma often originates from believing that our self-worth is defined by our needing to be needed. We may have received praise only when we looked after others; or have had no choice in developing a carer self. If we felt uncertain about making a career, we might have been relieved to settle for a role where we felt indispensable, and our worth reflected in everyday terms. It is gratifying to be needed; in being needed we often don't have to attend to our own needs, which may feel unmanageable. In communities where this 'service not self' is a shared practice there is more of a sense of balance, and a chance of everyone getting some of their needs met. But it is when our identities are caught up in believing we are nothing if not in the service of others that this dilemma can become a tyranny. We may even assume a 'holier than thou' pose, adopting a self-righteous and superior demeanour to save our inferior sense of self.

When we are looking after another and their needs, and have devoted much of our energy to this, we feel OK, and the reason for the dilemma is borne out. It is only when something happens (we are bereaved or told we are not needed any more), that we come face to face with our fears of coping with our *own* lives – in particular with our emotional and inner lives.

SALLY

Sally was the sort of person who could be guaranteed to look after everyone and their problems. She was a jolly, large, cheerful person, for whom nothing was ever too much trouble. She had four children, an unemployed husband, and worked as a nurse. In addition, she ran the Girl Guides and Sunday School, and looked after other people's children or pets when they went away. She filled every moment of her life with other people's needs.

During her forties Sally began to get irritated with people, to snap at them and then feel remorseful and guilty. She was depressed, and put everything down to the 'change', until one Saturday, when her husband and all the children were away and she wandered around a shopping centre wondering what to do with herself:

I sat down on one of the benches and looked at all the people milling around me. They all seemed to have somewhere to go, be doing something important. I saw my life as being one mad rush to get things done, and what for? I felt suddenly very frightened, horribly lonely, and I just started to cry, I couldn't stop.

This crisis brought Sally into counselling, where she needed to address her dilemma, be able to express some of her needs and understand that her irritation and bursts of anger towards others was not a 'madness' but the result of denying her own individual life and reality for so long.

Many people live with this dilemma in their relationships. Many women, particularly, have learned to be the carer, the one whose thinking is centred around another, who anticipates what husband, partner, family, group needs, and knows how to provide it. Many women receive an early training from their mothers in the role of serving and giving, and in how to respond to another's needs without ever thinking of their own (see Sheila, pp. 137–41). From this way of being we absorb a lot of good feeling and security, and find a useful place in the community. But if our responding to another's needs is not based on a solid sense of ourselves – who we are, what our needs are – our own desires will surface in some uncontrollable way, making us feel guilty and angry.

Over the years I have met several men who expressed their caring selves through being good providers and by making sure their partners never needed for anything materially. They tended to choose partners whom they secretly viewed as 'weak' and in need of looking after. Although this initially had the benefit of caring for the man's lonely 'inner female' self through its projection onto the partner, ultimately these relationships would become stuck. The female partner would become infantilised into being the weak, needy one who couldn't grow; the men remained in their loneliness, no nearer to claiming their neglected, lonely, young female selves.

Many people who have been busy carers admit that secretly they hope that if they give out enough, their own needs would be finally recognised, and the affection, attention and caring they had given would be returned in kind. But if giving out is based on a denial of need and the underlying message is 'I don't need anything', or, 'I don't matter', it is very hard to receive. If carers cannot bear to think of themselves as having needs then it's hard to reach them, and offers may be rebuffed. Some feel invaded and vulnerable if their own needs are discussed. Perhaps the ultimate fear for carers is that if they really show how they feel inside the outpouring would be unstoppable because the depth of feeling and need is so great.

Questionnaire: The 'busy carer or empty loner' dilemma

How much does the 'busy carer or empty loner' dilemma operate in your life?

How much of your daily energy is tied up with caring for others?

100%	75%	50%	25%	10%

How much of your caring for others is caught up in the 'having to please' trap?

100%	75%	50%	25%	10%

When people question your role as someone who gives out to others all the time, do you answer:

- ☐ 'I've no choice.'
- ☐ 'No one else would do it.'
- ☐ 'I can't let anyone down.'
- ☐ 'At least I'm doing something useful.'

Do you postpone your own enjoyment by saying 'I'll do this when ...'?

Can you list things you really want to do but daren't while you are in the role of carer?

Do you feel you have to do everything yourself all of the time and cannot ask for help?

Do you feel anxious and lonely if people aren't expecting you to do things?

Do you label wanting to do things for yourself as selfish? Do you want to be a selfless person?

Exercise

Begin to get to know your loneliness or emptiness. The next time you are about to fill a space by caring for others, pause for a moment and ask yourself what you feel. Does it remind you of anything? What does this feeling most need, and how might you offer this?

If you recognise that you are caught in this dilemma, and fear feeling out of control if your life and identity are not shaped by caring for others, spend some time thinking about how it came about. What is at stake now in terms of claiming the right to your own life? Your gifts for caring and giving will not go away. If you can start to free yourself to use your time creatively, your caring skills will be all the more nourished. You will be freer to give, and your giving will be enriched by choice. You will have a greater sense of appropriate boundaries and it's likely others will respect you more and demand less, because you are in firmer control of who you are and just how much you give out.

If we've given out but received little thanks or regard for it we might feel angry, or bitter. We might also feel depressed and wonder if it was all worth it. Some people may feel their lives have been wasted when they look back on years spent in the service of others at the expense of their own development.

Being centred, comfortable, knowing how to say 'no' without guilt, and having a quiet sense of selfhood, is freedom to give with a joy that is beyond price. If we allow ourselves to be dominated by this dilemma, we are tying ourselves to a life of slavery. There will be a build-up of underlying anger and resentment at the frittering away of our own precious life. Many murders are committed by wonderful carers who have suffered and been abused by their tyrannical charges, until the one time when they are pushed too far and boil over.

If as you are reading this you are getting in touch with your own anger, use it. Don't be afraid of it or consider it bad. Write down all the angry things you can think of; kick at the grass, throw sticks, logs or cushions, go into a tunnel and scream like Liza Minelli in *Cabaret*. Get it out. Find out what your anger is like before it turns in on you and swamps you with depression and self-destruction. (See Chapter 14, 'Techniques for working through the process of change, and how to hold on to change'.)

The 'bottled-up feelings or threatening relationship' dilemma

This dilemma is related to how we cope with our feelings and emotions. We either keep our feelings bottled up inside, or we risk hurting others and being rejected, disapproved of or humiliated if we express what we feel. For us the world of feelings is dangerous and unknown, full of frightening unstable volcanoes about to erupt. Unlike the cool, clear rational world of thinking and reasoning, the world of feelings can feel like a 'can of worms' and threaten our relationships with ourselves and others. Perhaps we were told to 'pull ourselves together' when we expressed something emotionally in early life. Maybe we saw others dominated by their emotions or making emotional scenes that convinced us never to get like that ourselves. Sometimes we are humiliated or laughed at for expressing our feelings, or made to feel weak, at the mercy of anyone with a command of words. So we learn to develop a rational response to life's demands because it feels safer, calmer and logical. We live in a society where words are the main currency. Feelings and emotions tend to come without words and are thus often misunderstood.

We usually bottle up our feelings because we haven't learned to express them, and we may be unaware of this because it's what we know. We may even presume we don't have feelings, but find ourselves weeping at something on the news or in a film, or find ourselves depressed and lonely for no 'good' reason. Many people who bottle up feelings store them in their bodies in backache, headache, chest pain, apprehension or anxiety. Although all these symptoms may well have other causes needing medical attention, sometimes they offer the only clue to a feeling life that has been denied expression.

PAUL

Paul, who was referred to when we looked at the social isolation trap in Chapter 4, would be overwhelmed by a surge of tears and sadness whenever he felt that someone was excluding him. His frustration came out in anger against others, which he was unable to express except by withdrawing into what others saw as a sulk. He experienced himself in a place where no one could reach him and all he had for comfort were the logic and facts of his encyclopaedias. He had learned no way to express his emotions, for in his early life there was no one to pick up the signals of what he was feeling or to interpret them. Thus, he had kept most of his feelings bottled up reasonably successfully for many years, through one marriage and its subsequent ending, and through the birth of his only child. It was when he really fell in love for the first time at forty that his bottled-up feelings welled up. His anxiety over making a 'mess' and suffering rejection of his new-found love overwhelmed him.

If you feel you recognise yourself in this dilemma, spend some time pondering over the next questionnaire. In Part 7 there are ideas to help you to anchor what you are feeling and learn how to cope with the feelings of others.

Questionnaire: The 'bottled-up feelings or threatening relationship' dilemma

In what ways are you aware that you bottle up your feelings?

- ☐ I keep everything inside, no one ever sees what I truly feel.
- ☐ When something emotional is going on I feel:

  - ☐ tense
  - ☐ afraid
  - ☐ hopeless

- ☐ Most of the time I am unaware of what I feel.
- ☐ I presume I don't feel anything.
- ☐ I experience physical symptoms:

  - ☐ stomach cramps
  - ☐ tightness in the chest
  - ☐ holding my breath a lot
  - ☐ 'lump in the throat'
  - ☐ difficulty swallowing
  - ☐ clenched jaw
  - ☐ grinding teeth
  - ☐ back pain
  - ☐ problems with eating, digestion, stomach

- ☐ I do express some feelings but not others. I find the following feelings very difficult:

  - ☐ anger
  - ☐ disappointment
  - ☐ sadness
  - ☐ envy
  - ☐ when hurt by others
  - ☐ when shown affection
  - ☐ love
  - ☐ jealousy
  - ☐ disapproval
  - ☐ embarrassment

(Continued)

(Continued)

If you don't bottle up your feelings what do you think will happen?

- ☐ I will get hurt by others who will take advantage of my weakness.
- ☐ It will come out all wrong and I will be embarrassed and want to disappear into a hole.
- ☐ I will be rejected. No one really wants to know what I feel.
- ☐ Everyone will see what a mess I am inside.
- ☐ My whole world will be totally out of control.
- ☐ Someone would get hurt. What I feel inside is out of control, intense, huge. If I really let out what I feel it would be unstoppable.
- ☐ People would laugh at me and try to put me down. They would call me names: wimp, cry-baby.
- ☐ Whatever I feel it always comes out as tears, and I can't stand it.
- ☐ Whatever I feel it always comes out as anger, and people don't understand.

On what sort of occasions are you aware of your feelings most strongly?

- ☐ When alone
- ☐ When with others
- ☐ After a row
- ☐ Days after something important has happened

Go to Part Six, 'Gathering Information', and ponder on how feelings were or weren't expressed in your early life, and with whom each feeling was associated. How were feelings discussed, and if not experienced within the family, how were feelings discussed in association with others outside? What kind of family sayings or myths did you grow up with?

The 'if I must ... then I won't' dilemma

Initially, this dilemma appears quite difficult to understand, but take a moment to examine the number of times when you have felt totally overcome by instructions or orders, or by 'having to'. They may come from inside you or from other people. Sometimes we feel so restricted by these requests and demands that the only freedom is not to do them. The feeling of restriction can be claustrophobic, and our only freedom is to not comply. This can operate in quite subtle ways: we may receive a letter which we ought to answer but don't, perhaps there is a telephone call we need to make and we keep putting it off. A more extreme and damaging example might be that we fail to turn up for an important job interview.

The seeds of this dilemma go back to restrictive former years, in family or school, where rules, regulations and obligations felt binding. We can feel so rule-bound that there is no room for self-expression. Our only self-expression is in saying 'no'. A graphic illustration of this dilemma comes in Russian author Ivan Goncharov's story of Oblomov, who lay in bed all the time because he couldn't bear any kind of obligations to get up and get dressed or go out. His dilemma consolidated itself to the point where he slowly dwindled away and died (a rather extreme form of this dilemma!).

Aspects of this dilemma operate in most of us because most of us have experienced restrictions during our early life. But when the dilemma is severe it becomes our default position and affects everything we do. It's not what we do but what we *don't do* that gives us a sense of control or power. But in time this backfires. Our inability to get anything done means that we are never able to develop a decent sense of self-worth or skill.

TERRY

In Chapter 4 in our discussion of the avoidance trap we looked at Terry's story and how the restrictions placed upon him in early life led him to avoid challenges to do with work. He felt restricted by the demands of others that he be both grateful for being cared for by people who were not his parents, and for his (later) inheritance. He felt he owed it to his grandmother, and the family who later on adopted him, to 'be good' and do well, but an overprotective environment meant that he hadn't developed the skills to deal with the challenges of outside life. These pressures resulted in him not doing anything.

When Terry came into money at age twenty-one, for which he was also unprepared, he took flight into heroin addiction. He could not cope with the demands the money made upon him, and he could not ask for help from those whom he presumed he had to please and be grateful to. He did not believe he was entitled to his powerful and mixed feelings of grief over losing both of his parents, and he felt disloyal for talking about them.

Since this time, several years ago, he has been courageous enough to get himself off heroin and to look at his life more fully. He has begun the painful process of grieving and mourning for his lost parents for the

(Continued)

(Continued)

first time, and is releasing himself from his restrictions in thinking about his life and what he was entitled to. As he began to have more choices about how to respond, and allowed himself freedom to take up choices about what to do, he has been able to release energy to put into tasks and training, has become professionally qualified and married. The energy that was tied up in the silent protest of 'if I must ... then I won't' has been well used.

If this dilemma is allowed to dominate it can take over and immobilise us, to the point illustrated by Terry's heroin addiction. If you find yourself saying 'I won't' when you feel obliged by someone or something, feel into what your own inner restrictions are. See how many ways you can find to respond to the perceived restrictions, other than saying 'no' or 'I won't'. You may find you need to be angry, to hit out, to be sad and grieve, to find a way of thinking about things that stimulate you and which you allow. You will need to go through the 'pain barrier' felt by restriction and to find yourself on the other side – your own freedom.

Questionnaire: The 'if I must ... then I won't' dilemma

How much does the 'if I must ... then I won't' dilemma operate in your life?

I respond to an obligation with 'I won't':

☐ all of the time
☐ some of the time
☐ in certain situations:

   ☐ at work, college, school
   ☐ with friends
   ☐ with family
   ☐ in relationships with men/women
   ☐ other

If I feel obliged, I feel:

☐ restricted
☐ caged
☐ controlled by others

This then makes me feel:

☐ threatened
☐ defiant

When I feel this way I want to:

☐ shut down
☐ run away

I see saying 'I will' as conforming to others' ways and ideas:

☐ all of the time
☐ most of the time
☐ in certain situations (name them)

Saying 'I won't' gives me freedom from restrictions imposed by others. I have put this to use by:

☐ creating my own life
☐ using my defiance to start something new

I am frustrated and feel I can only act 'against':

☐ I have been unable to create anything of my own.
☐ I feel the restrictions I feared from others have now turned against myself.

The 'if I must not ... then I will' dilemma

Take a moment to explore this dilemma, even if you don't relate to it immediately. Again, as in the 'if I must ... then I won't' dilemma, its concern is our response to pressures, whether they come from inside ourselves or are imposed by others, especially those connected to authority. It's as if the only proof of our existence is our resistance. In our protest, our fight against, we are struggling to be seen for our real selves. But all too often this dilemma results in harm to ourselves, and in punishment rather than acceptance. We begin to break rules – even our own rules begin to feel too restricting – and so our frustration and fury with life escalate. Sometimes our attitude becomes so entrenched that we feel we will lose face even more if we give in or change our pattern, so we carry on piling up negative responses to command, thus tempting fate.

Many of us will perhaps relate to this dilemma during adolescence, when we need to lock horns or try out our strength against those in authority. The 'cult' of protest is active, and usually appropriate, during this growing time. And many of us forge our sense of ourselves against such testing of authority, especially parents or leaders, for our views on religion, politics, social welfare, dress and addictive substances. We emerge stronger and wiser and go on to occupy those positions of authority we once had to kick against, developing rules or structures we once found so frustrating.

But this dilemma can become a way of life, piling up our anger and resentment without space to breathe or take stock. If it becomes entrenched, it may move us into circles of friends whose lives, behaviour and choices create a much greater force of 'must not'. Then the life itself can become like a brick wall which feels impossible to break down. Until properly revised and refreshingly challenged, this dilemma only serves to block our path and prevent us from having a life.

Sometimes we learn to resist as our *only* way of survival in a restricting environment, where our resistance ensures our actual body and soul survival. We learn to become guerrilla fighters in our own families or environment, living on our nerves, hiding, always prepared to be on the attack against the enemy. And while all communities need this fighting *for* aspect, to challenge authority when it becomes limiting and oppressive, we need to challenge when and if our fight *against* has become an unquestioned habit.

Many people do experience their lives as being oppressive in this way, as the hunted minority. But if and when the war is over, freedom is there to claim and celebrate. The skills and determination we have learned during our resistance will be needed for the creation of new rules and standards, where we are forging a life for ourselves rather than having to defend against an imposed position.

Questionnaire: The 'if I must not ... then I will' dilemma

In what areas of my life am I fighting the rule 'I must not ... '?

☐   at home
☐   at work, college, school
☐   in religious belief
☐   in my social life and sexual or moral conduct
☐   over money

Examine a rule you recognise as dominant: 'I must not ...'. Write it out. Experiment with different responses to it in your imagination.

How many times in a week do you say 'I will' in response to another's 'You will not'. Note the time, place, feeling, people or aspects involved. See how these tie in with the first question.

How much of your life is taken up living in a 'must not' cult? List the areas (friends, interests, etc.).

Does this serve your needs now?

Ask yourself what would happen if you examined your resistance more thoroughly? Try to communicate with your resistance now, and find out more about it. What are its qualities?

The 'satisfied, selfish and guilty or unsatisfied, angry and depressed' dilemma

This dilemma is to do with getting what we want. If we get what we want we find that any satisfaction is accompanied by feelings of selfishness and guilt. We feel like a spoiled child. At the other extreme, if we don't get what we want, we feel angry and depressed. This dilemma is related to our ability to receive something and possess it freely. At some point we have decided unconsciously that we are not allowed to have what we want. We may even have been told, 'Don't think you can get what you want,' or, 'You can't have your own way.' These kinds of statements, during childhood and at school, can be understood internally as 'if we get what we want there is a cost'. So we feel guilty, because we are not really entitled to it.

At the opposite pole, if we don't get what we want we feel angry and depressed and deprived. This can lead to a kind of spoiling mechanism. Because we feel guilty and childish when we get what we want, we don't allow ourselves anything – not even to receive from other people. But at the same time, we feel permanently angry and depressed precisely *because* we are refusing to receive anything, either from ourselves or from others.

Sometimes we get permission to get what we want only through being impaired in some way; we receive 'the privileges of the sick'. This might be through chronic symptoms or in minor repeated accidents where we need attention. This isn't to say that we make a conscious decision to become ill. It may be the only way we can receive something without feeling childish and guilty. But even when we have 'paid' the price, the dilemma dictates that deep down we feel we are not really allowed anything and guilt is just below the surface.

Identify as clearly as you can the areas in which you believe you should deny yourself satisfaction. Notice the feelings you experience when you go along with something that you actually don't want, but have not yet learned to say 'no' to. Note in your diary or notebook the times when this occurs and the feelings involved. Experiment with asking exactly for what you want as best you can and see what happens.

Questionnaire: The 'satisfied, selfish and guilty or unsatisfied, angry and depressed' dilemma

Do you feel that you get what you want:

☐   in relationships?
☐   with children?
☐   in working life?

If you feel you have never addressed this issue, take a few minutes to consider what you want in your life. Ponder on which areas in your life are satisfactory and which are not.

If you do get what you want, afterwards do you feel:

☐   selfish?
☐   guilty?
☐   greedy?
☐   triumphant?
☐   satisfied and happy?

Do you also feel:

☐   I will have to pay something back
☐   life or someone will get even with me sooner or later

What myths, sayings or 'old wives' tales' about being satisfied and getting what you want can you remember from your early life? Whose voice do you hear when you remember them?

If you don't get what you want, perhaps because of any of the above injunctions against it, do you feel:

☐ angry?
☐ sad?
☐ punished?
☐ envious of others who seem to get what they want?
☐ childish and want to cry?
☐ ill?

Do you recognise a pattern of illness after disappointment? Look to see if any of the above feelings could be hidden within the illness.

SIX   Snags and self-sabotage

'Yes, but ...' and 'if only'

Snags seem to operate when part of us is saying 'I'd really like things to be better, but ...' Or when we say, 'Oh well, I could never have a life like that,' or gaze very enviously at others and say, 'It's all very well for them.' We may also start to reminisce, 'If only I'd been allowed to do, be, have ...' Part of us has the desire to lead a fuller life, to have better relationships, to feel freer about ourselves, be more successful, to be more imaginative, but it's as if we have been found guilty and sentenced to a life of snag.

Part of us is saying 'if only ...' while the other part of us counters with 'but I couldn't ...' or 'I'm not allowed' or 'something bad would happen if I were to be happy'. It's as if we carry an eternal rebuke for being alive and well, as if we were responsible for bad things that happened early in our childhood. This is called 'magical guilt' for it is guilt for something we couldn't possibly have taken responsibility for or have reason to feel guilty about. It is formed unconsciously as an alternative to helplessness or overwhelming feeling, hence the word 'magical'. The 'magical guilt' we carry may be for things that happened in the past. It becomes fixed as if 'true' and seamlessly woven into our everyday repertoire without our questioning it. The things for which we have taken on magical guilt may be external, such as having a handicapped sister, or a depressed mother to whom we may, or may not, be able to express our frustration or be cross with. If not able, we turn our more aggressive feelings into ourselves, as if it is we who are responsible for the difficult, painful or lost lives of those in our early family.

As you read through this section, experiment with standing in your observer position as a third person in your inner exploration and dialogue. This is the mitigating 'judge' you didn't have when you were small, standing in for the new relationship you are trying to develop in yourself that does not blame or envy but understands the forces that formed you and forgives the past where they have become embedded.

Family myths

Sometimes this sense of 'yes, but' comes from powerful people in our early lives: 'She was always such a good child', 'He was such a clever boy', 'She was the one that kept the family together'. These can be very powerful myths and often prove difficult for us to challenge. We may be helpful and good and kind, but it may not be the sum total of who we are. We may also want to be fun, frivolous, exciting, naughty, cross and so on, but don't feel we can, or we will get punished if we try.

Another powerful injunction may come from the family myths themselves: 'People in our family never ... smoke cigarettes ... wear loud clothes ... shout a lot ... go into that kind of business ... marry outside their kind'. This means that hanging over us, imperceptibly (because we may not have realised it) is this idea that 'I'm not entitled to be anything other than what my family has made me'. Under this injunction we repress ways of expressing ourselves that don't fit in with what is expected. One woman said to me years ago that although she went through a very difficult patch in her marriage she never considered divorce, because no one in her family had ever been divorced. It was a completely alien concept.

Our attitude to work, friends, religion, health, ways of proceeding are governed by our early family and what the family accepts. Obviously all have an impact upon us. They may suit us well, but when we find that we are snagging ourselves as we've described above, we may need to look at our family's myths about us and what is 'expected'.

Families may also make judgements:

- People who think too much about themselves are self-indulgent.
- People who don't have a proper religion and don't go to church don't have moral fibre.
- Our race never goes with white/black/oriental people.
- Don't let anyone see you when you're down, they'll only take advantage.

Start making a list of the myths in your own family, from the smaller concerns like dress and appearance to the more major questions of politics, religion and relationships.

It may also be that the snags in our life develop because important people close to us actually do not want us to change. This may not be obvious, but remain hidden within a relationship. Ask yourself if the 'yes, but' in your life is related to what you anticipate from others. Sometimes we think that if we were to improve ourselves, become more successful, happier or healthier the people around us might not know how to deal with it. They may oppose it, because they feel unable to cope with what our changing means to them.

An example of this might be when one person in a relationship begins to enjoy success, while the other – parent, husband or wife, for example – becomes ill or depressed. It's as if they can only thrive when the other person isn't feeling so good. Thus, we may have become unconsciously caught up in the life patterns of another. Our reciprocal roles may be *merging/special* in relation to *merged/safe*, and to separate them feels threatening and betraying. What maintains the relationship is interdependency, where one partner thrives because, and at the expense, of the other. It is as if there would not be enough 'wellness' or 'goodness' to go around for both people.

You may not be consciously aware of snags because they operate unconsciously. Having read this section and completed the questionnaire, allow the concept of being snagged to be part of your thoughts, so that if you are actually snagged you can become aware of it. Be aware of how often you think or say 'yes, but'.

Questionnaire: Snags

I recognise that I snag myself by saying 'Yes, but' or 'if only':

☐ every day
☐ in certain situations (name them)
☐ in certain relationships (name them)

I always feel that others are:

☐ luckier
☐ more successful
☐ happier
☐ more attractive
☐ better than I am

Name any past obstacles you feel have caused a snag and prevented you from being successful or happy:

☐   if it weren't for ... I would be ... now
☐   my parents never let me ...
☐   I never had the chance to ...
☐   if only I'd been allowed to ... I would be ... now
☐   other

Look at these snags honestly and ask yourself: have I contributed to making these events worse:

☐   by resentment, bitterness, anger, laziness?
☐   by using them as excuses for not taking up opportunities?
☐   by letting anger and resentment get in the way of trying for what I would really like?

How much do family myths about how to be and what is allowed live on and influence your choices, forming a snag? (For example: 'There's never been a divorce in our family'; 'We never wash our dirty linen in public' (i.e. talk about our feelings to others); 'No one from this family has ever gone on the stage'.)

Do snags operate because you believe that if you make your own free choice of how to be someone important to you won't like it, or an important family value will be challenged? (For example: 'If I am assertive my marriage won't survive'; 'If I leave the job I hate and train to be a teacher my wife won't cope'.)

Self-sabotage

Other evidence of a snag operating is when we seem to arrange to avoid pleasure or success. Or, if we are successful and happy, we have to pay, either by depression or illness or our ability to spoil things. When success is within our grasp, we find we are not able to claim it. We may have achieved high marks in an exam, we may have got that important interview, we may have lost the weight we wanted, but we don't allow ourselves to fully have it – we miss the appointment, we immediately put the weight back on, we mess up the next paper of the exam – thus actually wiping out the good.

'Magical guilt'

Guilt becomes 'magical' because it is guilt for something we could not possibly be guilty for and magical guilt can have a very powerful underlying effect on our lives. As we saw earlier, it arises because in our families we felt more privileged than one of our siblings, or even one of our parents. We might be cleverer than them, or healthier. Magical guilt can also occur when a member of the family is ill or depressed or if someone dies when we are young. We may feel that this has something to do with us and it's our fault.

This is not a conscious thought, but a powerful undermining and unconscious process that can catch us like the undertow in an apparently smooth river. We then develop the unconscious, mistaken belief that 'I am strong at the expense of my brother or sister or my aunt, my grandmother, my mother or my father's weakness'; 'I am healthy at the expense of their illness'; 'I am well and fit and happy at the expense of their bad feelings and depression'; 'I am not entitled to my good fortune or my good luck'; 'My talent is at the expense of their misery'; 'If I am successful something bad will happen'.

Because we want to be attached to those early figures who are important to us, it's actually very difficult to manage all this when we are young. We unconsciously take on the burden of guilt, and live feeling (magically) guilty for our successes or happiness. Our only way to cope is to deny ourselves in some way, to deprive ourselves of our success – we may reach the point of claiming a lovely friendship, a good career, or a marvellous travelling experience, and we suddenly spoil it at the last minute. We either miss the boat, or we get ill or depressed or we do something quite extraordinary which prevents us taking it up. In doing so we are remaining within what has become a 'comfort zone' of avoidance and guilt. Shining the spotlight on these unconsciously maintained patterns takes time, and practice.

Envy

It's hard to acknowledge feelings of envy or that others may envy us. Envious attacks feel threatening and disorientating. But envy is a natural part of life and there is room for awareness of feelings of both healthy envy as well as malignant envy that wants to destroy.

A snag may operate in our consciousness because we've experienced envy from one of our siblings or a parent for our perceived good fortune, good looks, strength, sense of fun, freedom, abilities and skills. This may not be obvious and few of us are comfortable about actually acknowledging this. If you cast your mind back you may recall comments like 'I don't expect you to be able to do things like that', or 'A great girl like you! I would have thought you'd do a better job', or 'Trust you to do the most difficult thing there is', or 'I suppose with your skills you can have anything you want'. Such remarks are said in a slightly hurt, slightly belligerent way by people whose favours we want to keep. We then begin a process of learning to hide the skills and gifts we have, of jeopardising them rather than risking the wrath and envy of those people whose love we crave.

It can be quite upsetting when we eventually realise how much we are snagging ourselves in our lives and acting as if we aren't allowed to take up our gifts and skills. It can be quite painful to think that this comes from being actively envied in our early lives. We can only free ourselves from this pattern by making conscious all the instances and all the realisations, and seeing them clearly. We can then actually stop the pattern of self-negation and snagging.

Sometimes this is a hard task, because if we have taken on the idea that we were not entitled to what is in fact ours, it's quite difficult to start to claim to have something. When we do begin to claim our lives for ourselves we wake the previously unconscious fear we will be rejected or punished. We will *feel* the heaviness of guilt and the conviction that something really bad will happen. And some of those old voices that made us feel bad about our gifts will come back from the past: 'You're completely selfish', or 'You're a ruthless man', or 'No one wants somebody like that', or 'You give no time to other people' – all the kinds of accusations that originated from envy and jealousy that was not named.

DIANA

Diana suffered a breakdown after several gruelling years working as a singing teacher, a job she didn't really enjoy. She had been trained as a classical singer and taken part in major concerts, but, despite having a fine voice and being encouraged to take major solo parts she never felt able to accept them. She had to leave her operatic work when she lost her voice completely. During her recovery she started to write about her early life, where it was her grandfather who encouraged her to learn music. When she was permitted, she would sit and listen to classical music and go to concerts with him. But these visits were rationed and once back at home it was as if her musical life did not exist. Her mother and her older sister resented the space taken by the piano complained about the noise of her playing. They accused her of wanting to be special and showing off. Her father was absent a lot of the time so she had

(Continued)

(Continued)

no support. Over time she believed that if she did 'indulge' her passion for music she was 'nothing but' a show off and she could not bear the hostility this provoked nor the guilt she carried. Although she managed to study music and singing she had never allowed her real potential, to find her own voice. Her breakdown and subsequent revision of old patterns allowed her to realise the impact of her magical guilt at the family's envy for her gifts, and to begin to sing.

Questionnaire: Self-sabotage

Make a list now of the times and ways in which you feel you sabotage yourself.

I fear the response of others if I:

☐ do well
☐ look good
☐ win anything

I fear most the response from … (name the person or persons)

Because of my fear of others' envy through their (a) disapproval, (b) withdrawal, (c) sharp words, (d) criticism, (e) saying, 'It's all very well for you …', I play down what I know and what I can do:

☐ all the time
☐ in certain situations (name them)

I feel I'm not entitled to:

☐ success
☐ nice things
☐ happiness
☐ love
☐ freedom
☐ a good job

I feel that if I get things, others will be worse off and suffer. (Who will? Where does this feeling come from?)

If something good happens for me I feel:

☐ it's just luck
☐ I don't deserve it
☐ it won't last
☐ I could never create it for myself
☐ I could never keep it going

Once the way you are snagging or sabotaging yourself is clearer to you, you can see how important it is to free yourself from these old patterns. They are magical injunctions: *It's not true* that we are responsible for the depressed, miserable, negative, unhappy lives of those who have gone before us; and *it's not true* that we don't care. *We can care and feel compassion and also live our own life!*

It is possible to claim one's gifts without feeling guilty for them. As we embark on this journey we can only become wiser, more fulfilled and more comfortable in what we are doing, and able to summon up the energy needed. We also become able to inhabit a space where we can look back on what's happened, and particularly on how we've been caught up in these magical guilt processes of the past. We can free ourselves and other people from being involved in them. And of course we are facing these magical guilts from a different place, because we are that much older and the defences with which we had to protect ourselves from the harsh words or the harsh judgements of those around us are much less.

Realising how much we have snagged our lives or stopped ourselves being happy may be rather a depressing task at first. It's important to remember, however, that the way we coped was not stupid or bad, but the only way we were able to manage difficult feelings. But having recognised how this way of coping lives on and gets in the way, it's vital to understand that we don't have to keep on doing it.

By no longer 'snagging' we learn control, and this also changes the way other people behave towards us. We learn to stand up to those who, because of their own difficulties, do not want us to change. Sometimes others do resist the changes that we want for ourselves, particularly those who are closest to us. They might say things like 'You're not as you were', or 'All this psychotherapy is making you too inward', or 'I don't like what it's doing to you', or 'I think it's dangerous'. It's important not to underestimate them. Something quite important happens when we stand up consistently for who we are, and this can transform our relationships with others. If we're firm about our right to change, those who care for us will usually accept it. If they cannot accept, however, then we often do have to make a painful choice. Once we have faced the ghost, the ghost is never so frightening again.

Having completed this section, name those people in your life who wish you well. Begin to allow yourself an equal freedom and to allow yourself to claim your own life freely.

PART FOUR

The Tip of the Emotional Iceberg

Unbearable feelings, depression and symptoms

The painful distortions we sometimes have to make to survive, the areas of neurosis, of feeling stuck, are not viewed as a wound to be removed by finding a 'cure' but rather as a gateway into the psyche's attempt to heal itself. The particular qualities or symptoms are simultaneously symbols for what is required for healing ... listening to someone who has found meaning and come to peace with terrible suffering is usually sufficient evidence of how out of pain may come something priceless.

Nigel Wellings, 'The Wound In Transpersonal
Psychotherapy, Theory and Practice'
(Wilde McCormick and Wellings, 2000: 76)

SEVEN Unbearable and unmanageable feelings

Threaded inside the steps of our dance of reciprocal roles is core emotional pain, often hidden by our learned coping procedures. For example, within the dance of harsh critical judging in relation to criticised and judged will be core feelings such as crushed, hurt or bad. But we may never have named them as such. All we know is that this is how our life has always been – we might feel angry, hurt, misunderstood; we might feel just bad, or, we don't feel at all. Many of us long to be free to be ourselves, but don't know that this is what our longing is for. Finding a language for, and caring for our core pain is an important part of addressing our missing emotional experience. Within our dances of relationship, and in support of our hidden suffering, we become the kind, supportive, nourishing parent we didn't have. It is never too late. This missing experience can be discovered, named, supported and nourished.

Here are some examples of difficult feelings. See which of them resonates with you.

'Always feeling bad inside'

Our learned dances of relating incorporate implicit values about others and ourselves. Often we are not aware of how bad we feel inside. It might be that we experience others and life as bad, as against us, and things go wrong for us. Feeling bad inside might be a general description of core pain within the dance of critical, rejecting, judging in relation to criticised, bad and sad. Sometimes a way out is to reverse the roles so that the weight and hurt of it lessens.

Feeling bad inside might influence the relationships we make. We might feel we can only make relationships with people whom we consider worse than us. We don't like ourselves enough or feel free enough to know what we like, or to have relationships or friendships with people who are attractive or successful. The result of all this is that we feel depressed. It might be a general thin veil of depression and worthlessness, or, in more severe cases, deeper depression within which we feel trapped. We somehow manage to carry on, automatically doing things we feel we must do, but never really experiencing pleasure or happiness.

We may try to become 'bad' because, why not? People already think we are, so why not live up to it?

You may want to add to this list, naming for yourself what you recognise are your attempts to cope with feeling bad inside.

Sometimes in our early lives we are actually told we are bad and that 'nobody loves a bad girl or a bad boy'. We may pick up messages we interpret to be about our badness. Perhaps we don't come up to the standard required of us. We might enjoy doing things that the rest of the family doesn't, so we're labelled odd or difficult, selfish and therefore 'bad'. Feeling bad might be related to difficult feelings in our early life in relation to what happens to us. We might have experienced mental or physical cruelty or neglect. All people who have suffered physical or sexual abuse as children feel bad inside, they presume or are told that the abuse is their fault, and they carry this terrible feeling of badness deep inside. Sometimes this belief leads to destructive behaviours. We are made to feel even worse if we do start to express our feelings of frustration and hit out. When there is nowhere for bad feelings to go, we endure or bury them; sometimes they are projected onto other people and situations.

Feeing bad can stay inside festering, like a boil, for years. Although logically we may know we are not bad, we may feel in our core there is something wrong with us, something unpleasant and difficult. It isn't until something happens or we start thinking about ourselves that we realise we have believed that we are bad.

Exercise: 'Always feeling bad inside'

If you recognise that you feel like this, just spend a few moments quietly reflecting. See if you can get some sort of graphic image for 'badness'. Start with the phrase 'It is like ...' and let your imagination offer you a picture, colour, shape or image. It doesn't matter what comes to you, just

stay with whatever emerges. Examples could be 'heavy black mud'; 'squirmy tummy'; 'rotten apple'. When you feel you have a sense of it, make a graphic picture (drawing, collage) of what you have been carrying around.
Can you recognise any of the following?

- ☐ Heavy weight in my body, unexplained symptoms
- ☐ Feeling sick
- ☐ Depressed mood
- ☐ Always think the worst about myself
- ☐ Sometimes I believe I am evil
- ☐ I tend to move with a 'bad' crowd
- ☐ I feel that I am, and always was, unwanted
- ☐ If something good comes my way I only spoil it
- ☐ Because I never do anything good I must be bad
- ☐ I don't deserve goodness

Note any recognitions in your monitoring notebook. Try to notice, kindly, when and where these thoughts come in your everyday life. Monitor this process for a week to give you a pattern of what situations trigger feeling bad.

However many ways of feeling bad you identify, allow yourself to feel sad at this burden of badness, for it is sad when an innocent child – usually where this mistaken idea began – believes they are bad.

Next, start experimenting with a new idea, that actually, fundamentally *you are not bad; that, actually, YOU could learn to accept yourself JUST AS YOU ARE*. Challenge the critical, nagging voices from the past, whatever you have judged as 'bad' and whatever 'bad' behaviour you have felt caught up in. The habit of always thinking that you are bad might be spoiling your chances of proving to yourself it's not true. *It's a very old message and belongs to the past*. Try to find someone to talk to about it. Sharing the 'I am bad' idea is helpful, because the hurt and pain of the old belief are maintained by the internalised dance of *critical harsh judge* in relation to *bad and guilty*. Get some help to start a new relational dance of *listening* in relation to being *listened to* and use it to start listening to yourself differently. Look at the things about yourself that are not 'bad', however small. Reading this indicates that part of you is searching for change. Believe in that, that you have it in you to embrace something different from the old message 'I am bad'.

If you have done things you now regret, whatever the reason at the time, what about asking for forgiveness and forgiving yourself?

Not having feelings

We live in a culture where there is a growing emphasis on the imme-
diacy of publicising feelings and emotion. Whilst this can support
connection with others, it doesn't always honour the very personal,
tender and helpful nature of feeling that needs time to be heard,
respected and understood. Also, our feeling function may be intro-
verted rather than extraverted, which means that we feel things very
deeply inside but that's where feelings stay. Conversely, people with
extraverted feeling have no problem expressing and emoting.
Understanding this difference is very important in relationships!

When you are asked about what you feel, what happens? Do you
find yourself shrugging, believing you feel 'nothing'; or notice yourself
looking up, saying, 'I think ...' and struggling for words? This may be
because you have not been able to develop a language for feeling.

Sometimes we need to ask someone to write a list of 'feeling'
words for us to experiment with. Words like sad, anxious, lonely,
hurt, glad, open, happy. Another way is to start noticing what happens in your body when you are asked how you feel. If your answer
is 'I feel nothing', see if you can trace what happens in your body
when you repeat those words.

The use of images is also helpful, in support of our bodies leading
the way to help us find words. Descriptive words such as 'tight' or
'tingly' or 'cramped' or 'stuck' can be a good start to exploring more
about what you are feeling. Some people presume that they do not
have feelings, because their feelings are bottled up, unnamed. When
feelings have been shut away, unexpressed, we can appear cold. We
appear unaffected by the most devastating news as if we are dancing
to reciprocal roles of *cut off/controlling* in relation to *controlled/unfeel-
ing*. Can you recognise feeling *distancing* in relation to *distanced*, or
overwhelming in relation to *overwhelmed* leading to cutting off?

Feelings may start to emerge when something touches us really
deeply, or when we become more confident about having them and
are less under pressure from our contemptuous or dismissing inner
dance. Our fear of feelings, defended by denial or avoidance, may
wait for a 'safe' environment such as a long-term relationship, a
trusting therapy or a satisfactory job of work.

- We only get to know the range of our feeling and emotional life
  in a safe environment, where there is trust and respect. This
  needs to be built over time. We may have physical symptoms
  instead of feelings, as if our constrictions, our inflammations,
  were expressing our unbearable pain.
- We may try to contain our feelings by choosing a profession that
  will force us to operate only in our heads, using reason and logic.

- We may act out instead of expressing feeling, by driving fast, drinking too much, taking drugs, taking up dangerous sports and activities, gambling, fighting, stealing.
- When feelings are unbearable and unmanageable we may go numb and our rage, anger, jealousy or happiness is experienced outside of us, in other people, objects or as fantasy. This means that we cannot own them as our own and we cannot integrate them into ourselves as a whole.

If you recognise any of the above, just begin noticing anything that could be a displacement activity away from expressing feelings you presumed you did not have, but fear.

Exercise

If you recognise that you are suffering from not having feelings, ask yourself when was the last time that you 'felt' something inside? Where did you feel it in your body? What was that feeling? When did it occur? What was happening at that time?

If your answer to the last question was a long time ago (more than two years), what happened then? Did you express what you felt? How did others respond? Did something happen to make you decide you would not express feeling again?

If feelings have been damaged and battered, or if no satisfactory release for them is found, they may get split off into different states and so our sense of ourselves is fragmented. In Part Five we discuss this in more detail.

Exercise: Making feelings safe

Talk to someone about not having feelings. Begin to explore what feelings are and how other people express them. Become a 'student' of feelings.

Feeling WILL arise in its own time. TAKE TIME.

Focusing

Focusing can be an excellent practice for beginning to be with our core emotional pain; to be present with a direct experience of our emotions. This technique was developed by Eugene Gendlin (1996) (a student of Carl Rogers) and has a close connection with the energy generated by the practice of mindfulness. In its simplest form, focusing offers us a way of staying with a body sensation, a feeling or a word in a particular way that allows us to explore it without judging it or trying to change it in any way. In *Nothing to Lose*, Nigel Wellings describes it in the following way:

> focusing can be done in a moment and brings our awareness close to our experience. Right now I am feeling a tightness in my throat which is best named with a sort of growling word. If I stay with it I find that it reveals a more hidden panicky emotion which then slowly fades away. Thus with only a minute spent on the technique I have gained two things: knowledge of what was really bothering me and an experience of allowing myself to experience it directly and witness it passing away. (Wellings and Wilde McCormick, 2005: 178)

The following are steps that can be used for focusing, either on your own or in co-counselling:

1. **Clearing a space**. We ask: How are you/am I right now? This often evokes something of the 'story'. Concentrate upon what is underneath this by mentally scanning the body, particularly torso, chest, solar plexus, to see if a felt sense comes forward. If there is more than one, just stay with the one that demands more attention.
2. **Felt sense**. It's alright if the felt sense isn't clear. Just stay with it being diffuse and fuzzy. Go right up to it, but not so close as to become it.
3. **Handle**. Next we try to find the quality of this diffuse sense. Allow a word, phrase or image to emerge from the fuzzy felt sense. A word that describes the quality, such as sticky, tight, growling, shrinking, full. Stay with the felt sense as long as it takes for the word to emerge. (This is different from conceptually finding a word and labelling.)
4. **Resonating**. Then hold the word, phrase or image against the felt sense to check that they really resonate with each other. Changes may occur during this process. Continue carefully until there is a fit. An indication of this may be a small sigh or a feeling of 'yes'. Give it time, feeling it completely, the physical felt sense and its expression.
5. **Asking**. Sometimes the release of energy as we consciously connect with what is really going on in us gives us a deeper understanding of our situation. We can also try asking 'What

does this felt sense need?' It is important that the answer comes from the felt sense itself and not the rational mind. Give lots of time. A real felt shift comes when the answer emerges from the felt sense and there is a sense of physical satisfaction and connection.

6. **Receiving.** Acknowledge the process that has just been experienced or shared, however large or small. Be still at this point so that true receiving has time to take place.

7. **Returning.** Give time to return to everyday consciousness. In co-counselling check that your colleague is ready to do so.

Choose music and poetry, film or descriptive writing to express feelings. Can you feel for/with some characters? Music and poetry bypass the left side of the brain, which is our more rational, thinking brain, and touch directly into the right brain, the more feeling, intuitive, imaginative side. Allow yourself to be touched; and to move with, dance to, hold tenderly a tiny bud of feeling; to fire up in a blaze of anger or passion; to hear the sound of your own protesting voice and your own lost poetic soul. In *Finding What You Didn't Lose*, John Fox (1995) writes: 'when your poems become the "container" of your truest feelings, you will begin to experience and integrate those feelings more consciously'.

The void

Sometimes people describe having a 'black hole' or void inside them. Like the Little Prince's rose imprisoned in a bell jar. David Bowie's call: 'Anyone out there?' feels like a cry from the isolation of the void. It's a feared place – of being swallowed up, or ceasing to exist. It's the ultimate loneliness. Emotional life is on hold, waiting to be invited in. The dance of *'not there'* in relation to *not acknowledging* is powerful, as if 'denying the right to exist'. Because the nothingness of the void is so feared, ways of managing are to fill it with dreams, with people, food, drugs, work or social activity – anything external. We tend not to trust ourselves inside, and avoid anything reflective, or still. It's as if we are only defined or identified by our work, or our looks, or our role in someone's life, sometimes as a scapegoat or victim, like Julia Roberts in the film *Sleeping with the Enemy*.

ALISTAIR

Alistair, once he was brave enough to explore his experience of the 'void', had an image of a 'can of worms' containing everything he feared and loathed about his past and about some of his current feelings. (In Chapters 11 and 13 on writing our life story and working on our diagram, we will see how Alistair is currently working to cope with his particular void.) In exploring his 'can of worms' we met snakes who would come up and bite him in the form of an *accusing/judging* in relation to *judged/worthless* reciprocal role, and statements such as 'You'll never stay in the fast lane'. The feeling 'I'm unhappy' was strong and was suppressed as quickly as possible. Alistair first realised his particular 'void' when one day he caught himself thinking, as he rushed from one appointment to another, 'I wonder if taking drugs would help?' He believed that if he allowed himself to stop, he would fall into the vacuum and emptiness which he associated with the void. All his life he had coped with this feeling by being incredibly busy. We met when his body had begun throwing up symptoms – duodenal ulcer, anal fistula, chest pain – and he had become phobic about illness and death. One of his first tasks was to allow himself half an hour each day for reflection. He found this very hard indeed!

Sometimes the void can be explored through visualisation, through drawing. Often life itself plunges us into the void, and we have to face it the hard way – through a serious illness, accident, breakdown, or being left alone and isolated.

Questionnaire: How do you recognise a void?

- ☐ I feel as if I live behind glass. I see other people doing things, but I don't belong.
- ☐ I keep very busy with friends, relationships, work, eating, drinking, duties, etc., because I know that if I stopped, I would fall in the void.
- ☐ Inside I feel very lonely. Few people, if any, know this.

Just recognising a void is a first conversational step. We can get to sense we are either nearing or fearing the void. It's useful to find an image for it, like Alistair's 'can of worms'; or telling someone you trust about it. If the void has been created because when you were little you were mostly on your own, it may be that it is very hard for you to get close or trust anyone. We can befriend our sense of void, and find ways to soften its hard edges. Psychotherapy gives us the opportunity for a living relationship with another human being with whom we can develop trust. It is worth considering.

Unexpressed anger and rage

Unresolved and buried anger very often lies beneath depression, it is the underlying cause of most panic attacks, it is now a recognised risk factor in the psychosocial causes of heart disease and can also initiate many physical responses represented in stress-related disorders.

It can be hard to acknowledge that we have buried angry feelings. Fresh anger is usually a very physical experience, and like all feeling and emotion, involves our bodies. If you recognise after reading this section that you are carrying layers of unresolved anger and rage, just start noticing possible signs of anger, however small. It may be in clenching your jaw or a tightening in the small of the back; your anger may be in forced laughter, in speeded-up speech, in cold ruthless prose. You may hold your breath like Amanda (who we will meet in Chapter 8) or literally swallow your anger with food or alcohol. When you looked at traps, dilemmas and snags in Part Three you may have found out more about your own anger.

When it first becomes conscious, previously unexpressed anger can feel out of proportion and we will have the same fears we had when we buried it – that others close to us will hate or reject us; that we will be like the angry person in our life we feared; that our anger might take us over. This is quite usual. After becoming conscious of anger and how it has been buried under symptoms, we need to find a way of containing or expressing what we feel. One way is to write it out in our journal. Another way is to find a safe space to shout and jump up and down. The return from anger is to find ways to express it that are useful, freeing and creative, not destructive or harmful. And, most importantly, what is our anger about? What are the particular relational dances that draw our fire? What we really need – to feel protected, understood, accepted unconditionally – is often hidden under anger. Learning to find a voice to ask for these things is essential, once we have discovered what our anger is about.

A very high percentage of depressed and somatic symptoms are connected to the inability to express anger in a useful way. Understanding this, and finding ways to make conscious, name, express, contain or simply be with, previously unmanageable anger makes a difference. Some shadow of these feelings may always be with us, but we can learn to know and understand the shadows better and be able to use feeling more usefully. In her poem 'Anger's Freeing Power', Stevie Smith (1983) writes that it is the useful and enabling expression of anger rather than love, that frees her raven from beating himself inside the walls of his self-built cage. Also on this theme, the original Brothers Grimm fairy story about the Frog Prince had the princess throwing the frog she despised against the wall in a fit of rage, upon which he was transformed into a prince. Years later rage is replaced by the kiss, missing the point that sometimes the expression of love needs to be freed by allowing anger.

Many years ago I worked with heart patients as a counsellor in the cardiac department at Charing Cross Hospital with a consultant cardiologist whose work was to understand the link between unmanageable feeling and its somatisation in coronary heart disease. He was challenging to the patients he was trying to help, as in 'Did you not love your wife enough to be angry with her?' Giving permission for anger to be part of love and the expression of it as useful, was part of recovery from chest pain and its associated disease process.

We need to know our own anger and be able to express it and to contain it appropriately. Owning anger and learning to walk the talk of anger means that we have tempered the fiery dragons that once threatened us. Learning the limits of expressing anger and how to contain our anger and its more unreasonable or destructive side is essential.

Lying beneath anger is often hurt. And grief. If we have a fiery temperament, it's easier to rise up in anger and protest than it is to acknowledge we've been hurt or lost something important to us. We may fuel feelings of anger or resentment toward those who have hurt us, because the vulnerability of acknowledging hurt is too scary. When we are able to reach beneath the smouldering or hardened anger and touch the hurt, we have the chance to befriend and heal, using compassion and mindfulness. Pema Chodron, the American Buddhist nun, says, 'If someone shoots an arrow into your heart it's no good just railing at them. You need to attend to the fact that you have an arrow in your heart as well' (on retreat at Shambhala Mountain Centre, August 2002). Being able to grieve and mourn what has been lost or damaged, and forgive both others and oneself when appropriate, is an essential part of the process of change. The combination of being able to be usefully angry toward those who abuse power and finding skilful means can be the fuel needed for political action and much needed change.

Sometimes anger and assertion are confused and lead to miscommunication and misunderstanding. Assertion is simply asserting clearly something we feel or think, and if needed, with repetition, in relation to another who has perhaps not been listening. We do not need to become angry to do this, in fact, if we give in to angry feelings we have lost our skill at assertion. In this we might learn from the birds, who define their territory by singing on the boundary. When we can recognise that we have been caught in a reciprocal role of *overlooking/dismissing* in relation to *dismissed or despised* we can take our own feelings and responses seriously and we can find the words to say what we need. This is beautifully illustrated by Kayleigh in the next chapter. We need to acknowledge and learn the language of our own feeling and emotional need, and start expressing it in inner dialogue with ourselves, and then with others.

EIGHT How unmanageable feelings and beliefs become symptoms

We have seen in Chapter 7 how our feelings, embedded within the dance of relating such as *harsh/over-critical/judging/neglectful/abusive* in relation to *hurt, put down or crushed victim* may have remained unexpressed and unheard. Sometimes unmanageable inner feelings manifest in both psychological and physical form. This might range from feeling 'down' and in 'low mood' or having 'no energy' to becoming the unheard companions to many physical symptoms such as nausea, heaviness in the legs, headaches, tension in the neck and shoulders. It's as if our bodies are trying to speak for us; our symptoms are the voice of pain, and the symbolic language of symptoms are our body's poetic communicator – the broken heart; the stiff neck; the breathless lungs; the 'bag of nerves' of an exhausted nervous system; the wound that will not heal. Old beliefs such as: 'It's not OK to have needs' may have become embedded in our posture, our breathing patterns, the way we walk, or sit. Unmanageable anxiety, anger, fear and sadness may also be at the root of many eating disorders, in bingeing and starving; in self-harm; and in many presenting physical problems that are not organic in cause. Finding out what lies behind and then listening creatively may release some of the burden carried by the body.

Some provocative risk-taking behaviours, such as driving, drinking, smoking, dope-taking, flying, too fast, too much, too high, may also be a way of trying to manage unmanageable or unbearable feelings. There may be times when we spend too much money, or money we don't have, and buy things we don't need under the illusion that this will make us feel better.

Finding a way to survive and manage what feels so painful is vital and human beings are very creative. We may use food, drugs – prescribed or not – substances or different behaviours that give us temporary relief but do not deal with what we are feeling bad about, or help to make us feel less a victim, become more in control or complete inside. Our emotional dialogue may be waiting to be released.

KAYLEIGH

Kayleigh suffered from many difficult physical symptoms and from ME. She has generously written something of her journey for this edition and shared her artwork.

I was born on 8 December 1990, the fourth and last child for my mum, a very caring woman with a soft heart. I was also the youngest of ten cousins. My early childhood was very enjoyable. I had a lot of love coming my way. It wasn't until later that I started to notice the cracks in our family.

My dad was very hard working; he kept a nice roof over our heads but to him this was the beginning and end of his parental duties. When I was about seven I noticed that my older brothers did everything they could to avoid being in our house but then I did not comprehend why.

At ten I was very confident, but as soon as I went into secondary school I turned into a very anxious, self-conscious girl, who suffered terribly with intimidation. I was so shy I would hardly talk. When I was thirteen I started having trouble with some of my friends who had turned into my bullies. This situation caused me to suffer with depression, depression so bad that I had two years off school; I spent the whole time in bed. My mum and my doctor were extremely concerned but no one else in my family believed I was ill. They don't talk about their feelings so they expected me to be the same. They would make horrible comments and ignore me, making me feel worse. When you're suffering with severe depression, you feel the world is against you, you really need your family's support.

(Continued)

(Continued)

When I was sixteen I slowly started to climb out of the black hole of depression. I decided to get into work as I didn't want to go to college; I didn't want to be around anybody my own age as I didn't trust them. Unfortunately when I went to work I started to suffer really badly with anxiety and depression again. I was basically on a knife-edge 24/7, which was no good for my health but I felt I had no choice; I could not take time off so struggled through each day. Everyone in my family works no matter how ill or bad they feel and they expected me to do the same. The mental torture I got from being called a skiver was a lot worse than the physical pain I was in, so I carried on working.

A few weeks before my eighteenth birthday I had a week off work because of a throat virus, and after this I got irritable bowel syndrome, extreme fatigue, tiredness and a general feeling of being unwell. I had test after test but nothing came back and the doctor's conclusion was that there was nothing wrong with me. I felt that no one believed me, even the doctor, so I kept working until I couldn't take it any more, I felt pushed into a corner. Then I tried to commit suicide. It's sad, but after my failed suicide attempt some people started to believe me and I was referred for further tests to try to find out why I felt so ill.

A year later I was diagnosed with ME. The professor suggested a special kind of therapy to help with my depression, anxiety, tiredness and stress. I welcomed this as I knew I wasted a lot of time worrying. I knew that my childhood affected me in a lot in ways I didn't understand.

I found it quite slow at the beginning of CAT but after a few weeks I started discovering things that astonished me. I had no idea how much my family and their ways affected me. Because I'd lived with them for so long I almost accepted that this was the way that everybody lived.

My struggle with self-confidence originated with my dad. He had had a tough upbringing and suffered with low self-esteem, so the way he made himself feel better was to pick on us so we felt worse than him.

It wasn't until I had CAT that I started to realise that this was not normal. It was not OK for them to treat me the way they did.

Goals of CAT

When I realised that my family put me down to make themselves feel better I decided to work on not letting them put me down any more. My way of dealing with nasty comments was to laugh them off or put myself down. I didn't want to cause a fight with my reply I just wanted to stand up for myself, so I worked hard and found some reply that would do this. I first needed to realise there was nothing wrong with me. Being prepared helped me a lot. I would prepare myself for the comments in advance. It was hard to begin with but with each comment and reply it got a little easier.

One day my sister-in-law made a comment and my response came before I had the chance to think about what to say back. Afterwards I realised what a huge accomplishment this was, my prepared and quick reaction was my first example of how well I was doing with the CAT exits. What also happened after I answered my family back was that those who had put me down started chucking compliments my way and this just made me see how weak they were.

Another thing I struggle with is perfectionism. Mum told me that when I was younger if I went just a tiny bit over the line in colouring I would screw up the picture and start again. (I must not have finished any pictures.) After talking about this I realised that being a child who never got any attention or praise from my dad I would work extra hard to try and get some. I never did get any praise but what this situation left me with was trying to be perfect in everything. **It even affects my ME. I was advised to pace myself and walk a few yards a day, slowly increasing until I can walk a fair distance. But I would either walk really far and wear myself out so I wouldn't be able to do any more for the rest of the week, or I would do none. When I got to the point where I should stop for the day I would feel so disappointed, judging myself as pathetic that I could only walk this far. On the days where I felt exhausted and thought about walking the recommended distance I would think I'd rather sit here and do nothing than walk and feel like a failure.** [emphasis added]

I started to find ways to challenge this bad habit. My therapist suggested doing some visual work, so I made a poster [see Figure 8.1]. The poster is about two different extremes: fanatical exercise or too lazy; too hot or too cold. The poster helped me re-educate myself on how to think about extremes. Life is about finding a healthy balance: I discovered a saying which is 'froth at the top, dregs at the bottom but the middle is excellent'. I use this quote when I either find myself being too much of a perfectionist or when I'm being a lazy bum. It really helps; it reminds me of all the things I learnt during CAT.

CAT has seriously changed my life. I discovered the things that were buried deep inside me from childhood. I really did rediscover

(Continued)

(Continued)

the innocent child inside and learned how to reconnect with her. I realised that I still had the right to be that child. We are all born free with a clean slate, it's the people around us that make that clean slate dirty and make us feel like we have chains around us. My course of CAT has removed those chains and I now feel ready to achieve my wildest dreams.

(A complete case study for Kayleigh appears on the companion website to this book.)

Figure 8.1   Kayleigh's poster

Exercise: Symptom and symbol

If you would like to know more about the language of your symptoms try the following:

Spend a few moments concentrating first on the feel of your feet on the floor.

If it feels comfortable allow the rhythm of in-breath and out-breath to settle and imagine that these two movements are forming an invisible circle inside you.

Now turn your attention to the symptoms you have in your body.
If possible, place your hand where you experience pain, discomfort or physical symptoms. Notice:

☐ [Language] Does it – burn, stick, ache, pulse, throb, vibrate, linger, stab?
☐ What colour or shape does it have?
☐ Do you have an image for it?
☐ Does it remind you of anything?
☐ If it could speak, what would it say?
☐ What does this image/sensation most need?

If an image arises, such as cool water for a hot skin, or oil for a rigid joint, then allow your imagination to play and experiment with bringing this helpful image into the painful area. Whenever you feel pain or symptoms, notice them kindly and accept them and then place whatever emerges from this exercise right next to what you are experiencing, holding the image or new words in your awareness.

Depression

Depression is an umbrella term for a whole range of difficult and unmanageable feelings that have been turned inwards. In Part Three we saw the 'trap' created by depressed thinking and that recognition of the circular nature of the trap and the creation of 'exits' helps to focus upon and bring about change. When depressed thinking and feeling start to merge into the more blanket term 'depression' it is harder to get to the root of the internal patterns underneath. *But it is vital to do so and not to waste time.* Antidepressant treatment is needed for some cases of severe and disabling depression that has biological components such as are described below, alongside learning about the underlying psychological patterns. It is very sad that depression and drug treatment for depression are so widespread in Western nations. Very few people need long-term medication. People who have periods of depression and also periods of being high ('manic depression' or bi-polar disorder) need carefully managed medication, but can also benefit from psychotherapy focusing on underlying beliefs and self-management.

In *Mindfulness Based Cognitive Therapy for Depression*, authors Segal, Williams and Teasdale (2002) write:

Depression is rarely observed on its own, it includes anxiety, and panic attacks are 19 times greater than someone without depression. Simple phobia and obsessive compulsive disorders have increased odds. Depressed patients spend statistically more time in bed than patients with lung disease. Work loss is five percent greater than non depressed patients. Suicide risk increases with each new episode. Major depression tends to be recurrent and the biological characteristics are: sleep disturbance often with early morning waking, gloomy desperate ruminate thinking in the mornings and a constant overactive neuroendocrine system creating the arousal associated with cortisol. These experiences are not varied with life circumstances such as taking a holiday or getting married. (2002: 10)

I like to imagine a rainbow-shaped graph called 'the arc of depression' for the different experiences of depression, with 'grey melancholy' at one end and 'dark abyss' at the other.

Grey melancholy is a term for when we feel persistently sad. It's the term I use for those long grey stretches of time that can follow bereavement and illness, and which accompanies transitions.

Part of the human condition is to feel 'down', sad, blue, low in spirits, melancholic in response to disappointments, loss, difficulty and to the awfulness of world events. In our melancholy we have time to be with ourselves. Melancholy can be seen as a necessary time of slowing down to aid recovery and gives an opportunity for healing. For artists, poets and writers, the melancholic state is often a necessary place within which to create. The half light dims the glare of everyday demand. (Wilde McCormick, 2002: 131–8)

The blanket term 'depression' can feel overwhelming, and add to our sense of hopelessness. But in between grey melancholy and dark abyss is our own unique experience. It's important to find our own language, context and description, and our experience varies, it is not always fixed. And any experience of depression is not just about not coping! It helps first to look at where we are on the rainbow graph and to find a context.

1. Depression may be grey melancholy, a natural response to a life event – the needed twilight following bereavement, illness or loss; the wasteland experience of rites of passage during adolescence, mid-life, retirement where change in identity is taking place.
2. Depression may be directly connected to a life situation – poor housing, chronic poor health, family disruption, no money, racial discrimination, violence.
3. Depression may be a response to unconscious self-sabotage – a safer internal choice to whatever is feared from success or happiness or from the consequences of expressing anger and rage.

4. Depression may result from a long period of exhaustion – too much, or too little work or contact with others and no way out or to say no.
5. Depression is a form of breakdown – the breakdown of the way we have been before and seen as 'normal'.

Maintaining our depressed response may be restricting, and self-limiting reciprocal roles such as *disallowing/envious* in relation to *magical guilt; punishing* in relation to *punished; critical judging* in relation to *crushed restricted*. There is often the dance of demanding bully and helpless unseen victim, both within ourselves and with others. The core feeling held in the internalised dance is often a *punished, flattened, crushed* and *restricted self*, and repressed disallowed rage. This is maintained by the tight hold of the *punishing, belittling*, or *judging internalised 'other'*. Other people will also be invited to join this dance until revision and new reciprocal roles are learned.

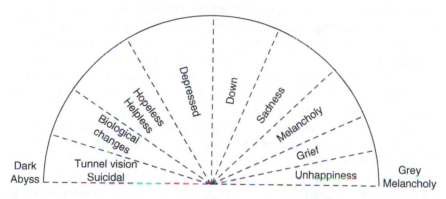

Figure 8.2   The 'arc' of depression

Questionnaire: Recognising depression

Answering 'yes' to more than three of the following may help you to recognise a depressed response.

I feel and believe that:

☐   my needs will never be met
☐   there is something wrong with me
☐   I'm worthless, useless

(Continued)

(Continued)

☐   there seems no point in anything
☐   I feel miserable but I cannot cry

Metaphors can help us clarify our experiences. The following metaphors are often used in relation to the experience of depression. Do you experience yourself as being:

☐   in a cage?
☐   in a prison?
☐   stranded on a high cliff?
☐   stuck in the desert?
☐   doomed and drowning?

When depressed, our feelings often include confusion, heavy-heartedness, sinking sick feeling, feelings of exclusion, a fear of our own and others' anger and rage, the feeling of being trapped with something alien, inscrutable and intransigent that does not want to budge. And often deep, deep sadness and loneliness. Depression is also very physical: heavy body, legs at times unable to move, head tight and fuzzy, sick in the stomach.

Treatment for depression will be varied. Finding our own way, with help, is vital. The practice of mindfulness has been found to be valuable in patients with more than two episodes of depression. The CAT diagram creates an accurate description of problematic reciprocal roles and repeated procedures that maintain a depressed response.

AMANDA

Amanda has kindly written the following account especially for this book to illustrate her experience of depression. She has had a long history of depression, which has included hospital treatment as an in- and out-patient, and also CAT and learning the practice of mindfulness. Her diagram is included in her account (see Figure 8.3).

Depression arrived suddenly and without warning. I was assured by doctors that once the right dose of antidepressant was reached I would soon be fine again. Unfortunately it didn't work like that and I was referred for psychotherapy.

At first I was unable to focus on what the therapist was saying or asking. I had continued to work full-time and I was exhausted. Over many months we looked at the snags, dilemmas and traps that I was falling into. I wasn't quick to grasp their significance. The diagrams and cycles of thinking centred largely on my anxiety about most things, but in particular about my work and with my inability to deal appropriately with my own and anyone else's anger. It also took me a long time to realise that I needed to understand the processes involved. I could understand it in theory but much harder in practice, finding it difficult to 'exit' at an early stage in the process. We also explored visualisation and, for me, the image of a lifebelt, which I could recall in times of need, was enormously effective. Much later, after a third stay in hospital and a long course of ECT, which improved my energy levels but not enough else, I returned to therapy. The lifebelt was still there for me but all too often I still felt desperately low. Suicide was frequently considered and I had started to try to self-harm even though I knew that the exit points of the main diagram were to talk to someone, to be kinder to myself, being 'good enough' and not constantly striving to 'get it all right'. But this felt all too elusive. Now, in addition to the CAT was the introduction to the practice of mindfulness.

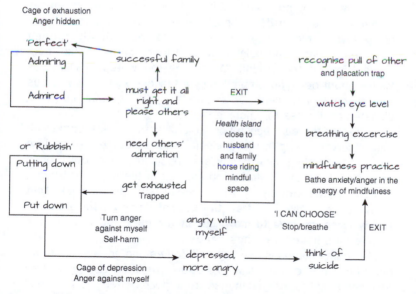

Figure 8.3   Amanda's diagram

(Continued)

(Continued)

On the very first session with Liz, she pointed out that I was holding my breath before I spoke. I had been going to yoga classes with different instructors and all would say, as we attempted a posture, to 'keep breathing'. Breathing appeared to be more difficult than I had thought!

Practice of mindful breathing became a daily part of my life. It was difficult at first to let go of thoughts that constantly entered my head, something that in yoga I had yet to fathom. To my surprise, just by saying to myself 'there's thinking' or acknowledging whatever was happening in the background, letting go of it was much easier. Even if my mind wandered for a while it was OK and returning to the breath was even a matter of congratulations.

Sobbing uncontrollably has been part of the practice too. Each experience of practice is different but that is all part of it. Sometimes the mind wanders a lot or it is particularly difficult to settle but it really doesn't matter. That is where its beauty lies, especially for me, whose mind tends to be on full alert to what is going on all around. I can use the breathing to give me mental space and to break the negative process from the diagram that I now know so well and recognise my difficulties for what they are.

Last week I walked into the town centre and started to feel very heavy in my body and mind. I decided to sit in the Abbey gardens and take in the calm of the beautiful park. There were only a few people about so it was easy to find somewhere to sit and breathe. At some point I realised there was a broken beer bottle lying on the ground. William Styron writes in *Darkness Visible* about being accompanied by a 'second self' who watches 'with dispassionate curiosity' as one 'struggles against oncoming disaster, or decides to embrace it'.

Sitting on the park bench I could look at the broken bottle with this observer, taking in with curiosity what I intended to do. Like taking pills, cutting my wrists was a considered idea. But I found myself thinking about what I had learned in therapy, that I had a **choice. It was entirely up to me as to what to do next. That choice in fact gave me strength to resist doing anything except slowly force my legs to move out of the park and back to the respite care hostel**. [emphasis added]

My depression hasn't gone yet. It comes and goes as it always did. I hope that one day it will go away completely as innocuously as it came, but for now I can manage it much better. I can still feel desperate. I am lucky to have many loving friends and family. Talking to someone can do much to calm me, but then I have the thought that is so welcome; that I can give myself a few minutes of the space and peace that mindful breathing can invoke, however I feel and wherever I am.

If we have had to bury feeling because it has felt unmanageable, when we begin to touch it again it hurts, and we can feel just as we did when we were small, just as frightened and helpless.

Take it slowly, knowing that you can now call on practical help to accept and process what you feel. This is to be not so much concerned with story, as with the emotional pain you feel and the ways you have learned to manage. See the pain as evidence that your flesh and blood feeling nature is still alive and needs your help with containment and nourishment. Allow it to emerge, flow and flourish, to find words for feelings. Trust it to show you what it most needs.

Depression in elderly and other carers

The Psychotherapy for Older Adults Service (PTOA), based in Newham's Mental Health Care for Older People team, is made up of clinical psychologists with expertise in both dementia and psychotherapy, and provides psychotherapeutic interventions to carers. CAT, having been developed within the NHS as a time-limited model of psychotherapy with an explicit focus on problems in relationships within the social context, helps to make sense of how the caring role can trigger unhelpful coping patterns in the carer, which can be linked to early experiences as well as the wider social and cultural environment patterns that do not work well.

Sheila's story has generously been offered by Dr Michelle Hamill and with Sheila's permission.

SHEILA

Sheila was in her seventies and described herself as a 'typical East End working-class woman' who put her family first. She had many physical health problems but had decided to care for her husband at home rather than place him in residential care, against the recommendation of social services. Consequently she had been labelled as 'difficult' by some members of the team, who attributed her depression solely to the practical burden of caring for her husband and which could be 'sorted out' by placing him in long-term care. Some of her children agreed that their father should move into residential care while others agreed with Sheila's wishes for him to remain at home.

Sheila was experiencing a range of painful emotions – grieving for the man her husband had been as well as for the man he had not been,

(Continued)

(Continued)

exhaustion and frustration of caring and immense guilt for sometimes wishing he would die and free them both from pain. She blamed herself for not being able to take better care of him due to her own poor health. As the condition progressed he became more suspicious, restless, agitated and confused, no longer recognizing her, leaving her distraught.

Sheila had grown up as the youngest child of a very large family and sometimes felt invisible. Her mother was a caring and dedicated woman who worked hard to provide for her children. She described her father as a 'horrible husband', a drinker who had numerous affairs but her mother stuck with him. Sheila described her own husband as 'an aggressive, controlling and possessive man' whom she felt sorry for as he had experienced a very abusive and neglectful upbringing. Sheila married him in spite of her mother's concerns. There was a sense of history repeating itself, with both women experiencing neglectful and turbulent marriages to unreliable men but bound by sense of duty to stay and care for them for the sake of their children regardless of their own suffering. Despite the difficulties, she reported loving her husband for the children they had together.

Sheila reflected that she had been 'depressed all my married life'. She had never opened up about herself to anyone.

The letter drafted to her (CAT reformulation given at session 4) read:

Growing up in a large family you learnt to keep your feelings to yourself. You also described hating having to rely on others for fear that they will take over. You seem to have taken after your mother, putting other's needs ahead of your own, deriving your self-esteem from caring. You explained that you have 'never been one to look after yourself' as well as expecting little from men as husbands or fathers. So although you may feel in control, your own needs and wishes get neglected. Now you feel as if you are 'in prison', trapped by your own body, your husband's deteriorating health, your house, family and professionals, everyone telling you what to do and taking over your life. It seems that your dilemma is that either you are independent, in control but ultimately neglected (always put others' needs ahead of your own), or dependent, controlled and helpless (others making decisions for you but it may not be what you want), either way your needs go unmet. It is as though you are the young child again struggling to be heard, invisible and lacking control ... My hope for you in this therapy is to create a space for you, about you, where you feel heard and work towards you finding a balance between others doing for you and looking after your own needs as well as exploring these feelings of loss, which surround you at present.

Sheila's diagram helped her in her day-to-day life and to make links with her early experiences (see Figure 8.4).

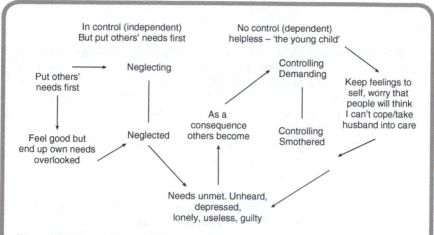

Figure 8.4   Sheila's CAT diagram

It was the manifestations of these patterns within the therapeutic relationship that formed the focus of the work. In the initial stages it was unclear whether Sheila would allow herself to trust and rely on the therapist due to her fear of being taken over and controlled, as well as the risk of opening herself up to another loss when therapy finished. In the second session her therapist reflected that her being there for herself might be difficult when she was so used to being there for others and ignoring her own needs. Her eyes welled up and she said that she had never let anyone see her cry and 'did not want to be thought of as soft'.

The therapist told her that she thought she was brave for having taken a chance in displaying her emotions and accepting this time to reflect with genuine sadness on her feelings of grief. Sheila was also able to voice her worry that the therapist might also try to take over or persuade her to place her husband in care. Her diagram helped her to make sense of this in relation to her worry of being controlled and her subsequent neglect of self. When Sheila developed an infection on her leg she reported that her leg 'just won't stop weeping' and required frequent changes of bandages. The therapist suggested an emotional meaning and that her leg was symbolic of how she was feeling; that perhaps she was worried that if she thought about her situation too much, then she may not stop crying either. Sheila thought for a while before saying that she was scared of breaking down, just like her body appeared to be doing. In allowing the therapist to attend to her feelings of grief and fear she could develop an internal resource to self-soothe. A few weeks later she said that she had cried during the week and was surprised when she experienced some relief afterwards.

(Continued)

(Continued)

Sheila was able then to explore alternative possible coping strategies, 'exits', that she began to internalize and implement, attending to her own needs and receiving support from others as well as speaking up more for herself. Her response to using these alternative strategies was touching. She expressed surprise at how she was beginning to feel less overlooked and more in control in addition to attending to her feelings of loss. This healthy dependency on others enabled her to feel stronger in contrast to her fears of being taken over.

In her goodbye letter to mark the end of therapy Sheila wrote:

I did not think that I could tell a stranger so much about myself. I think I will find it much easier to talk to my daughters now. Believe me, I think I have already started to look at myself in another light.

The therapist's goodbye letter to Sheila read:

I hope that our relationship has shown you that another kind of relationship is possible – where endings can be managed differently and feelings expressed and thought about. I hope that you can continue to find a balance between others doing for you and looking after your own needs as well as acknowledging and facing your ongoing feelings of loss. It seems that whatever decisions you make regarding your husband's care, there will be painful and difficult consequences. I hope that you can continue to allow yourself to experience the range of feelings that arise as things change.

As she completed therapy Sheila had improved in recognizing her patterns of feeling controlled and self-neglecting, and was beginning to practise new ways of relating. She was being firmer with voicing her opinions to both her family and health care professionals and was learning the importance of using the time when her husband was in respite, to which she had newly agreed, in order to recuperate, catch up on her sleep and better attend to her own emotional and physical needs without feeling so guilty. Although she continued to report fluctuations in her mood, her appetite and sleeping had improved. These gains were maintained at her 3-month follow-up.

Sheila's daughter contacted the therapist a year later to say that her father had moved into residential care a couple of months before and that Sheila's health had deteriorated considerably. The first thing Sheila said on her return to the therapist was that she had lost her 'voice' again and how much at a loss she felt since her husband had moved. Reflected back to her was the fact that, in requesting her daughter to call the therapist she had found a way to attend to her own needs in asking for help and that, in no longer having her husband at home, she was all the more confronted with her own increasing health needs and sense of dependency on others. Sheila said she worried that he was not being well looked after and how painful it was accepting that she could no longer care for him. The therapist wondered if she was also worried about who would care for her as her needs increased. She said that she wanted to die at home and that she needed to talk to her daughter about this. She agreed to six fortnightly booster sessions to go back over some of the themes from her therapy and create some space and containment around these feelings.

Sheila once again engaged in this process. Her extended family began to visit more frequently and, at the time of the second goodbye, she spoke of finding joy in spending more time with her grandchildren and holding in mind both her feelings of loss in addition to a sense of pride in having raised her family as she had done.

Sheila's husband died in late 2009. Sheila's daughter got in touch a few months later to say that her mother had died peacefully at home with her family around her, and expressed her appreciation for the CAT involvement over the previous couple of years.

[A complete case study for Sheila appears on the companion website to this book.]

I am grateful for permission to publish excerpts from 'The long goodbye: Cognitive Analytic Therapy with carers of people with dementia' by Michelle Hamill and Kate Mahony. The full article appears in the *British Journal of Psychotherapy*, August 2011.

Eating disorders

Eating disorders represent an abnormal preoccupation with food and weight, where food is no longer a simple substance for sustenance and pleasure. Underneath the symptoms of eating disorders are usually preoccupations with issues of control, submission, placation and perfectionism. This preoccupation becomes a means of communicating unmanageable feelings and emotions. It can be seen, as Anthony Ryle and Ian Kerr report in *Introducing Cognitive Analytic Therapy* (2002), as a covert way of communicating or coping with feelings of not being heard or being pressurised to 'perform'.

In eating disorders we split food into 'good' and 'bad' food, with which we have a love/hate relationship. 'Bad' food we binge on may accentuate the badness and ugliness we feel inside and have to get rid of in order to feel clean; the control of food to the point of starvation gives the anorexic a 'high' and can become addictive.

Too often groups or websites for eating disorders concentrate upon the management of food without attending to the underlying reciprocal roles such as *controlling* (neediness and mess, as in unmanageable feeling) in relation to *controlled/withholding*, and *conditionally excessive/ rigid controlling* in relation to *empty controlled/worthless and angry*.

Finding the meaning behind a preoccupation with food is essential for the process of change. And the process of change may be slow, for eating disorders are the end result of many years of struggling with unbearable feelings and emotions, or feelings that have been dismissed or disallowed.

Claire Tanner, a CAT supervisor and therapist with a wealth of experience in working with eating disorders, writes:

> Patients with eating disorders are so often caught up with their problems around food and body image that they find it difficult to step aside from the symptoms and understand the meaning behind them. Many eating disorder services focus on weight gain in anorexia and on the diminishing of symptoms, which is of course helpful. But for patients to really recover they need to understand how old beliefs about themselves and emotions play an important part, particularly when they have become unbearable or been disallowed. In my 20 years' experience, at both The Bethlem and Maudsley Hospitals Eating Disorders Services, I have found that when patients can reclaim their disallowed feelings and begin finding skills to express themselves other than through food, avoidance of food, bulimic rituals or any other eating disorder symptoms, their recovery begins to take place. These changes involve relating to themselves and others differently, and finding continuing acceptance and nourishment in manageable ways. I encourage all mental health professionals and patients to use the relational focussed CAT structure, in therapy, and as outlined in this book.

FREDA

Freda came into therapy because of her depression. Her eating problem only emerged later, as she had been ashamed of it. Also she had failed to see it as a 'problem', even though she always ate a limited diet alone, and took laxatives that were seriously affecting her digestion. We made the following chart of the presenting problem, its underlying procedure and the aim for the therapeutic work. You will see that the aim is always directed at the procedure, not the problem. This approach gets us away from only recognising symptoms and being caught on the symptom hook.

Problem 1: Depression
Procedure: I don't think much of myself and get into the 'I'm worthless' trap. There doesn't seem much in life for me, because others' needs have always been more pressing.

Aim:	Every day to monitor negative and depressed thoughts. To allow times for music, countryside and my friend Molly that put me in touch with my 'healthy island'.
Problem 2:	Placation trap, 'doing what others want'; needing to be needed
Procedure:	People can easily tyrannise me, and I tyrannise myself by giving in and judging myself harshly.
Aim:	To be aware of the times when I placate or create tyrants. Recognition of *feeding off* in relation to *fed off*. To risk saying 'no' or having a different view. To trust what I feel I want to do or say.
Problem 3:	Eating compulsively, then starving and bingeing
Procedure:	Recognition of *tyrannising* in relation to *tyrannised*. I long to be 'full' but feel bad if I have anything, so I have to get rid of it.
Aim:	To monitor feelings prior to, during and after eating compulsions and binges. To recognise where in my body I feel 'longing to be full' and offer kindness.
Problem 4:	Guilt
Procedure:	Self-sabotage due to irrational guilt about dead brother and mother's depressed life.
Aim:	To let go of the family's disappointment and misery. To say, 'I am allowed to have a life' without feeling guilty.

Freda took up her journal-keeping enthusiastically. She said it was like having 'permission to live, even if only inside a notebook'. After a few weeks her depression began to lift. As she challenged her placating, her eating problems got worse. She noticed a craving for food and an intensity of feelings of 'high' followed quickly by heaviness and despair where she sought food for comfort. She found that she could express herself in images, finding visualisation and drawing helpful, and a colourful language emerged, linking early life memories with her current need to starve herself in order to experience control. During one particularly moving session she expressed previously hidden feelings related to the death of her brother when he was six days old. There was an image of her mother's flat stomach, and the intensity of her weeping (which she showed only to Freda). The four-year-old Freda felt caught by the despair in her mother's eyes, believing that she had to make it better. She saw that she had taken magical responsibility for trying to fill the space left by the dead baby.

Freda described how she felt 'eaten up' by her mother's needs and demands, which returned later when her sister developed anorexia and Freda was once again expected to fill an empty space. One of her drawings showed a huge open mouth into which tiny fish were being shovelled by a thin witch with a child's broken-handled spade. In one of

(Continued)

(Continued)

her dreams her right hand was being bitten by a wolf. She drew a picture of the wolf, and came to associate this animal with her own emotional hunger and need, her 'wolfishness' that tyrannised her. The wolf would nip her, reminding her of her own hunger (for something which she needed to name) and of the devouring and tyrannising quality of her mother's neediness, from which she was struggling to free herself. This needing to be needed, or *feeding off* in relation to *fed off* was also recognised in several other relationships – husband, sister, children, family.

Freda was encouraged by her friends' new respect for her holding her own ground. Two key phrases – 'selling myself short' and 'I am allowed' – helped her to have the courage to express herself fully with other people, especially difficult people like her mother, to whom she felt duty-bound.

Exercise: Mindfulness of feeling

When you decide to practise with feelings, just take a minute and experiment with the following.

Soften: Mindfulness of feeling requires us to soften into it. This will sound strange because, after all, we've spent most of our life trying to get away from feeling, which is how our learned procedures develop! When you have named the core feeling that has until now felt unbearable or been disallowed, just take the word or description for that feeling – hurt, afraid, sad, crushed – and sit with it. See if you can locate the feeling in your body. Place your hand there if possible. Keep breathing. If you can, take the in-breath into that feeling, allowing it to soften.

Accept: Now offer to that feeling acceptance, just as it is. You might like to say 'Hello, my fear. I know that you are there.'

Befriend: Offer this feeling kindness and friendliness. Try 'I am here for you. I will take care of you. I will love you.'

You will find that it's hard to stay for long on difficult feeling. Choose an anchor such as the in-breath and out-breath, or, if the breath has difficult associations, an image or object that offers a steadying energy, and alternate your mindful awareness between the two points. Each time you return to place your kind attention on the difficult feeling you will get to know more about it. You will be giving it the attention it has waited for and the nourishment it needs. Remember that you are not doing, but being with. There is nothing to prove and nowhere to go.

Exercise: Mindfulness of eating

Next time you are thinking about food, or about avoiding food, sit down and place your hand on your diaphragm. Breathe in and out allowing the diaphragm to rise and fall. See if you can get a sense of where your hunger is. Is it in your belly? Your mouth? Your heart? Is it nowhere at all?

Stay breathing in and out of any responses to the above. Note any sensations, feelings, words, images. Some might be from long ago.

Write down any responses in your notebook.

When you want to eat, choose a raisin. Have a look at the raisin, notice its colour and shape, its smell, the way it feels in your hand. Think of where it has come from and how many people have been involved in the work of getting it to you.

Place it slowly in your mouth and note what happens. There will be the slow sensation of saliva arising and different taste sensations. Try to go as slowly as you possibly can, noting any sensations, thoughts or feelings you have. There may be memories or images from the past. There will probably be strong feelings.

Anytime you feel overwhelmed, return to breathing in and breathing out.

You will note that these exercises aren't designed to achieve anything or 'go' anywhere. They offer a way of safely and kindly helping you to touch those places that have been locked away leaving you with emotional discomfort and fear. This tender process is best shared with another person if possible, someone who can stand in for the missing voice in your emotional dialogue with acceptance and kindness.

PART FIVE

The Emotional Roller-Coaster

Mindful self compassion means holding difficult emotions – fear, anger, sadness, shame and self doubt – and ourselves – in loving awareness, leading to greater ease and well being in our daily lives.

Christopher Germer, www.mindfulselfcompassion.org

NINE   The challenge of shifting states

Whilst we all notice shifts in mood, sometimes the way we feel about ourselves can be very unstable, such as switching from one state of mind to a completely different one, often without knowing why. Until this is pointed out to us we may not know it is happening, especially if some of the states are accompanied by intense feelings. We also may not know how we got into an intense state.

We saw in the earlier chapters that if we have internalised harsh relationship dances such as neglecting/abusing in relation to deprived/abused our patterns of inner and outer relating will reflect this. If we have suffered emotionally unmanageable experiences when we were small, as a result of neglectful or punitive early care, we learn to shut down emotionally in order to protect ourselves. Our core, and chronically endured emotional pain comes under an umbrella term of unmet emotional need. Our survival mechanisms in the absence of care are extremely creative and useful, and operate through our capacity to switch off from painful emotion, often through dissociation. There are two forms of dissociation: one form is experienced as going blank/detached and unreal; the other is called structural dissociation, or fragmentation. Here it's as if we were built out of lots of different but separate pieces, described in CAT as **unstable states**. The shifts between the states are often abrupt and confusing to us and to others. They may appear unprovoked but usually follow perceived repetitions of threats of abuse or abandonment or the failure to get the desired response from the other person. Stressful situations and remembering past abuses can also provoke state switches. But the different states are not static, they are animated by the different ways we have learned to survive, our learned procedures.

Without dissociation we would not survive. When we stop to map our learned coping procedures we are able to name the emotional states more clearly. Then we are able to find new, equally creative ways to support ourselves and be with emotion differently.

Some people describe switching from one state into another as being on an emotional roller-coaster. If you imagine the tramlines of a series of separate roller-coasters in a park, it's as if we swing up or down one tramline and then find ourselves right on the other side of the park on a different tramline, with no idea how we got there. All we know is that we end up feeling either confused or overwhelmed or intensely upset with things going wrong around us.

All of us have differing senses and experiences of ourselves in different situations. If our movement between the different parts of us is fluid – we notice when our mood or sense of self has changed and can reflect on what brought this about; if we are able to allow our different self states to rise and fall, we retain flexibility and choice. With normal maturation, the integration and modulation of states is established, but this process is vulnerable to trauma. Most of us, however mature, when subjected to extreme stress and exhaustion or traumatised by an event, can experience intense and split-off emotional states. But if we have experienced the traumatisation of neglect, violence, abandonment early in life our self-organising and self-stabilising mechanisms are not established. We live more closely to our animal defence reactions to severe threat: fight/flight or freeze. We feel as if we are always living on a series of mini roller-coasters. This may be illustrated in our outside life by lots of unconnected movements – many different jobs and relationships, never staying in one place for long or completing anything. Inside we may have volatile mood swings – extremes of idealised longing or reckless abandon and utter despair and self-harm. Each of the different states of mind is a knot of relationship, governed by a usually harsh reciprocal role internalised from early life such as *powerfully neglecting, absent and unpredictable* in relation to *feeling powerless, fragmented and neglected*. If it becomes too frightening for us to make relationships with other people, our search for safe attachments may be with objects such as cars or clothes, substances such as food or drugs or alcohol, and activities such as work, sport or sex. Or with animals, groups or causes that give us a sense of containment and meaning without risk.

Because we have not been able to internalise a sense of continual self – the 'me' that sees all the 'me's – our sense of ourselves remains fragmented, and our longing for real care is idealised. Whenever we try to seek connection and therefore risk intimacy, or of being safely close or loved by another, we tend to raise hope and expectation to impossible levels – as if this person, object or substance will save or transcend all our suffering.

Of course, no one person or substance can do this and so we are continually plunged into feeling neglected, abandoned, abused, and the violence we have internalised will be directed both at 'other' and toward ourselves. Impossible idealised hope is raised only to be dashed over and over again.

When we are on an emotional roller-coaster our different states of mind are accompanied by intense, extreme and uncontrollable feelings such as feeling intensely guilty or angry with oneself or being unreasonably angry or hurtful to others. In some states we may feel intensely angry towards ourselves, wanting to hurt ourselves, and sometimes this intensity can be projected out toward others, wanting to harm them. We may sometimes find that we feel blank or unreal, feeling muddled and confused. Sometimes the only way to cope with confusing feelings or 'forbidden' anger is to blank off and feel emotionally distant. Quite often there are headaches or other physical symptoms. There is little space to develop a 'healthy island' from which to reflect on our predicament, and our potential for connecting with the life of a healthy self will be in eclipse.

Writing in *Reformulation*, Steve Potter (2004) says: 'I think of states as little knots of relational intelligence waiting to be loosened. Some clients will describe them in terms of behaviour; others in terms of predominant feeling, others in terms of the role played for self and others.' The CAT model offers a clear way to name and describe our different states and their procedures, and for fostering a self-observing mindful self that can see all.

If you find yourself identifying with the description of different state switches, our first shared task is to notice them. That is all we do at first. Then we will find creative ways to describe them. Then we will make a map of them. In this simple process we are already opening a potential space for creating a witnessing 'other' inside us. This is the beginning of a new and helpful reciprocal role that could be described first as developing the 'I' that sees if not all, then most of, 'me', however many 'me's there are. This step alone can have a stabilising effect on the more extreme states. Over time, as the healthy island grows a little more, this 'I' can develop observational skills, and a further step is to become *helpfully witnessing and caring* in relation to *being seen and cared for*. This new self state we will be building over the next few pages has our general co-ordination at heart and is a way that helps all parts live together as consciously as possible.

To help this process, below is a list of descriptions of states (originally formulated by Anthony Ryle, Hilary Beard and others), some of which might apply to you. The list is only a beginning. It's good if you can add your own from your experience of just noticing what happens to your mood through one day and finding words to describe it.

Identifying our states

By a 'state' we mean a way of being and feeling which is clearly distinguished from others and which is only present some of the time. Select those states from the following list which more or less describe states that you experience. Add others when they occur to you:

- ☐ **OK state** A more or less normal state of coping with life and feeling the common range of moods.
- ☐ **Victim, abused state** Feeling that other people use and abuse you, do not respect or care for you, threaten or bully you.
- ☐ **Soldiering on state** Getting on with what has to be done, coping, doing what people expect of you without pleasure or satisfaction.
- ☐ **Rage state** Crazy, out of control, dangerous, feeling violent to self and/or others.
- ☐ **Revengeful state** Angry, self-righteous, violent, envious, wanting to get your own back.
- ☐ **Zombie state** Blanked off from emotion, indifferent to others, 'on automatic', unreal.
- ☐ **Bully state** Without pity, hurting others, contemptuous of others, hurting yourself.
- ☐ **High state** Speedy, energetic, efficient, happy, over the top.
- ☐ **Cloud cuckoo land** Blissfully happy, close to others, safe.
- ☐ **Dismissive, contemptuous** Feel better than others, special, deserving admiration, intolerant of weakness in others, intolerant of weakness in self.
- ☐ **Powerful caretaker** Helpful to others, strong, needed, in charge, resourceful.
- ☐ Other

You might like to choose one or two states and keep a diary for a week, noting each time you recognise them. As you look at what you've written see how far you can trace the state back before discussing this with a therapist or co-counsellor. A helpful companion to this process is to try to find a glimpse of a safe or kind space. However small – it might be a fleeting memory of the smile of a stranger, a piece of music or a song with lyrics that support you; the voice of the friendliest person you know; or an image you have seen somewhere that is very beautiful. Being touched in this way, through the senses, and however brief, is a lifeline. Practise returning to it, its energy and feeling; if it feels OK, notice where you feel it in your body. You might like to carry a reminder with you in support of bringing some kindness to yourself. This then can become part of the extended OK state that will grow into a healthy island.

You can continue with this process of understanding by working through the **State Description Procedure** on the companion website to this book. This helps describe what happens when in each state, how we feel toward ourselves, toward others and how others feel toward us. From this exploration we are able to identify and name our reciprocal roles in each state.

Exercise

Remember to be really gentle as you make this exploration. Keep returning to whatever is the safe enough moment.

Feet on the ground, touching the earth

Experiment with feeling your feet as they touch the ground, either in sitting or in walking. Bring all your awareness into the contact between the soles of your feet and the ground. Think of it as a silent and wonderful communication between your feet and the earth itself. Let them speak to each other. Keep practising and see if this activity helps you to safely become more into your body and its sensations and feelings.

Whenever you can, just keep noting the times when you recognise you are in one of these mind states. Whenever you are able to record your experiences find a few words to describe the state you recognize, and the thinking, feeling and body sensations you experience.

Over time, see if you can add other words that describe the states you find. Perhaps: furious, confused, upset, lost, afraid. There may also be colours, pictures or images. Sometimes when we do this actual memories arise of earlier times when you felt this way. Don't be alarmed. Just record them in your notebook and return to them when you are ready. As you are naming and describing, you might also like to ask 'what do I need right now?'

The next step is to see if you can recognise the relational knot within the state itself. For example: if you are wanting to hurt yourself whilst feeling hurt and humiliated you may recognise the pull of being *violently rejecting/dismissing* in relation to *abused/rejected/crushed*. If you recognise craving, wanting to be lost in bliss, you might describe a *perfectly admiring* in relation to *specially held* reciprocal role.

In the rage and hate of 'monster' you might find *belittling/punishing* toward others or yourself in relation to *punished/humiliated/shamed*. The reciprocal role of *judging/blaming* in relation to *blamed/put down* may have kept your natural anger repressed and feared as 'monstrous', leaving you unable ever to express natural anger and only either to turn it on yourself as self-harm or to threaten others in distorted ways.

The diagram from Graham, who had a long history of drug abuse and self-harm, illustrates the internalised reciprocal roles at the beginning of therapy and, in bold lettering in Figure 9.1 (which represents red used by Graham in his diagram), the new roles he learned to develop through self-observation and reflection. As his self-observation grew, he started to feel more in charge of the different states and their sudden switches. The pull of the dissociated states felt less extreme. There were fewer episodes of blanking off and feeling unreal and cutting himself. But without the states to contain his shifts in emotion there came lots of very painful and difficult feeling. Through monitoring and recording, then pondering, he found the description 'gritty grief' that most fitted his felt sense of longing, despair, rage, loss of innocence and hope for good things. He wanted to kick out at the helpless little ducklings in the park in spring, squeaking and following their mother. He longed to cry 'a normal bucketful' for his own helpless little duckling but was too scared at being overwhelmed. He wrote about his lost childhood spent in numerous foster homes.

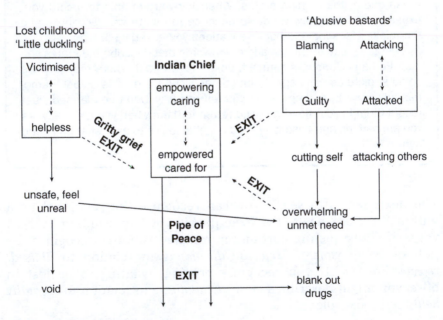

Figure 9.1   Graham's diagram

In the centre of his diagram in bold type is an 'Indian Chief'. This figure, an image representing a new self state, is made up of one of the few good figures in his life: an institutional chef who once befriended him and taught him snooker, and a Native American tribal chief in full headdress who appeared to him in a dream. In the dream, toward the end of therapy, the 'Chief' showed him how to ride through a herd of buffalo. He understood this as an indication that he could learn to ride amongst his roller-coaster states with greater consciousness and also be in charge. This was the beginning of the creation of his 'healthy island'.

The energy of this dream figure also allowed us to talk of different 'pipes of peace' from the crack cocaine that had long been his habit. At follow-up he was finding some benefits from meditation and had joined a group that met weekly.

Whilst all of us have times when our familiar way of being in the world is in eclipse and we feel 'on the edge', living with emotionally unstable states means that our relationship with ourselves and others is highly charged and unpredictable. Until revised we feel at the mercy of sudden moods and impulses, as either 'all good' or 'all bad', and may seek desperate measures to bring about relief. We feel perplexed about the effect we have on other people and them on us, and can swing from a state of ideal longing and bliss, often projected onto others or ideals, into in a bitter, dejected paranoid world of disillusion and unhappiness.

Trauma and complex trauma

Psychology has now integrated a lot more information from neuroscience about the effects of traumatic stress on the brain, body and mind. We understand that the old reptilian part of the brain responsible for fight and flight stores 'memory' which is not available to cognition. It remains hidden. If as an adult we suffer from the trauma of an accident, and are able to utilise our fight or flight response, we are less likely to suffer Post Traumatic Shock Disorder (PTSD). If we have been able to develop inner resources, and recruit the support of family and friends we can find ways to process our shock and grief and not become 'traumatised'. But if we have not been able to fight or run away we move into a freeze response where what has happened cannot be processed and recovery takes longer. When we suffer early trauma as a child, our natural survival fight/flight mechanism is compromised because we are too small and helpless to either fight or run away – and we move into freeze. This may dominate our fragmented emotional states leaving us cut off from being able to relate comfortably with others or ourselves. The trauma will be recorded in body memory and nervous system. If past abuse memories are triggered by associations or reminders, by smell, sound, image, the freeze mechanism shuts them down immediately for protection.

Dr Alison Jenaway a consultant psychiatrist and psychotherapist uses CAT combined with EMDR (Eye Movement Desensitization and Reprocessing) to help patients understand and process their trauma history. She writes in *Reformulation*:

> Listening to patients' histories through a 'trauma lens' gives a different perspective on reciprocal role enactments. These are not just understandable because they are repetitions of internalised relationship roles – it is possible to give a much more convincing explanation of, for example, why raised voices are unbearable and you have to avoid conflict and please people at all costs. The raised voices are a trigger to memories of being physically abused as a child and to your primitive mind it is as if things are about to 'kick off' exactly as they did then. (Jenaway, 2016)

Memories of traumatic abuse can begin to emerge from freeze at any time, such as when a committed relationship is attempted or during a therapy. Then it is a challenge for others to support the helpful release within the body – not by retelling the story, which can re-traumatise, but by allowing the body to come out of freeze safely and complete its fight/flight response.

If any of what has been written in this chapter triggers an uncomfortable memory or feeling related to the past, or any time you find yourself becoming overwhelmed by feeling or thoughts, focus on an image that represents a 'safe place' for you that is referred to in Chapter 1. Sometimes holding a simple object such as a stone, pebble or crystal helps us to feel steadier when we are in the grip of powerful emotion. Placing our concentration on our feet as the ground holds them is another way of contacting a place of safety.

But if you notice really difficult feelings as you read this section the best step is to consult a professional who is trained to work with the results of trauma and there are useful addresses of professional associations at the end of this book.

When we have never had a safe environment within which to grow a flexible and manageable repertoire of relatedness, our inner world can become severely fragmented. As we saw on page 35, major inconsistencies and abandonments, not explained or understood, leave us out of dialogue, alone, lost and unconnected. Some people describe this as 'feeling in bits' or as having many parts. Patra's drawing illustrates this (Figure 9.2). Often there is no

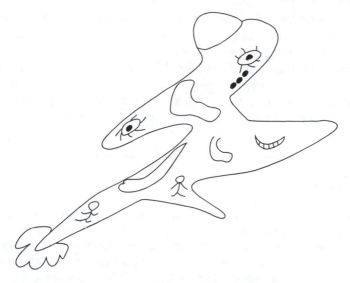

Figure 9.2   Patra's drawing of herself: 'All in bits'

communication between the different parts, which seem walled off as in structural dissociation, leading to one part acting in ways others are unaware of. Many people compensate for their earlier losses by developing a high functioning self, and as a successful, 'apparently normal person' (Minton et al., 2008) who goes to work, cares for others and functions in the outside world; but inside there is turmoil – multiple states dominated by the biological responses to earlier trauma of being in a dangerous world: fight, flight, freeze, submit and attach.

It is usually in the areas of personal relationship, which demand intimacy and trust, that our more emotionally primitive states emerge, often surprising us and others. For in these close encounters it's through our bodies that we are brought back into the same territory where we felt terrorised, hurt, numb with fear, in the silenced rage that has never been able to find a voice. Symptoms and behaviours are, until released, the only voice. And this voice is frequently misunderstood, misinterpreted, threatened once more and punished. There is no 'window of tolerance' in the multiple state system. It is possible to name and collect the fragmented pieces in one place. After recognition of the states and their reciprocal roles, we need to recognise the biological basis for our most traumatised selves. These scripts and tensions are met and released slowly through skilfully listening, tracking and finding ways for the body to speak in order for the natural self-regulatory processes to come to life. Then the body and nervous system is able to find healing.

If, when you looked at the states description list above (or the more detailed one on the companion website to this book) you marked several shifting states, spend a few moments looking at how much these states dominate your relationships. It may be that your shifting states are active in only one part of your life and you can ring-fence them in order to study them. The very act of observing yourself in this way is the beginning of developing the 'observing eye'.

MURIEL

Muriel was referred for CAT therapy by her psychiatrist, who she had been seeing for depression. She had made one serious suicide attempt and had recently started having 'flashbacks' where she 'froze'. The trigger for her 'freeze' state was the image of 'an angry face with a huge mouth'. The flashbacks gave her and her therapist an image, the emotional state of terror, and they were able to identify a reciprocal role of *terrified help-less victim* in relation to *violent bully*. As the therapy progressed, Muriel was able to open a window on the impact of a summer of terror when she was sent to stay with an uncle whilst her mother was in hospital. She was nine years old. Each evening the uncle locked Muriel inside a small utility room at the back of the house, tying her to the electricity wires. He told her she was a devil's child because she had red curly hair and freckles and this had to be cleansed by the electric force, but that if she struggled the force would electrocute her. On Sundays he would subject her to long sermons from the Old Testament.

When Muriel returned home her father had left and her mother was frail, having suffered a complete breakdown. Muriel's responsibility was to care for her mother and to keep control of the home. She had been silenced by threats of what would happen to her if she 'told' and felt powerless to say anything to anyone, especially now that she was her mother's main carer. She threw herself into school work, which gave her control and relief. She did well and 'forgot' the incidents. She never told her mother, even when the uncle was sectioned under the Mental Health Act a few years later. She developed a high functioning and 'apparently normal personality' and was admired for her control at home, cooking for her mother after school, passing all her exams and being very neat and polite. Her liking for colour and design helped her later on to become a successful garden designer.

But the terrified self state froze when she attempted closeness with men, with whom she could not hide her freckles. She became socially isolated and depressed. She was phobic about churches and electricity, not trusting computers and writing everything out in longhand. Her suicide attempt came after she had plunged into the unbearable and unmanageable feelings of attack and hatred following a rejection.

The work of therapy was to help her find a self state of trusting and safe in relation to safe ground and she found the Grounding Exercise (see the companion website) useful. During one session, when her breathing became panicky and irregular, the therapist helped her to remain safely with her shaking and trembling in order for the autonomic nervous system to release the terror held in her body. As her breathing became regular she sat very still. During that moment of release she had a memory of the tiny skylight in her uncle's utility room. There were branches high above the house, waving freely in the wind, that had helped her to form a 'safe world somewhere out there self' and survive her ordeal, and which probably contributed to her choice of work as a gardener. The image of the tree became her 'safe place' for the journey of therapy and a place to return to as she discovered other parts of herself that had been dissociated. These two prevalent split-off self states, one terrifying and the other potentially healing, were both hidden from the view of the apparently normal person.

Sometimes people are unable to find any resolution to their inner emptiness or terror and are unable to develop an 'apparently normal' personality or enough reasonable functioning to live a life and earn a living within the society in which they find themselves. Then other solutions are sought to find a way of life that appears to control fear and terror, such as joining the armed forces or vigilante groups or in courting the edges of crime and addiction. In *At Hell's Gate*, Vietnam War veteran Claude Thomas (2006: 71) writes: 'I was trained to cut myself off from my emotions, to repress them. This created a separation from the essential life force that is our humanity and enabled me to kill. I learned to see myself as a separate self, not connected with anything, and the ruler over all things.' In the years since returning from Vietnam he has become a peace activist and monk, travelling to countries at war. He writes that we all have our Vietnam, our own experience of violence, and about mindfulness and compassion and how it is possible for all of us to find healing.

'Touch and go' practice

This practice draws on work by Pat Ogden and Dale Asrael and takes just one fragment at a time of traumatic affect to be 'touched' and then the 'go' is to step immediately into the resourced place. It is best shared with a professional or in co-counselling. But it is safe to try for yourself.

Make a circle on the floor with golden thread or ribbon. Spend some time inside this circle, nourishing all your resources – holding safe objects that have meaning for you, imagining kind helpers alongside you. It is helpful to practise in this circle so that you can draw on it inside wherever you are. Whenever a traumatic response is activated it is possible for it to be just 'touched' by awareness, before stepping inside the golden circle, either actually or metaphorically, so that we immediately resource the wounded self. Practising in this way can help us build our resources around the traumatised self so that it is gradually released safely.

PART SIX

Gathering Information

A person's consciousness awakens wrapped in another's consciousness.

M.M. Bakhtin, *Speech Genres and Other Late Essays* (1986: 138)

TEN · Examining the impact of our beginnings

In this section we look through our notebook of patterns of thinking and responding and seek to find out more about where we are rooted. Focus on what feels right for you. **Push where it moves**!

Some memories will feel painful. It's the pain you have tried to manage all your life. Whether you are reading this section in co-counselling, or you are on your own, call on your courageous self to help you, and take breaks with mindful breathing. Use the diagram in Figure 1.3 (p. 21) to keep yourself in the 'window of tolerance' by monitoring your body responses to what you are exploring.

Understanding where our conflicts are rooted helps us to see how our fears, often unconscious, keep us behaving 'as if' the circumstances that produced the original problem are still in full force. We still behave as if: unless we please, avoid, cut off or act in a particular way, our emotional life is threatened.

No book can hope to step into the place of a living person met each week in the privacy of the same room and time. But these pages may offer a beginning for the safe exploration of our misunderstood self, challenging old assumptions and messages, and facilitating the discovery of previously hidden parts of us that we come to value.

Am I odd?

Another reason for looking into the past is that we often take what we feel for granted. Many people say to me 'Doesn't everyone feel like this?', as if they were trying to find what was 'normal'. Am I odd? Am I making a fuss? Freud tells a story of a young man who visited him early in his career. When Freud asked the man to describe what he did each day he said, 'Same as everyone else … get up, throw up into the toilet, dress, go to work …'.

Claiming our uniqueness is part of allowing ourselves to be real and to put our experience into context. When I suggested to Freda (see p. 142) that it sounded as if she had had to grow up quickly and become a 'little mother' when her brother was born and her mother became depressed, she responded with relief. Suddenly she had an explanation for why she felt responsible for everything. She could then choose of her own free will how to take up responsibility or not.

Sometimes we need to express fury at what appears to be the unfairness of our lot. Sometimes we find understanding, even forgiveness: of a mother or father who we learn was immature or ill, given little or no help, dominated by others, and living in poor and inadequate housing. While it's important to experience those feelings that have become blocked or split off by our need to survive earlier life events, it is equally important to let go of feelings about the past when they stop us maturing.

As you reminisce about your early life, make notes or draw or paint any of the feelings or memories that come to you. Let your own imagination speak.

If you notice that you have blanked off, become stressed in your body, or desperately want to eat, just note this feeling. Write about it in detail as much as you can.

Early life review

Prebirth

There is an increasing awareness that intrauterine conditions affect the relationship between mother and growing infant. If a mother is stressed by depression, anxiety or trauma her cortisol levels are raised and so are her baby's. If these levels are not able to be regulated, it can mean that the growing person is born with anxiety that is not understood.

Birth stories and reciprocal roles

The late psychotherapist Angela Wilton made a study of birth stories – the actual birth as well as the earliest postnatal experience – and their link with the reciprocal role procedures. She asked people to tell the story of their birth and its impact on the family, using any anecdote, story or image from any source – parents, siblings, doctors, midwives. She included jokes, myths or catch-phrases, as well as any actual memory of the birth itself.

As she worked with different birth stories she began to notice how the atmosphere around the birth story was often mirrored in the person's ways of relating to others. For example, a mother exhausted and angered by a long, arduous labour might be less able to bond with her baby than a mother who found giving birth exhilarating. This birth story would carry an atmosphere of pain and struggle, inducing possible hidden and 'magical guilt' in the child. These feelings might well be carried over into other relationships. Parents who hope for a child of a certain gender may have difficulty covering up their disappointment when their baby turns out to be the opposite. This disappointment may give rise to the person feeling worthless, especially when they get close to others, and to the belief that they have to strive to justify their presence.

Sometimes when a baby is born after a bereavement or loss, he or she becomes associated with this rather than greeted in their own right. As a result, the person grows up believing that they were 'born under a shadow' or have become a 'replacement child'.

Over half of the people in Wilton's study felt they had damaged and hurt their mother during the birth, so burdening them with a relationship dance of *damaging in relation to hurt* (as if to be alive is to damage others), evoking guilt and a need to make compensation. Another theme was 'just we two', where an easy birth was followed by close and uninterrupted bonding between mother and child, with the father absent. This emphasised an idealised central and perfect position in relationships, from which there could be, in reality, a long fall! Relationships in adult life with the 'just we two' emphasis could be over-close and dependent, mutually admiring, with a tendency to over-idealisation; or, if this was not met, a crash into feeling rubbished or, conversely, rubbishing anything too 'ordinary' (see Figure 3.1 on p. 51).

The 'unwanted' theme was also prominent, leaving the person with a sense of ambivalence about commitment and an anticipation of rejection: the *rejected/rejecting* reciprocal role.

HELEN

Helen came into therapy because of difficulties in close relationships. She had a pattern of desperately trying to get close, getting close for a minute and then fleeing. The myth in her family was that she always had

(Continued)

(Continued)

her 'knickers in a twist'. It turned out that she had been a breech birth, in spite of being turned before birth to come out head first. She had turned again to find her way out. Her mother always felt that she 'couldn't win' with Helen and thus was born the relational dance of *stubborn/ defeating* in relation to *defeated/depressed* with the resulting feelings of anger and resentment that made intimacy and acceptance hard.

Facts of our birth used to be shrouded in mystery, but today this is changing. My grandson Harry told me, aged three, with a serious look in his eye, that his mummy had to be cut open in order for him to be born, but that there were lots of people there and when they pulled him out they all shouted 'It's Harry!', and a huge smile came over his face.

I have found that when people begin to ask friends and relatives about their birth or their early life, a few things start to make sense. It also offers a chance for corresponding with or meeting relatives who may have been scattered over the world, as well as the family 'black sheep'.

Sometimes the atmosphere of our birth seems to accompany us on other transitions. We can sense a 'long difficult birth' when starting a new job or relationship, or in moving house; or impatience as if we have to get out quick, as in premature birth. People who experienced slow and difficult births perhaps need to recognise that this may be the way we go into new things, and accept it for what it is. In knowing it consciously we can choose whether to get help to push ourselves on a bit, or whether to let the slow, difficult way take its own time.

The following questionnaire is to help you ponder on the nature of your own birth and the atmosphere into which you were born.

Questionnaire: Birth and prebirth

Our time in the womb is our first experience of containment and unconditional being. How much time do you allow now for being rather than doing? How does your need for containment – a house, room, building – reflect itself in your life? Does the place you live in suit you?

How much care do you take of yourself – warmth, safety, protection, and rest and sleep?

How much do you know of your actual birth? Were you breast-fed or bottle-fed?

Multiple births

This means that several lives share the same space right from conception. Sometimes this creates rivalry for attention; and strong feelings. Multiple-birth children are actually deprived maternally, however hard the mother works: those moments of being alone and special to Mum are rare.

Many multiple births also include deaths, especially today with *in vitro* fertilisation where several embryos may be implanted. The gratitude for the survivors can eclipse the impact of the deaths, for the parents and the survivors. There is anecdotal evidence that if you have had a twin who has not survived you are subtly aware of it; there also may be uneasy feelings, such as survivor guilt. Fearing we were greedy will not be conscious, but might subtly be undermining our freedom to live.

Adoption

In adoption we are carried by one woman and then nurtured by another, or many others, during our first years. We come to each one as a stranger with whom bonding has to be achieved and new signals learned. People who have had many different 'mothers' seem to suffer most in terms of insecure or disorganised attachment and lack of self-esteem. But sometimes, if there has been one central kind influence, even the most deprived early backgrounds can be compensated. During the process of self-exploration, people who have been mainly in touch with the negative side of their backgrounds do often unearth the memory of someone who showed care and helped them to feel valued.

JAMES

James, who had had several difficult fosterings before living in a reasonable children's home for several years, kept his life very ordered and unadventurous, not making many friends and not risking relationships. He had a fine sense of colour. He would wear coloured socks and have an attractive tie and handkerchief. When I commented on this he looked startled and embarrassed. Teased for his 'foppishness', he had tended to repress this side of himself, but on exploring it further he did acknowledge his love of colour and design, and his attraction to beautiful things.

(Continued)

(Continued)

He had a knack for picking out small objects, like glass and silver, at markets, but he felt it to be 'wrong' in some way. What we discovered was the influence of an old lady he used to visit as a community service 'punishment' during his early fostering days. He hated being associated with the 'cast-offs' of society – babies and old people who weren't wanted. But this old lady had a room that resembled an Aladdin's Cave, and when he showed an interest (which he had in him naturally) she encouraged it. It was the only concentrated attention and appreciation he received during his early years. The memory of it was buried underneath years of basic survival in a difficult competitive world that revolved around who was going to get the best parents or foster parents. It was a moving moment when he realised how much kindness he had received, and it raised his self-esteem. He started to value his appreciation of colour and shape, and took it seriously enough to begin an evening course in design.

Many people who are adopted carry the sense of rejection all through their lives. In an interview with Anne de Courcy in the *London Evening Standard* in June 1995, the writer John Trenhaile explained that many adopted children are overachievers, struggling to compensate for some sin they are not even aware of having committed:

> ... the feeling that you have failed a test you didn't even know you'd been set ... In my case I felt I had done something so unspeakably wrong that my own mother gave me away. But it took a long, long time to realise this.

Sometimes people who have been adopted carry an *abandoning/ rejecting* in relation to *abandoned/rejected and worthless* reciprocal role. This may express itself as an obsessional interest in security, being attached to objects or rituals of checking, or fear of emotional commitment. Or, the dance of *conditional* in relation to *striving* may include rebellion, testing out all attachments to see if they will last, to prove oneself 'lovable'.

Some people split their biological and adoptive parents into good/ bad or ideal/second best. Biological parents may be idealised and the split between the two sets of parents may be reflected in later relationships, or form a 'snag'. For example, a pattern of allowing a 'second-best' relationship while yearning for the unattainable idealised 'real'. Now that adopted children can search for their biological parents this split has a chance to be healed, both by the reality of finding actual parents less than ideal, as well as healing through self-exploration or therapy.

Do you recognise that either of the following underlie your feelings about yourself?

- I unconsciously behave as if I'm about to be:
    - abandoned;
    - rejected?

Questionnaire: Our first reception

- ☐ Were you expected, wanted?
- ☐ Did it matter if you were a boy or a girl?
- ☐ Were there any miscarriages, stillbirths, other children who died but were perhaps rarely referred to?
- ☐ Was much expected of your presence, for example as the first boy, girl, grandchild, mixed race child, child for generations; or as the heir to a title, fortune, family business, etc.?
- ☐ Was your birth an attempt to redeem lost other lives or disappointment?

Development of a sense of oneself in the world

Infancy

The dance of relating begins during infancy when our world is experienced through our bodies – hot, cold, wet, soiled and uncomfortable, hungry, empty, full. Then, held gently, firmly, roughly, not held at all; stroked gently, soothingly, lovingly, roughly, angrily, harshly, or not at all. Because we are so dependent and vulnerable when we are infants we experience a great deal of anxiety if our safety is threatened in any way. Donald Winnicott (1979) uses the term 'primitive agonies' to describe the unbearable anxieties of the infant in fear of falling forever, of being abandoned.

When our early infant life is adequately provided for, our fears are allayed and our anxieties do not get out of proportion. We learn to trust that what or whoever goes away will come back; that it is safe to know love and be loved, and to know and love oneself; and that there are parts of us we can trust to be safe and to where we can retreat. We form appropriate boundaries between ourselves and others as we grow from infancy into childhood, a process that takes from the time of birth to between two and three years.

When the early environment is experienced as non-nurturing, but neglectful, hostile or inadequate, our development is thwarted by anxiety. We learn to adapt in order to accommodate, and, before thought process, and before we have separated what belongs to ourselves and what belongs to others, our only defence against what is experienced as a hostile outside is to compartmentalise our experiences. This might involve states where we withdraw, become zombie-like; or states of unmanageable feeling. We may also split off the things that are unpleasant and experienced as 'bad' from the good experiences, setting a pattern for later of things appearing as either totally good or totally bad, with nothing in between.

Projection

From birth to about the age of seven the ego needs to grow healthily and be of use to us as a lens through which we see and operate in the world, and for this we need a 'good enough' background. We need to feel that we are loved and therefore lovable; liked and therefore likeable; accepted and therefore acceptable. We need to know that however 'bad' we are, we will not be rejected; to discover that we, and others can be angry and love someone at the same time; or to receive someone's anger without feeling hated. If we split 'good' and 'bad' we may project what feels 'bad' onto others, thus experiencing them as bad or against us, as chaotic or hateful. We then invite others to live out for us the unresolved difficulties or rejected parts from our early life.

If our early years are accompanied by a 'too tight' environment, where a parent or guardian is too attentive and protective, we get little experience of the outside world and therefore lack the tools to cope with adult life. We tend to grow up to be afraid of life and our instincts, unwilling to take any risks, avoiding challenge and thus isolating ourselves. Our reciprocal roles tend to involve *restricting/controlling* in relation to *restricted/crushed* and we may recognise the dilemma 'if I must, then I won't'. We may be drawn to want to merge with another.

If there has been too little interest, too loose a soil, we feel ungrounded and 'dropped', which can emerge later in depression and a lack of ego strength or self-esteem, a sense that we inhabit a 'nowhere world'.

Recollecting early life and influences

The following section offers exercises and questions for gathering together and reflecting upon your early life.

Exercise: Family tree

Figure 10.1 shows an example of how to lay out your own family map. Make your family map or tree in your own way. Use different colours for different people and different shapes. Alongside each person put their date of birth, occupation, any anecdotes or personality traits, and any other description you feel is significant. See if you can find words to describe the reciprocal roles of the family members in your map.

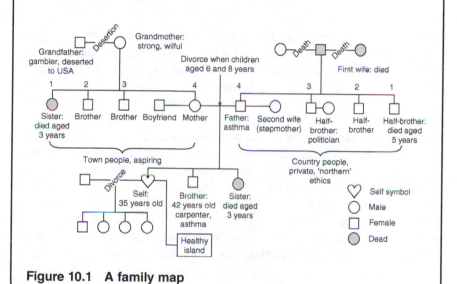

Figure 10.1   A family map

Exercise

Many people have few or no early memories, although sometimes early memories start to come back during therapy or self-questioning. What is your earliest memory? Picture it, in all its colours and shades. What is happening, with whom, who is there? Set the scene for yourself down to

(Continued)

(Continued)

the tiniest detail – what everyone is wearing, the texture of the cloth, smells around you, sounds. Again, closing your eyes, feel into your own place in the recollection. Feel your feet on the ground, feel how small you were, actually become yourself as a small person in that picture. Write down what is happening, and what the feelings are. When you look at it now, what do you sense are the reciprocal roles being invited?

When you have got this memory, anchor it by writing or drawing. Make another, of the early life you would like to have had, painting in all the feelings, objects, ideas, atmospheres. See if you can begin to understand the world you inhabited as a child, and the kind of choices you had to make in terms of survival. Make a note of the parts of you that went underground or unnoticed and undeveloped.

Ponder on where you fit in the family network and on how this position has influenced you. Eldest children are 'King or Queen' until a sibling comes along. As the eldest you had 'new' parents, inexperienced at the art of parenting. Sometimes the eldest or only children are expected to be more 'grown up' than is appropriate for their age, and are given responsibilities way beyond their years.

Second children are often treated more leniently, because parents are by now experienced and more relaxed. If the elder sibling is making a success of things and fitting in with the family network, a second child may feel they have to keep up. Or, if the eldest has in some way disappointed parents and family expectations, the second (and this can apply to any children who come afterwards) can take on the position of the eldest, making the eldest feel redundant and a failure.

If you are a middle child then there is a sense of having to 'jockey for position' in a family, often feeling in between or in a 'no place'. Youngest children may have a lot of freedom, but can also be neglected or taken for granted. Sometimes they are babied longer than is appropriate because they are the last to leave the nest. If overprotected, they may find it difficult to grow up and lead their own independent lives.

Researching signs of our 'healthy self' in early life

Play

Were you allowed to play as a child? See if you can remember games, toys or stories. Notice the quality of this remembered play and how it made you feel. Play can often be creative and nourish our imagination, our sense of colour and shape. It may also have been a way in which we safely expressed difficult feeling. Telling off dolls or teddies or mending them with bandages sometimes tells us about our internal world. Burying things in the garden, learning to punch, throwing darts may help us see our natural defences emerging.

How do you play now?

Longing

How have you experienced longing? For what have you longed? See if you can follow where your own natural longing, or your own heart, has been trying to lead you.

Happiness

Write down the times in your life when you:

- felt happy
- experienced joy
- realised you were being taken seriously
- felt you mattered

Note how you experienced these feelings:

- in your body
- in feeling words

How might you write about these good feelings now and about what you received?

Connection

Write down the number of times in your life when you have felt connected to someone – person, animal, situation or group, part of nature, belief. Note the feelings around this sense of connection.

Note also the times when you have found it easy to understand something without learning as if your own natural wisdom is speaking.

Spiritual awareness

What are your spiritual practices and how do you nourish them as part of your everyday life?

Healthy self

Whatever you discover about your healthy self, make a space for it in all your writings, diagrams and in your own self-monitoring. When, later on in the book, you make a diagram of the problematic reciprocal roles, remember to put your healthy self on to your diagram.

Exercise: Using objects to create our family map

Have some fun by gathering a number of objects – for example, shells, stones, plates, glass – that might depict your family members. Choose a favourite object for yourself and place this on the floor first. Then gather objects that represent other family members, including steps, fosters, aunts, grandparents and any animals and neighbours if they were part of family life. Move the objects around to indicate times of change. For example, if one parent left, became ill or died, when you went to school, when siblings were born or other people joined the family. We can often remember something happening in a certain house, but not how old we may have been.

Allow the objects to show you something of your early family atmosphere.

Relatives

- Who got on well with whom?
- Family feuds: what was their nature? What was the history, story, mythology?
- How were relatives treated who had not 'made it' or were different?

Religion

- What was the family religion or belief system?
- Were you allowed to have your own view as you were growing up?
- Was religion important to you?
- What lives on today from your early experience with religion and religious ideas?

School

Take either primary or secondary school or both:

- What was your first day at school like?
- What lives on in you today that comes from early schooldays?

- Did you feel different from other children? If so, why? Was it:
  - clothes?
  - hygiene?
  - where you lived?
  - colour of skin?
  - religion?
  - being clever or not clever?
  - speaking in a different language?

- Did you get rewarded for achievements, or did no one notice or seem to care what you did?
- If things went wrong at school – bullying, fights, teasing, taunting, unfair treatment by staff – who did you talk to?
- If things went wrong at home, was there someone at school to whom you could turn?
- How did it feel to come home after school?

Friendships

- Were you allowed to bring friends home?

Money

- Was money important for:
  - saving?
  - basic survival?
  - having power?

How do you feel now about money?

- Do you feel you never have enough; or you have to hold on to it if you have it?
- Are you afraid of it?
- Are you comfortable or embarrassed about talking about money matters?

Talents and gifts

Many people grow up not knowing that they are really good at something because this is never appreciated and mirrored back. In Chapter 6, 'Snags and self-sabotage', we looked at how envy of skills or gifts can lead to magical guilt. So talents remain hidden and undeveloped, sometimes making us feel thwarted in some way and envious of others' successes.

What gifts do you feel you have? Make a list. Include things like good listening, patience, kindness, ability to analyse or put things together, intuition, as well as being good at sport, writing, science, selling, making things, reading, storytelling. Add this to your healthy island.

How did the family remark on your gifts?

- encouragingly
- took no notice at all
- said 'Don't let it go to your head' when you did something well
- compared you with others, themselves or their ancestors

The things we are good at may also not be properly understood by our parents. Sometimes our talent or interest is dismissed because they can't see where it will lead. In a school report, a teacher wrote about Barry Sheene, the champion motorcycle racer: 'Barry has got to learn that fiddling with motor cycles won't get him through life!'

Go back to the time of your early growing-up period – age four to twelve – and think about what your own interests were then. Write them down. Include the ones you might be tempted to dismiss.

List the things you were drawn towards then that are still part of your life today.

- If they have been driven underground how can you resurrect them?

Sexuality and gender

- What was physical touching like in your family? Was it:
  - encouraged?
  - not allowed?
  - allowed too much so you weren't sure of the boundaries between what was acceptable and what was not?

- Were you helped to feel good about your body or were you ashamed of it?
- At what age did you first become sexually aware?
- Could you talk freely about sex in your family? Did you want to? If not, what did you feel?

- Were you told about sex:
  - at school?
  - at home?
  - via a brother or sister?

- In the family's attitude, did sex mean one thing if you were female and another if you were male?
- Write down some of the myths you received about sex as you were growing up.
- If you discovered you were more attracted to people of your own sex, when did you become aware of this and how?
- If you were sexually abused as a child, how does this affect you now?
  - feeling guilty and contaminating/contaminated
  - unable to feel safe enough to get close
  - sometimes drawn into dangerous sexual situations

There are many special agencies to help survivors of sexual abuse. Finding a therapist who understands these difficult and painful wounds and whom you trust is an essential support for the journey of healing. Someone who will treat your story with care, confidence and compassion. There is information on finding a therapist in Appendix 3.

Illness

- List the instances and dates of illness and hospitalisation within your family.
- If you were ill, who looked after you, and how? How much did you know about what was happening to you?

When small children are admitted to hospital they sometimes 'forget' who their real parents are and attach themselves to nurses or other staff members as a way of protecting themselves from abandonment. Sometimes parents do not believe us when we say we have a pain or problem, either because they are afraid, or they need to go to work. Either way, if we are not believed we feel neglected.

Parent's illness

Children may have learned to fear 'Dad's heart' or 'Mum's wheezes', and believe they can make it worse by their behaviour. They mustn't laugh too loud, be rowdy, play tricks, in case they cause deterioration, or worse, death.

- Did their illnesses become barriers to your being with your parents and having fun with them?
- How much has your experience of other people's illness affected your own attitude to health?

Accidents

Accidents often stand out in the memory during childhood. Being scalded, falling, grazes, swallowing foreign bodies, being bitten. How they were responded to can influence the way in which we subsequently take care of ourselves. We may become overcautious or, in defiance, reckless. Childhood accidents are often accompanied by parental anger and blame – 'I told you not to take your bike on that road/play with the neighbour's dog' – can actually convince us that we cannot trust ourselves, we are bad or foolish.

Abi had been struggling for over a year with depression. We came across an old memory she had buried, of being twice scalded badly, and in hospital for several weeks when she was under ten years old. The most powerful visual and emotional memory for her was the fear and worry on her mother's face, overwhelmed at being burdened by a large number of children and now a child suffering from burns. Abi vowed that she would never complain, that whatever happened to her would be her own fault, and she must not burden anyone with her feelings. When she did become unwell with exhaustion later in life she had no way to speak of what she felt or ask for help, and her depression followed.

Death

Were there any deaths in your family during your childhood or adolescence, which made a big impact upon you? (If the person who died was your mother or father, look at the sections that deal with this in more detail below.)

Write something about the person you lost, what you learned from them about the world and about yourself, negative and positive:

- Were you told how they died and where?
- Were you allowed to go to the funeral, take part?
- Could you talk about the death, or were you told to be quiet?

As you flick back the memory album, see yourself as a small person in whose family someone has just died. Imagine yourself, in a room in your house. Get as strong a picture as you can of that small person and then sit beside them with kindness. Keep noticing if you did any of the following:

- go silent
- scream and yell
- have nightmares
- find yourself clinging to another adult, soft toy or place

How much does the impact of these deaths live on in your memory, or have they been blanked out?

Sometimes when a family death occurs early in our life, and we are not allowed to discuss it or mourn, it can produce 'magical guilt' (magical because we couldn't possibly be guilty), which may unconsciously undermine our later life (see snags p. 104). We may have had negative thoughts about the person who died, and because we are small and our thinking is not sophisticated we presume these negative thoughts contributed to their death.

We may also develop a sense of magical guilt because of our own survival. Do we deserve to survive when they have not? We feel as if our health, or success and happiness, is at their expense, that somehow instead we should be limited or damaged as they were. It's a very uncomfortable idea that our happiness has only been achieved at the expense of someone else's unhappy life. And so it lives on unconsciously inside us, coming out as self-jeopardy, self-sabotage, arranging things so that we do not fulfil our potential or really embrace fully what we can do.

Loss of a father

Men who have lost a father early in life do sometimes have difficulty relating to other men, particularly older men, and this is more so if there were no other good male figures after the father's death. Grown-up masculinity can feel 'on hold'. One man said to me, 'I still feel as if I'm waiting to grow into a man ... and I'm forty-five.' Some men strive to overcompensate for not having had a father, taking on powerful roles and responsibility to make up for the loss; trying to fit into dead men's shoes that they cannot possibly ever fill. Left behind is the lonely 'fatherless boy' inside them. Until he is recognised and related to, he will remain sad, cut off from a possible mentor and mate – possibly dominating inner and outer relationships. Developing a dialogic connection with this fatherless boy is an important part of mourning for the loss, which may never have been accomplished and moving forward as a man.

A girl who loses her father early in life may later on have difficulty relating to men, because of fear of another loss. If her father has become a hero through his death she may search for the 'perfect' man only to feel more and more disappointed, but without realising why.

A parent's death may also cut a child off from that side of the family, their values and lifestyle. I have known many people who knew nothing of their father or mother's family because they had died early on. The remaining spouse either could not bear to be reminded of their deceased partner and did not keep up with the family, or remarried and lost touch. Sometimes in rediscovering what a dead parent was really like, by using old photographs or writing to anyone who knew them, people reclaim the character and flavour of their lost parent and can also claim that connection for themselves.

KIM

At forty-eight, Kim discovered a host of relations in Russia whom she had never met because her mother had lost contact after her father's death. She found they shared her love of music and dancing, of colour and of melancholy verse, qualities her mother had criticised in her and which she had come to feel were undesirable, extrovert and pretentious. Finding that she did indeed carry some of the essence of her father was a real gift to her.

ANNE

During therapy, Anne brought many old photographs of herself as a child with her parents. Her father had killed himself when she was three, and the subject was never referred to. He was made out to be a 'bad lot', unstable and generally no good. She was convinced that not only was there a poor quality running in her blood, but that her father hadn't cared enough about her to stick around.

By writing to one of his friends, whom she had discovered quite by accident, she was able to piece together her father's last few days, when he was hospitalised and suffering from shell-shock during the Second World War. He had believed he was responsible for killings in Germany and France which his conscience could not tolerate, and in a frenzy of self-hate and acute misery he had leaped out of an eighth-floor window. This friend went on to describe to Anne some of the horrors of war and the lack of help available to people, such as her father, who were sensitive and conscious of what they were being asked to do.

Anne was herself a pacifist, and this realisation changed her given view of her father's character. One day she brought to the session some old photographs (discovered in the drawer of her aunt's desk) of her father holding her as a small child. Her arm was firmly round his neck and she was smiling radiantly. He was the image of a proud Dad, holding her as if she were the most precious thing on earth. Suddenly tears welled up in her eyes: 'I feel as if I was loved by him,' she said, 'even though I didn't have very long with him!' This realisation made a profound difference to her, and although she had to work through her ever-present fears of rejection from men, and her habit of reading rejection into everything that happened, she had begun the process of building a more solid core to herself, upon which could be built other profound experiences.

Loss of a mother

When a small child loses their mother it is an extremely sad day. She represents our link with care and nourishment in the nursery years, the person who makes our emotional and physical world safe. Although others may take her place, we have lost our link with someone who, whether liked or disliked, was the centre of our world. As she is often the actual centre, family life is seriously disrupted when a mother dies and children may be fostered or farmed out to other families while help is found.

The loss of a mother may live on throughout the following years like a yawning gap. Part of us may stay 'on hold' internally from the time of our mother's death. Our instinctual, emotional and intuitional life may remain undeveloped as we struggle to survive in what to us is an alien world. Later we may look for 'mothering' influences to allow us to complete the unfinished work of our development. We may seek quickly to become mothers ourselves, or conversely, avoid mothering, because we know the excruciating pain of loss.

A man who loses his mother early may be deprived of a feminine influence. He may not be able to develop his feminine side and build relationships with women. Whatever the way of compensation, the wound inside will be deep and the need for appropriate mourning and release of sadness important.

Questionnaire: Loss of mother/loss of father

- ☐ How old were you when your mother/father died?
- ☐ Describe your world until that point if you can – where you lived, your own room, toys, school, atmosphere.

(Continued)

(Continued)

☐ What is your most lasting memory of your mother/father? Paint this picture if you can, with all the details you can manage.

☐ Do you feel you have properly mourned the death of your mother/father?

☐ Is the mourning process held up in some way:

　☐ by the lack of knowledge of facts of the death – time, date, place of burial, nature of death?

　☐ by not talking enough about her/him, about how you felt for her/him, what you miss about her/him?

　☐ because part of you has not let her/him go, not accepted that she/he is dead?

☐ How does she/he live on in you? By the nature of:

　☐ how you live, work, family, place
　☐ religion
　☐ ambition

☐ Does she/he have an unconscious presence in your life:

　☐ through dreams?
　☐ through ideas of how to 'be'?
　☐ through 'magical guilt'?

☐ Do you feel you have to compensate for her/his death?

☐ If someone else took on the mothering/fathering, what is your relationship with that person or people now?

Take a fresh page in your notebook and write down the positive and negative aspects of the mothering/fathering you received after your parent's death.

How much have you been able to take on 'mothering'/'fathering' or looking after yourself? Are you:

☐ kind?
☐ encouraging?
☐ neglectful?
☐ demanding?

Can you change this if needs be?

Divorce and separation

Children always suffer when there is a marriage or partnership failure. They too feel rejected, betrayed; they wonder if it is their fault. The practical aspects can hit hard also – moving, having to adapt to new places and faces, travelling between one parent and another, each with different new agendas. There is frequently financial hardship.

If your parents divorced or separated:

- How old were you at the time?
- Who told you what was going to happen?
- What were your first thoughts? Did you voice them? Did you get heard?
- How much did your life change at this point – at home, at school, with friends?
- Did you carry on seeing both parents?
- Did you feel you had to take sides?
- Did you feel angry inside? Do you still feel angry now?
- Do you feel it was anyone's fault?
- If you grew up with only one parent, what were your fantasies about the absent parent?
- What do you feel about being the child of a single parent?

  - different
  - deprived
  - ashamed
  - it was special

- If either parent remarried, did it change your relationship with either parent? Were there new family members, step- or half-siblings? How did you feel your place in the family changed?

PART SEVEN

Making the Change

What is newly understood within us may be unformed in words and remain unseen by others until we find a language for it. Integration is helped by our conversations with ourselves and by recording the new words that are emerging within us in regular journal keeping. This written communication to ourselves helps us to bring what has been inside into the outside.

Nigel Wellings and Elizabeth Wilde McCormick,
Nothing to Lose (2005: 162)

ELEVEN Writing our life story

By now you have a notebook with lots of writing, some pictures and some ideas of how your life has been so far. You are getting to know yourself and have begun a new inner dialogue and will have been noticing how this operates, both with other people and within yourself. There may be painful life issues you were previously unaware of. Trust your own natural self-regulatory processes. Remember what it was that made you pick up this book now and look at your life more closely.

This next stage shows ways in which we will put together all that you have been through in a useful and creative way. You are going to be listening to the different dialogues within yourself and writing out how things have been for you and how you have coped in the only way you knew. As you write you will be extending and nourishing your healthy island.

Some people protest that they could never write anything about themselves, and are so daunted at the prospect that they don't even begin. It really is amazing how this fear (perhaps arising from school, where we are judged) simply melts away when we allow ourselves to play with our images and understandings and get involved in our own creative process. This next section is for no one but you. You need not show it to anyone unless you are in therapy or co-counselling. No one will be awarding gold stars or dunce's caps. Once you allow the ideas, images and metaphors to inform you, the sentences will form themselves.

How to start

Get one large sheet of paper or several small index cards. Take your notebooks and cast your eyes down the pages. Take the words, images, or phrases that leap out at you, or any particular words you seem to have used a great deal. Don't worry about being dramatic or self-conscious. The simpler the phrases you can find to describe something the clearer will be the picture of your life and development, and the more powerfully the images will stay in your mind as you begin the process of change. Some of the phrases that come up in the six examples of life-story writing that follow are:

> Sitting on a volcano – Death waiting at my shoulder – Wild Janet and Controlled Janet – Black hole – Ostrich attitude – Can of worms – Stolen child – Busy Lizzie – Child behind the chair – Anxiously skidding away – Puppy dog – 'What … little me?' – On the treadmill – Scared rigid – On automatic – 'Knew inside'

Take your own examples and either brainstorm them onto the large sheet of paper, or write each one on a card. When you feel you have enough, begin elaborating upon each phrase or image. For example, 'I grew up in a family where ...' or, 'All my life I have felt that ...' or, 'Early on I remember feeling that I was ...' or, 'I have few conscious memories of my early life, but having begun to question myself I can guess that I took on the position of ... early on'. Give as much detail as you can. Facts, memories, realisations.

When you feel you have the important experiences and facts you need, put on your 'observer' hat. Reflect upon the impact of your early environment and your response to it. Notice the impact on your thinking about yourself, and the way you act in the world. The process needs to go something like this: because of 'a' and 'b' I believed that I had to be 'x' and 'y'. This has led me to having an 'e' attitude to others and to behave as if 'j', 'k' and 'l'. Your story might then begin something like this:

> Most of my life I've been afraid of other people thinking I was stupid. This seems to go back to the time when I was very small and the youngest, with brothers who were all very clever. They used to call me 'slow coach' ... I felt helpless and upset. I tried to keep up by running after them and pleading with them to let me come on their outings, but they only laughed and said they could never have girls around. Both my parents were out at work all day and were too tired to listen. They expected my brothers to take care of me when they weren't there. I feel these experiences have contributed to a pretty low self-esteem, which I fight by being quite aggressive and macho. I play the toughie and tell crude jokes, but inside I am hurt and sad and wish someone would notice. But things don't happen by magic and I have to learn a different way of being with others, especially men. I would like to risk taking off my tough mask from time to time and just seeing what came out. It's a risk, but I've got to get something to change how things are or I will remain on my own, the butt of others' jokes. I drink far more than is good for me, and I know this is related.

Remember to write something about what has helped you through the difficult times, those qualities you can now see are valuable and have aided your survival. Write also about what you have done well and feel good about. This helps to establish a link with your healthy self.

The final process is to end your story by writing about what changes you would like to make and how you might begin to achieve them. Which reciprocal roles do you feel are most problematic and restricting? Which do you need to develop? There may be a need to recognise and challenge traps such as avoidance or pleasing, isolation or thinking negatively. In dilemmas, we must change from living lopsidedly to being more balanced, finding a third position from our extremes. In snags and self-sabotage we need to learn to recognise times when we unconsciously arrange to spoil our happiness. Making a diagram of our shifting states helps settle confusion. All change means embracing the things we have learned to fear, and reframing our experience by challenging the 'as ifs' that live on from the past. What we are changing is our perceptions and our habits.

You may wish to write your story in prose form, or you may prefer to illustrate it with sketches, drawings, cartoons or colour paintings. Alternatively, you may like to write poetry or write in a stream of consciousness. Another way is to use a flow chart or tree, showing the passage of your life from roots to branches, with images or words to illustrate what has happened during growth.

Writing the story of our life is always a powerful experience. It can be very moving, especially when we hear it read out loud during a therapy session or in co-counselling. Usually it is the first time we have heard our life laid out in full, how it has all been, and how our early formed attitudes to ourselves and others have contributed to our present difficulties. And we begin to understand how, by changing these attitudes, we can move away from what we may have believed were indelible footprints or entrenched habits over which we had no control. It may be the first time we have a glimpse that we can be in control of our life.

Six examples of story-writing

The following are six examples of life stories taken, with their permission, from people working in therapy. Names and professions have been changed to protect identities. You will see how varied they are and how completely individual. They may help you to get more ideas about how to write your own story.

SYLVIA

I grew up as the *wide-eyed eldest child*, taking everything in and not always sure that things were right for me. I felt special love from my father – when he was home – and from Grandma – when she was allowed to show it to me. But otherwise I don't remember there being a readily available lap or someone to pick me up when I fell. I felt like *the child behind the chair*. It seems my mother was not very enamoured about having children, and perhaps we were a hindrance.

Because now feeling things deeply is very painful for me, and because I didn't have a safe framework in which to express feelings, I have developed ways of keeping feelings at bay. I do this either by *showing off* intellectually, observing and commentating, often very astutely and with flair, but in the head, or by *controlling things rigidly*. This control also extends to relationships, when I sometimes feel anxious and threatened and prone to angry outbursts unless I am in control. I feel as if something is holding me back from claiming my life fully for myself. Perhaps the *child behind the chair*, who represents my deeper and more painful feelings, is wanting recognition, and I perhaps need to relinquish some of my tactics for keeping feelings at bay, even if experiencing feelings is painful. Then I can be more rounded and integrated as a person and move forwards to claim my life, without *anxiously skidding away* from real feelings.

JANET

I grew up in a lovely family where I was the youngest and felt *special*. We were very close and I feel upset when anything happens to break that closeness. When I broke out to 'do my own thing' it hurt my family and I feel really guilty about it. I feel God is punishing me for it by letting bad things happen to me.

I live now as if I have to keep my *feelings bottled up* and bend over backwards to please people and be a good mother, wife and daughter, so I don't hurt people. I feel that if I make trouble, they might stop talking to me, and that is terrifying for me. It reminds me of when I was seven years old in hospital after I had my tonsils out, and when my sisters weren't allowed to see me. I can remember how lonely and frightening that felt, and perhaps that is why the panic attacks I get now often feel as though something is stuck in my throat (like the pain after the tonsils were removed). Sometimes it is as though anger and strong feelings, which I'm frightened to express, get stuck in my throat too. But I daren't let them out because they would hurt people.

In the past two years a number of things have happened that have threatened the safety of my *special family*: my mum's illness, Mike's [husband] dad's death, and the dog biting Siân [daughter]. This has shaken my security and I feel 'anything could happen', as though I am *sitting on a volcano*, or as though *Death is waiting at my shoulder*. I'm very frightened that something bad might happen and that I might die. This probably causes me to have panic attacks (sometimes sparked off by outside events like the boy getting hurt in the playground). At times I have experienced a sort of *black hole*, feeling there's nothing there, as though the anxiety and fear are so great that it makes me cut off from the world around me.

Perhaps I also have this fear of death because I feel my life is passing by and that I'm missing out. Although I like being a good mum, etc., I don't really do anything for me. Perhaps deep down I feel if I do what I want it will hurt others, and that I don't deserve to put myself first. But I also believe that there are parts of Janet that want to come out and express themselves. I have tried to blot out *Wild Janet*, but perhaps I need to feel that it's OK to be my full self, and accept all of me, to like myself and express my feelings. And I need to realise that, by doing these things, I won't be hurting people and the world won't come to an end.

STEPHANIE

I was born into a family where I somehow seemed to be carrying the pain of generations. My father was born twenty years after a 'black sheep', his father died when he was eight and his mother died in front of him when he was fourteen. My mother came from a family who avoided conflict. Like my father, she was the only graduate of the siblings, and her older brother and sister died young, so she may have had to make up for them in some way.

In our family, Barry, my brother, and Jennifer, my sister, had special places. Barry is the boy and the oldest and he is like the

(Continued)

(Continued)

prodigal son who returned from the threshold of death. Jennifer is special because she is the youngest and there was a belief that everyone must be nice to her because she is fat.

I am in the middle, and it feels as though the bad fairy at my birth wished that, no matter what I did, I would never be good enough. Spilling the orange juice as a very little child is still an unexpiated crime for which I cannot gain forgiveness, no matter how hard I try. I was labelled clumsy when I was six and that label has stuck – as 'exotic', 'difficult', etc. Since then, I have always felt that I'm treading carefully, trying to negotiate a minefield laid by my father. I'm aware of this little bright face, eager to live, eager for approval, always being knocked down, bouncing back, but somehow being left behind. So it feels that I have never been able to flourish: I am the shrivelled bud of my poem, who has never been nurtured or allowed to grow properly.

As a result of this, I have become caught in a trap of 'trying to be perfect'. In order to be acceptable, I aim at perfection. I never feel good enough, but still try to please, and eventually feel let down and out of control, which reinforces my sense of worthlessness. So I try again, even harder.

Another way I have of coping is by taking all the knocks on the chin, trying to bounce back no matter how much I've been knocked down, keeping the face bright, even if bits of me are left behind. But in this cycle, I come – more and more – to expect to be hurt, and I have begun to believe that I don't deserve anything good.

In some ways, this is what happens in my relationships. With men, it seems that I recruit those who fulfil the '*prophecy*' of my never being good enough, of deserving nothing for myself and of expecting to get hurt and abused. Getting herpes is like a physical manifestation of this, an emblem of the transaction where I try to give everything that's good and joyful and get back an increasingly more threatening sexual disease. They leave me, and that's my legacy – so now I feel completely diseased. It's the same feeling as I exposed in the 'letter' to my father: 'I tried to think of an image to describe how it felt to be your daughter. What came to mind was that when I was small, over a period of time you slit me open, placed a box of maggots between my heart and my stomach and slowly and deliberately sewed the scar away. Your living legacy was that I could never again feel peace, goodness, satisfactions; just rottenness at the core ...'

In my relationships with women, it sometimes feels that, in the give-and-take equation, the only part available to me is the giving, and I have learned to interpret this as being as valuable as actually receiving. I have the image of me as a plant that grows legs and moves out of the range of any nurture that may be intended for me – so convinced am I that I don't deserve to receive. Perhaps therapy is an opportunity to change this pattern. With a few women, it feels that they are strong enough to force me to receive, although then I feel controlled and trapped as if medicine were being forced down my throat.

One of the family sayings is, 'Stephanie has only one problem and that's Stephanie.' And I have come to believe it in some way, as though I am eternally snagged in trying to be fully myself. I have the feeling that I have never been heard and that I therefore have never been really connected with someone. Deep down I am still the deprived, needy child craving recognition, warmth and acceptance for who I really am. But I daren't show this neediness, so I try to behave well and please and give, treading carefully and thinking before I speak, terrified that the neediness will seep out and make a dreadful mess and doom me to more verdicts that I am clumsy and impossible. I wanted to star in the play, but ended up being cast as the ugly, grunting troll.

I often intellectualise my feelings – carefully releasing words so that I don't overwhelm people. But I am entitled to experience my feelings fully, even if they are very painful. And I do have some profound self-knowledge, as, for example, expressed in my poetry. There are some good bits on which I can begin to build the full, real, lovely Stephanie: my closeness to Barry; the warm, creative and admirable part of my mother which doesn't seem to judge me and is also close and very special to me; and the newly acquired sense that I have an '*angelic overview*' of the minefield – as an allegorical picture of a Tuscan field, with my father laying mines as I fly above, unseen, blowing raspberries at him!

I need to believe in the shrivelled bud – that it is good and valuable at heart, that it will and can grow, that I am the one who can nurture it and allow it to flower, and that I don't need to find ways of being special other than as the 'fortunate victim'.

I need to start learning to take as well as to give, without feeling I need to spit out the goodness. I need to feel I can stand tall; the little, bright face can become the full, bright Stephanie.

ALISTAIR

I have very few memories of my early life, and it's possible that much of my feelings from that time have been buried under my need for control. I saw my father as a strict authoritarian, a hard-working research scientist who was rarely at home. My mother seemed to spend most of the time in bed depressed, and was always trying to leave. I followed my very clever brother to boarding school and felt the pressure of expectations to continue in his footsteps. Just before boarding school, at eight years old, I had a frightening experience of racing in the school playground with another boy – the fastest boy – and slipping and hitting my head so badly against a brick wall that I was hospitalised for two weeks and at home afterwards for several months. I have no memory of my parents visiting me, only an overwhelming sense of loneliness and fear of being made to go to school. The one positive element was my nanny, who waited to get married until I went away to boarding school so that she could look after me.

I think that probably the early part of my life was quite deprived emotionally, with the feelings of the child I was at the time unexpressed and unexplored. The natural response to *depriving/ rejecting* in relation to *deprived/rejected* is feeling hurt, angry, abandoned, and also needy, jealous, vindictive and destructive. There was no place for expressing any of these feelings. I coped by learning to control everything connected with feelings. The only way I hoped to receive anything for myself was through my achievements. I constantly tried to win. Mother said, 'Let feelings out,' but I didn't believe it. Father said, 'Chin up, son.'

I felt in control and good about myself later on at school, because I could do things well and be in charge. Life at home was extremely difficult, because I was trying to keep my parents together during their increased threats to divorce. And again I felt alone and lonely, and took responsibility for the adults, missing out on getting help for myself over the choice of career.

All this has led me to have an *ostrich attitude* to my inner feelings and needs. I feel that I have to strive constantly to win, that if I stop I have failed. And even when I do win I don't feel satisfaction or pleasure, but the despair of feeling I have to go on winning. I have tied my life up in such a way that I have to stay *on the treadmill*. There is little room for self-reflection, for connecting with the imaginative artist in me, or the creative dreamer. This self-deprivation has resulted in my being terrified of illness, loss and death, as if this were a metaphor for my own creative, free life being snuffed out by the desperate need to control my own life and win. I feel that if I let go it will all go wrong, or be a dead end like the brick wall.

I was recently intensely moved by a piece of music. I found out it was called 'The Stolen Child'. I would like to be able slowly to get in touch with some of the pain of my early childhood feelings, allow them space and air, through therapy, talking or through drawing and painting. I would like to make this vulnerable area within me less anxious and afraid, less the *can of worms* I fear it to be. In doing so I realise I may have to face the fear and sadness and lose some of my more controlling side for a while, until a more appropriate balance is restored and I feel freer to make more comfortable choices for myself as a whole. I would like to be brave enough to open the can of worms, rather than spend my life trying to run away from it and putting myself at risk of exhaustion and ill health.

MARTIN

It seems as if in my early years I was the centre of my mother's life. My parents married late and I was an only child. My father was away travelling for much of my childhood, and when he was around, took little interest in me. He's still a difficult and uncommunicative man. My mother felt he wasn't intellectual enough and often ridiculed what he said and did. It feels as if she looked to me to fulfil her ideals of what a man should be, in her eyes. I was forced to be centre stage, feeling unconsciously that I must conform and be hard-working and good, perhaps to make up for my mother's disappointment in her husband, perhaps to ensure that I was loved and accepted. As a result, I was often lonely and anxious. I couldn't let it show, but I was intensely bored and bit my nails ferociously, both of which made me feel very ashamed. Negative or angry feelings were a no-no, and I learned early on the habit of pushing away anything negative that might come into my head. I learned to be vigilant about all my actions, to judge myself constantly and to fear things that came into my mind that did not conform to the image I believed was mine to live up to and upon which my survival was placed.

It seems as if in some way I have remained on the *treadmill* developed out of my early life through my professional training, repeating the pattern of trying to live up to what I believed was my lot through excessive hard work. I have believed that I must be all

(Continued)

(Continued)

things to all people in order to be a good, caring professional. It seems as if I have felt it necessary to provide what is expected of me from others or I will not be recognised and valued.

Since my mother died, the pattern of things in my life has begun to change. The feelings I have never allowed to the surface have made themselves known, and the natural resentment at having to live my life entirely for others in order to be recognised has made its point. I am frightened by my angry and negative feelings; they seem to rock and threaten my entire equilibrium. I find I cannot control my thoughts, which swing from one thing to another. I can understand that many of these feelings are ones that have been repressed since childhood – they are natural and ordinary feelings. But because they were not allowed earlier on, they still carry with them potency and fear. I find I desperately want to gain control of what is happening to me inside. Some days I want a 'magical cure', when I will wake up and it will all be over; other days I feel despairing and hopeless and am plagued with guilt about what is happening to me, and seek reassurance that all will be well.

Some days it is very difficult for me to acknowledge what is happening to me and that I can have an active part in the transition from survival self, which was very restricting, to being more real, saying what I really think both intellectually and emotionally. I need to believe more in my own capacity to make change, to use my own insight, to listen more directly to the voice inside which allows stillness. My religious faith says: 'Be still ... and know ...'. One of my biggest hurdles is to get over feeling bad and guilty when I am angry, envious, cross or impatient with anyone. I would like a more active relationship with everything that is happening to me, so that I may use some freedom of choice and get to know sides of myself previously in eclipse. The reciprocal role of *powerfully controlling* to *guiltily submissive* is the hardest for me to work with. I sometimes take refuge in helplessness and then my controlling rituals begin. I am working on trying to be noticing/accepting/supporting in relation to myself in order to feel accepted and supported for myself as a whole. Warts, feelings, problems and all. I do know that the strength I have is something of my own which is flexible and not dependent on others.

SUSANNAH

Susannah came into therapy because of issues in relationships where she felt merged and lost her own separate identity. This made her feel frustrated and used. She had recently separated from her partner of fifteen years and was feeling the loss of this closeness and the pull to return to the relationship for the wrong reasons – in order not to have to see her ex-partner suffer or because of her loneliness. She felt that her 'bid for freedom' to be herself was a breakthrough, but it meant she had to face many unresolved issues around close relationships with others and patterns from the past. The following are extracts from the reformulation letter we created together:

> We have shared some insights into your experiences in relation-ships and understood a reciprocal role of striving in relation to a conditional 'other'. Also the dilemma of being either close but taken over and losing a sense of yourself; or, free but alone and cut off. You are particularly in touch with the feelings around this dilemma since your separation from Pete [your partner] last June.

> Possible roots for these patterns would appear to be in your fairly strict childhood. You were a shy child kept on reins by an anxious mother. There was a sense of keeping your natural self-expression back in order to please her and keep her happy, as well as yourself safe from her withdrawal if you were not as she wanted you to be for her. This, and the controlling sense of order in the household, may have contributed to a fear of 'making your mark' and 'going over the mark' in your life generally.

> The ending of your marriage to John was devastating and the deeply upsetting feelings of hurt and betrayal are still fresh for you, feelings that perhaps you bottle up for fear of mess. The ending of your marriage pressed your fear of 'not being up to the mark' and you seem to have taken more blame and responsibility than is your share. You felt guilty and ashamed at your children not having the secure background you wanted for them.

> After your marriage ended you felt vulnerable to your next partner, Pete, and his need to merge and be close was at first comforting. It gave you the 'arms' you longed for and for many years the sense of safety and comfort was welcome and often creative and happy, but you were always aware of the more stifling aspects and your need to be and express yourself differently.

> To balance the restricted feeling of needing to please is the need to break free of constraints. Sometimes you recognise 'if I must, then I won't', in relation to joining clubs and networks where con-formity is overt. You can be anxious about being 'up to the mark' at work and can envy colleagues who get ahead. Breaking free also carries the fear of hurting others and being seen as mean by those you care about, and it also leaves you with a deep sense of loss and loneliness, and unresolved feelings about your own unmet need in close relationships.

(Continued)

(Continued)

I feel that our work together needs to concentrate upon helping you befriend the anxiety about your own self-expression, your own 'mark' either with others or at work, in order to have a more robust relationship with your own power, self-expression and skills. This will entail recognition of when you restrict or place conditions upon your own response or go along with others' conditions in order to keep the peace.

I feel that the conditional regard for yourself which has led to a restricted striving sense of self needs to be loosened to become unconditional. This may mean experimenting with new responses in order to revise their feeling and impact.

The dream you had early on in the sessions, of you and your manager measuring feet against each other and finding them to be equal, gives us a positive and hopeful image of the authority already present in you. Your description of the qualities of the manager – sharp, open and very nice – can be seen as a reflection of your own robust and lively self that needs permission and space in order to flourish and find her own mark.

At the end of Cognitive Analytic Therapy both therapist and patient exchange 'goodbye letters' that reflect their work over the sixteen sessions. My goodbye letter to Susannah refers to the dream:

At the end of the reformulation is the image from the first dream in therapy, of you measuring your feet with the manager and finding them to be equal. We spoke of this dream as containing a positive and hopeful energy, symbolising the robust and lively authority already present in you, and that one of the goals of therapy was to give this authoritative self permission and space, and to experiment, to learn to make her mark and become integrated.

We have shared a lot of sadness connected with the ending of your relationship with Pete. You often connected with this in the few minutes' mindful space at the start of the sessions. There has also been the anxious questioning – 'have I done the right thing?', followed by connecting with your very strong need to 'break free'. There was the sadness at losing the intimacy of the 'arms' followed by the realisation that the arms could at times be 'conditional tentacles'. There was the fear of being seen as 'mean' and seeing Pete suffer, followed by realising you had merged asking for your own needs to be met with being mean or unreasonable.

So the work of therapy has been to recognise your relationship with 'other' and how you can lose a sense of yourself and the reality of your own feeling by disappearing into others' needs. We imagined that this was a pattern of relating learned from your relationship with your anxious mother, for whom you had to make things alright, whose arms were there only if conditions were met. It was hard for you to develop a safe sense of your own needs and voice, or to make your own mark without feeling guilty or selfish. In allowing an understanding of these patterns you have opened to the harshness of the 'stolen ease of being' and begun to allow a kindness to yourself. You could also see that the gap left by unmet need had been filled with an idealisation of how things 'should' be in terms of duty to others, in order to feel alright yourself. From this position you were able to articulate the wisdom that came from the recognition and acceptance of your own feelings. You said: 'Freedom comes from within myself, in accepting the reality of what I feel and seeing things as they are rather than how I feel they "should" be. Right now there is too much anxiety, sadness and longing in me to be comfortable. So I need to wait.'

At session 8 you had the dream about the stolen bag. We shared a lot of sadness at the feeling of this dream, of having to plead to have back what was rightfully yours. In the dream you did get back fully what was yours. And this dream was followed by two others that seemed to reflect both your fear of danger and also, like the first dream, a balancing factor. In one, under pressure from others, you were climbing along a ledge over the sea and were frightened. Then after rounding a corner you drop down onto the sand and the feeling was of relief at being finished with danger.

The reciprocal roles of conditional/controlling/merging in relation to restricted with 'stolen sense of ease', and critical bully in relation to hurt victim, have softened and a new psychological position of playfully caring for yourself in relation to meeting your own need joyfully and growing your own 'arms' has been created.

So the post-Pete part of therapy has been about consolidating this new sense of self. We made a new diagram that included 'growing my own arms, supporting my needs separately from others; being mindfully free to make my own mark'. There is the image of your own kingdom, your own path and an ease of being. You are also aware of putting more energy into making your mark at work and making plans to travel next year and deciding what you would most like for yourself.

And last session there was the opportunity to re-explore the way you can experience a 'silenced emptiness' when you fear not knowing what to say and the 'other', me in this instance, is in the position

(Continued)

(Continued)

of being judging and demanding. I was glad that we had the time to share this reciprocal role and the understanding that rather than being empty and not knowing what to say, it is when you get hooked into the reciprocal role of being emptied by 'other' that you lose your voice and a hold on your liveliness.

Susannah wrote the following in her 'goodbye letter':

Two significant dreams brought me in touch with my own desperate longing, indeed, pleading, to reclaim my precious, lost, stolen, self. I liked 'ease of being'. I dreamed of escaping from danger, fear and demands, by 'breaking free' from the narrow ledge above the raging sea by jumping down and experiencing the safe, firm sand under my feet. I went on to see my own vast kingdom in front of me, green, irrigated and open for exploration into the far distance, with no set paths or restrictions. Depicting this marked the reawakening interest in painting.

If I had checked my lung capacity before therapy and again now there must be an increase in volume! I am learning to breathe in as well as out, and to channel the air, nourishing in itself. Getting to the end of therapy made me wonder if I would manage alone and last week heightened how vulnerable I am in relation to questions, demands or expectations of 'the other' and how I can feel anxious and depleted. I know, however, that what I have experienced in therapy cannot be taken away, that the kingdom is all around me and I am walking on … The concept of Maitri has been important. I have never known the unconditional in my life, let alone the unconditional acceptance of myself – thoughts, emotions, reflexes and behaviour. Some of the time it eludes me, but when I can enter this freeing, caring place I am filled with tears of relief and gratitude. Thank you for this gift. I know it is mine forever and what better way to navigate a new journey – to navigate a change of path.

You will see that everyone's story is quite different, that the images, phrases and what each made of the different experiences was highly individual. **Your story is your own and you need to claim it as your own story**. It is an important start to reflection and gaining control over making manageable goals for change.

TWELVE   Targeting the procedures that create problems and deciding on aims for change

We have been seeing throughout this book how we can find ways to name early unconscious beliefs such as 'Only if I behave in a certain way (please others, cut off, avoid action) will I survive' and that this keeps us lonely and in a placation or avoidance trap, restricting choices of how to be and possibly depressed. Whilst they are all important survival mechanisms, these old beliefs and procedures shape our everyday sense of ourselves, our behaviour and restrict us.

This chapter is devoted to naming the restricting procedures that we take for granted and setting realistic goals for change. We will look at how Sylvia and Alistair made charts of their problem procedures and developed their aims for change; how Linda's aim was to develop trust through the therapeutic relationship. In Chapter 13 we will see how Alistair, Martin, Freda and Susannah also made use of diagrams to focus upon the way their procedures grew into the sequences that led to problems.

Once our individual targets have been created, it is useful to carry them around, so that we can turn to them when feeling stuck, or feel the old responses coming on. Recognising where we are in our learned sequences is the beginning of change, however far down the sequence we have travelled. **It is never too late to stop, revise and reverse!** When you have read this and the next chapter, choose the best way to set about focusing on the areas in your life that need revision and change.

It is important to remember that what we seek to change are the learned procedures that maintain the traps, dilemmas, snags and unstable states that limit our life and cause problems; and to focus upon these rather than the problems the procedures create. For example, our problem may be an eating disorder, but the procedure underlying it may be that we bottle up feelings for fear of making a mess, or we stuff down anger for fear of being rejected. It is the procedure we need to address and change. We must stay off the symptom hook!

It's important too to be realistic and to start with what we *can* do rather than go for trying to sort out something large. Once we begin to change even the simplest thing, other changes follow, like the ripple effect of a stone on water.

SYLVIA

Problem procedure: Either, in touch with the child and feeling and being in pain; or, using my 'telescope' to avoid.

Aim: To feel safe enough to let the child come out from behind the chair and be part of adult Sylvia.

Procedure: The 'telescope', a performance trap.

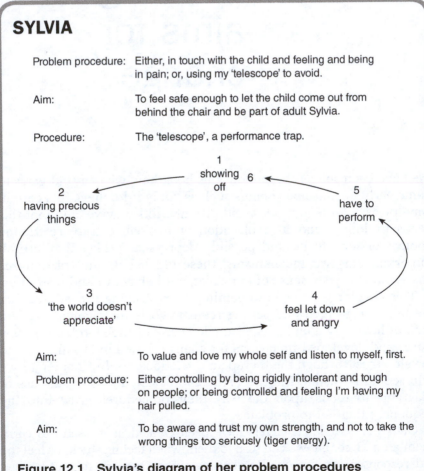

1 showing off 6

2 having precious things

5 have to perform

3 'the world doesn't appreciate'

4 feel let down and angry

Aim: To value and love my whole self and listen to myself, first.

Problem procedure: Either controlling by being rigidly intolerant and tough on people; or being controlled and feeling I'm having my hair pulled.

Aim: To be aware and trust my own strength, and not to take the wrong things too seriously (tiger energy).

Figure 12.1 Sylvia's diagram of her problem procedures underlying her angry outbursts

Sylvia's target problem procedures and aims are shown in Figure 12.1.

Sylvia decided to look at her life when she began to have angry outbursts with people at work. She had also been aware for some time of feeling depressed and sad, and of a sense of meaninglessness in her life. As she worked with her reformulation (p. 190) she became aware of her inner creative spirit, her 'tiger'. Being in touch every day with her tiger has helped Sylvia to feel more 'whole', to become less depressed and to give up her 'performance' self. She has been much less frustrated and is less likely to burst out angrily.

ALISTAIR

Alistair's target problem procedures and aims were as follows:

Problem 1: High blood pressure and exhaustion.
Procedure: Overwork to stave off anxiety, fear; no time for myself, anxiety leaks out in the car, at weekends.
Aim: Make space for some anxiety and fragility to be accepted. Practise stopping with three breaths.
Problem 2: Eternal treadwheel and depression.
Procedure: Constantly striving in order to win, to cope with feelings of failure and inadequacy.
Aim: (a) To recognise 'can of worms'. Recognise when activity is accelerated in order to cope with 'can of worms'.
   (b) To find a container for these feelings. To take half an hour every day for reflection, and writing in the journal.

Alistair also made a map for himself (see p. 213), which describes his main traps. His story is recounted on pp. 194–5.

Begin designing your own chart for change after writing your life story and focus on which target problem procedures you wish to revise. Each week, mark on the chart how you have managed, first in terms of **recognition**, then, second, in terms of **stopping and revising**, and lastly, the **aim. The symptoms or problems are not our primary aim at first**.

The aim may be simply to be more aware of the procedure itself, or it may be just to give yourself half an hour a day for self-reflection. Once recognition of the issues is stronger we can be more specific about the aim. For example, Susannah found that whilst her initial aim was to bear the anxiety of 'longing to merge' in relationships and her fear of hurting the other by being separate, she found that after a few weeks of practising awareness, she was able really to listen to what her own feelings and intuition were telling her. She said, 'I can just feel right now that I am not ready' and the value she could place on her own authentic feeling was vitally important. This is what happens when we start to recognise and challenge old habits: our healthy island starts expanding. The space and awareness we gain helps us in ways we could not anticipate.

Alistair is aiming to move from his half-hour a day reflection to allowing a space for the feelings he has never had time for. He has chosen to use music and poetry to help him with this and to keep writing about what happens. His next step will be to accept and then integrate the feelings trapped in the can of worms and to live more harmoniously with them.

LINDA

Linda's targeting of problems involved relating differently, to trust another human being as well as her own internal world of healthy emotion. She has generously written the following account of her therapy:

> I came to CAT therapy very confused and muddled; 'screwball' was how I described myself. I couldn't understand why my life had turned into such a horrible mess. My childhood had been very difficult as my father suffered from a severe mental illness, and I had to help and support my mother. Also, I was teased terribly at school.
>
> In my late 'teens I developed anorexia and depression and I have struggled ever since. Depression is debilitating in itself, but for me it was the grips of anorexia that caused irreversible damage to my body and controlled my very existence. Many people think it is all about being figure conscious and that the remedy is just to eat anything stodgy. Everyone was concerned only about weight gain, even medical teams. This is an important aspect of the illness, but I had become 'Linda the anorexic'. I no longer knew who or what I was. I found relating to people extremely difficult and seemed to have no emotional connection with anybody. I became a recluse, living with my parents, holding down a part time job, that was it!
>
> After a few meetings with the CAT therapist it became obvious there were a lot of issues from the past that I had not understood and dealt with. I had developed many behaviours to protect myself, and was still using them. Slowly as the sessions progressed I began to let down my guard and my confidence grew. It felt so

freeing to pour out all the things that had whirled around in my head for years. My highly critical internal dialogue contributed so much to my own lack of self-worth and reinforced beliefs of my being stupid and mentally incompetent which perpetuated a sense of hate towards myself.

Laying out my past for another to see was difficult and I was surprised to discover that I was still accepted. The reformulation letter I received highlighted: *'I don't know how to trust anyone sufficiently to develop an adult relationship.'* I would set out to gain approval from others, making sure that I got noticed. As long as I was in control of the interaction I could cope. But as soon as I felt others were looking for something more in a physical way I would become fearful and run away or reject their advances. This would then lead me to feel remorse and become self-critical.

The second dominant procedure was: *'I have learned to cope with my fears alone but cannot contain them.'* This related to my father's illness. When I was young I took responsibility to protect my mother. Dad's illness was never talked about for fear of making things worse, and never mentioned outside for fear of the stigma of mental illness and people judging us. I had to stay strong, and contain all my emotional feelings, alone. Unfortunately endless doubts crept in and disrupted my self-control. I avoided intimate situations and developed defences, including health problems that then restricted my world.

We worked on finding new ways I could relate to others, where I could express the real Linda and not have to be someone I imagined others wanted me to be. We did not concentrate on my illness, we only talked about my health if I was feeling down.

It made me realise I was not just 'Linda the depressed anorexic'. My symptoms had deep underlying issues connected to the avoidance of unmanageable emotions from childhood trauma, having a dad who was so mentally ill. I just could not handle these feelings in any other way. This understanding in itself was like music to my ears, someone was treating me as a real person, not a statistic, was looking through the illness and seeing the real me. I remember one of my biggest fears was that I too was just mentally unstable and that there was no hope.

As we worked together I began to realise not only did I have a soul, but also a heart and could experience useful emotion. I discovered that I was able to express this through my creative skills of photography and poem writing which just seemed to flow out of me freely, from 'the real Linda'.

(Continued)

(Continued)

Another area we worked through was that no one or no thing is 100% perfect. I was always looking for this so when it fell short I felt disappointment. So we discussed the words 'GOOD ENOUGH'!!

One of the most important things I learnt throughout my time in CAT was that I am allowed to have a voice, and I do not need to contain all my problems fears and emotions inside. I learnt there 'are' trustworthy genuine people who will accept you for you, and any problems that you have. My task was to find people like this to collaborate and share stories with.

On my last session I wrote a goodbye poem as my way to express my sincerest thanks for the time and work we had covered over the twenty-four sessions. We had built up a great rapport and he encouraged my personality to shine through!!

My goodbye!

I don't know what to say … a dear friend you have become

But again I face the world alone as our work is said and done,

Our meetings have been insightful, I guess some I already knew

But it has been a privilege and honour to come and talk to you.

One thing I have realised. my responses can be straightforward

Not always such a drama queen and I've gone way over board

With 33 years of self doubting and harsh criticisms to my name

It was easy to believe I am no good and hold my head in shame.

I was worried I would develop an illness similar to that of my dad

And with such evil thoughts, it's easy to see why I thought I was bad.

So Steve having you there to confide in, over the last 24 weeks

It's given me chance to air my thoughts, a total freedom to speak.

I never realised the importance that opening up would set me free

Instead I've battled alone in silence, which in fact it was hurting me.

Have realised I live with a delusion of seeking out that perfect thing

Even knowing it doesn't exist, it's the let downs in my life that ring.

So how do I move on, to that new place, the one on my map?

Where you have stated 'Good enough', the one I discounted as crap.

I wish we'd spent more time, looking at ways that I could do this

And now not having you there to talk to, I am really going to miss.

I'm worried what'll happen as I have yet to find that replacement friend

And with all my thoughts and troubles my life is so tough to mend

But now at least I can accept why my family can't heal my pain

It's to be someone on the outside, which is fresh like the pouring rain.

I hate those words 'goodbye', it's like you've gone and passed away

Yet even though you're still alive you cannot feature in my day.

I've not agreed to everything that we've said, as that would not be me

I like to have a challenge, a laugh and joke, as you've come to see.

It's been good to meet someone that accepts me for the person I really am

And not repulsed by my sinister flaws it's almost like having a fan

I'm slowly realising that I don't need to be ashamed for the way I act

I shouldn't need to go and hide; people should accept me for that.

I just want to say 'thank you' for understanding all about my past

To share my deepest thoughts and also to enjoy those many laughs

But your acceptance of my personality struck a chord in my soul

Given me confidence to reveal another side, to be proud and whole.

(Linda, 2009)

[A complete case study for Linda appears on the companion website to this book.]

THIRTEEN Making maps and diagrams

This chapter looks at how to map the way we have learned to cope with inner conflicts so that we have a map that illustrates our inner and outer dialogue with thinking and feelings.

Mapping is a fluid process that invites us to find our own words that fit our felt experience, and to check out the fit. Steve Potter refers to the shimmering ability of words to help us move between open and closed positions (Potter and Sutton 2006). Language is a continuous process of finding self-expression and communication, with wider meanings being closed down to make a point and then opening to be re-dialogised. Our task is to draft which words fit what we feel to form the current map of our inner and outer dialogue. Maps illustrate the country, but they are not the country! They can be built upon, decorated, like the British Ordnance Survey maps that are famous throughout the world. They show how to get from A to B and also what we might find along the way, the various signs and symbols that indicate character, past and present.

First we find words to describe our core pain and the problematic reciprocal roles that maintain this. Then we need descriptions of how we have managed, such as striving or placating. Many of these routes become a trap, dilemma or snag, a management loop that maintains rather than releases us. Sometimes we are able to describe the nature of our core pain by first outlining the learned reciprocal roles that maintain it. For example, a demanding perfectionist role may be our way of coping with, but also maintaining, a harshly judged self, where core pain is experienced as humiliation and worthlessness.

Start mapping your diagram by drawing out two or three boxes that look like the example in Figure 13.1. Choose two or three of

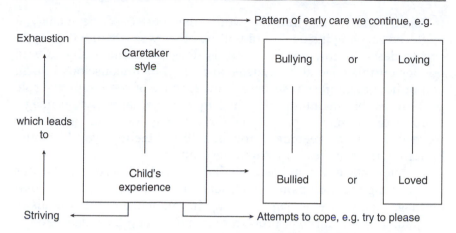

Figure 13.1 'Caretaker style and child response' example of learned reciprocal role

what you feel are your main problematic reciprocal roles. Draw out one box for your 'healthy island' and healthy reciprocal roles, such as *listening* in relation to *listened to, giving kindness* in relation to *receiving kindness, caring* to *cared for*.

You might like to consider how you would describe core emotional pain. Freda described her core pain of worthless/rejected as being maintained by the reciprocal role of *deprived* in relation to *depriving*. And *feeding off* in relation to *fed off*. She received no unconditional love from either parent and very early on took the position of the 'parental child', taking responsibility and magical guilt for her mother's loss and depression. She also recognised the *tyrannising/controlling* in relation to *tyrannised/controlled/restricted* role where her anger was turned against herself and the only way to manage this was through her eating disorder. Here she was in a cycle of *rejecting* in relation to *rejected as worthless* and *controlling via placating* in relation to *controlled/kept guiltily caught*.

To find words for your core pain feel into what best describes the feelings you have worked hard to get away from through the learned procedures.

Some of the following examples might help you find your own words:

afraid, terrified, lost, abandoned, forgotten, deprived, abused, left, rejected, lonely, in pain (physical, mental and emotional), angry, furious, in a rage, spitting, shrieking, yelling, crying, screaming, dropped, teased, tantalised, tyrannised, longing, waiting (to be held, loved again, picked up, nurtured, for Mum/Dad/other), hungry, starving, empty, needy, intense

Spend time feeling into the words that best describe what you might be carrying inside. There will be other words you will wish to add to describe how you feel. If this does not come easily to you, ponder on this page and its ideas, and let your unconscious inform you of how to address your core pain. A sense of the reciprocal role procedures that maintain the pain may emerge naturally: an image, word or dream may come to you. Or you may just come across the word you need by keeping in touch with the feelings you have and by letting them indicate the right description.

The next stage in making your diagram is to describe the means of surviving the core pain, which leads to forming traps, dilemmas or snags, and to use arrows showing the sequence of what tends to happen. The self-survival procedures tend to loop back again to the core pain.

FREDA

You will see illustrated in Freda's diagram (Figure 13.2) that she coped with her inner pain of rejection and deprivation first by pleasing others, and later by overeating when placation no longer relieved her feelings and the core state feelings included depressed and worthless. The diagram shows how each of her procedures, or coping tactics, while useful when she was small, in adult life trapped her in an actual circular trap, or were split into a dilemma. Each old coping pattern ultimately led her back to her inner pain.

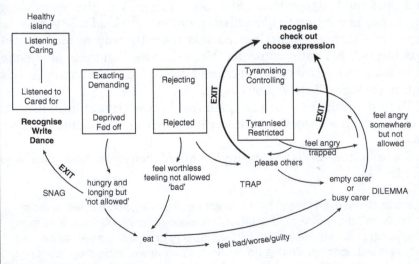

Figure 13.2   Freda's diagram

Freda could see how the 'doing what others want' trap led to the perpetuation of her depression and restricted her own life. By using the diagram every day she could see exactly where she was at a time of difficulty or conflict. The eating to cope with the emptiness and feeling 'bad' made her guilty, for which she was self-punishing, and then felt alone. She 'snagged' her life in a way that deprived her of using her own creative skills. Her way out of the map, the exit point, was through recognising her ability to be able to cope, as she had done all her life. But instead of using it in a placatory way for others, she began looking at it as a natural skill that could be used to create a better framework for her attitude to herself and for her life practically.

Always try to keep your diagram simple. The most important thing is for it to work for you.

If you recognise that you avoid things, work out the feelings you are trying to avoid and plot the way you continue avoiding them in your life, as shown in Martin's avoidance diagram in Figure 13.3.

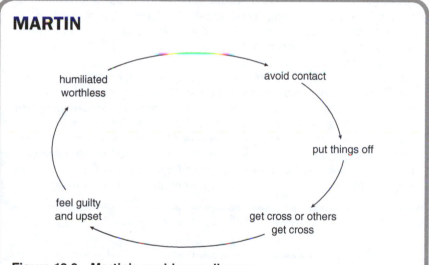

MARTIN

Figure 13.3 Martin's avoidance diagram

Martin had great difficulty with swings of mood and with obsessional thoughts, in particular his preoccupation with the word 'baptism', which emerged only in the middle of his therapy. He had been baptised a year before the onset of his depression. This was very important to him and an expression of his own need and devotional attitude. But he had always felt guilty about it because he believed it went against the wishes of both his wife and his mother. His chart showed how his survival-self

(Continued)

(Continued)

mode was either to please others he considered 'perfect' and strong, or to work excessively hard to meet 'perfect' standards. Both survival modes restricted his healthy island and natural development and contributed to making him dangerously exhausted. He was caught between his desire to be himself truly and the guilt he felt when this conflicted with the two most important and powerful people in his life, his mother and his wife. The most intense period of his depression began after his mother died. Although free of her very tight hold, it was still inside him in his self *restricting* in relation to *restricted* reciprocal role. This contributed to panic and guilt for wanting freedom to be himself. His guilt was unconscious and his map helped him see how much guilt he carried for every negative thought about anything or anyone. Every time he had the tiniest negative thought he would punish himself with feeling bad or by tormenting himself with the word 'baptism'.

One of the most wonderful experiences about the nature of suffering is that within the nature of the suffering is the key to the way out. Although the word 'baptism' could be used obsessively and as a punishment for not being 'good enough', Martin also needed to be 'reborn' into his real self and initiated into the adult freedom of choice about feelings in full range, without guilt.

Martin has managed to contain the extremes of his mood swings, and has been able to explore with his wife ways in which he restricts himself within their relationship and how she can be invited into the restricting role initially occupied by his mother. Restricting can make him feel contained and safe, and he panics when he is apart from his wife or with nothing to do; but restricting also makes him feel furious and trapped and he once again becomes the 'little boy'. Over time he has processed this change and now has a wider range of feelings without guilt. He does not have to be 'perfect' or centre stage in order for life to be meaningful.

ALISTAIR

Alistair is currently working on his life story and diagram (see Figure 13.4). Because he has organised his life through excessive striving and control he has had no time for reflection, for letting his natural, spontaneous thoughts come to the surface, or for following his ideas. He had to suppress all of his vulnerability early on in life, mainly because of a very tense family situation and because both his parents were largely absent. He had a very clever older brother, and he picked up early on that if he did not strive to win he would be left behind and regarded as a 'failure'. Thus, any feeling of which he was not in strict control has

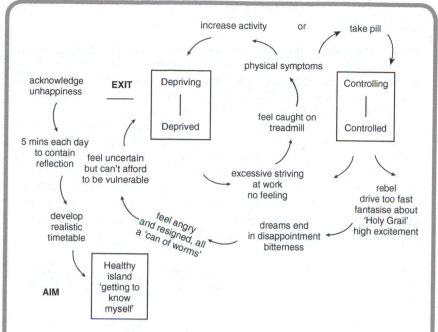

Figure 13.4   Alistair's diagram

come to be seen as a failure. When we met he was so afraid of the out-of-control feelings that he had shut them off completely. They would 'leak' out, through 'odd' thoughts, dreams, irrational fears for his own health and a great flood of fear when two close friends died suddenly.

Alistair is now able to acknowledge how unhappy he has been and to look at what this means in terms of his life. This acknowledgement alone has allowed him to review the job he does (he works a fourteen-hour day every day, starting at 5 a.m.). Previously he had been 'on automatic', and his internal needs had reflected themselves in health problems such as a duodenal ulcer and abscesses. He could not allow himself proper time to take care of these matters, or to look holistically at the implications of his symptoms for his general stress level. Had he continued to deny his needs and difficulties, he may have developed an even more serious health crisis.

KAREN

Karen's diagram is shown in Figure 13.5. Karen was recommended for focused therapy after taking a number of overdoses. She had a pattern of making intense and immediate relationships with men that

(Continued)

(Continued)

ended explosively after just a few weeks, when she would then make an attempt on her life. Karen was only eighteen, but had had five admissions to casualty over the previous two years. Her family background was unsettled. She had been fostered at age four, then adopted by a couple who split up when she was eight. She was 'parcelled round' to family and friends, but never settled anywhere. Two 'uncles' had sexually abused her and she had also developed a pattern of bingeing and starving as a way of trying to control her confused feelings. As a result, by the time she began secondary school, and all her peer group were pairing off, she felt worthless, unlovable and that no one really wanted or loved her. All she could identify with were stories from romantic novels or an idealised longing for what we called 'perfect care'.

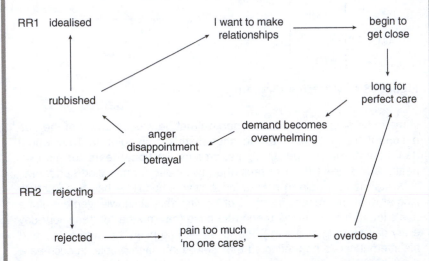

Figure 13.5   Karen's diagram: two reciprocal role (RR) patterns

A diagram helped her to see the pattern of her responses to relationships which had led to her overdoses. This gave her a certain degree of stability, so that she could see why and how the patterns had emerged and begin the work of receiving 'good enough' care for herself. This diagram helped Karen see what patterns were involved in her starving/bingeing routines. What she began to work through in her therapy was how her idealisation had become a substitute for her grief at the loss and deprivation of her early life, and how it prevented her from receiving something that was 'good enough' for her needs.

SUSANNAH

We read Susannah's story in Chapter 11. In diagram (a) we see what she worked on in her therapy. Diagram (b) reflects how she was now exploring and nourishing her healthy island through mindful awareness, and using 'her own arms' symbolically to care for her emotional need. Susannah kept this second diagram in her pocket to remind herself each day of the focus on mindfulness connected to her own separateness and self-care.

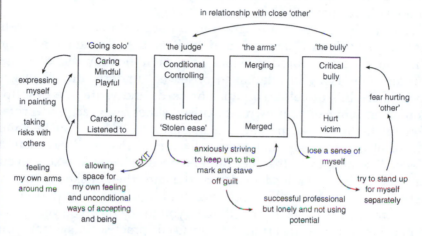

Figure 13.6(a)   Susannah's first diagram

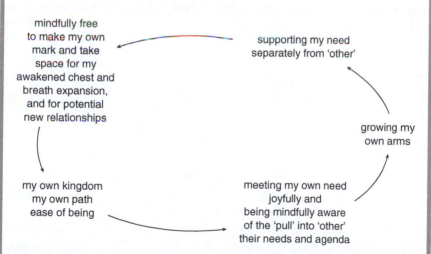

Figure 13.6(b)   Susannah's post-therapy diagram: the healthy island

Go over each of the diagrams in this chapter again and see if you can follow them clearly. Each stage should result in the next one by following the arrow. In a trap, the way of coping leads back to the core emotional pain, sometimes after quite a detour. A dilemma (the either/or, or if/then) results in a lopsidedness that also causes a return to the core pain. And a snag tends to keep the core pain as it is all the time. The exit point begins when we simply **stop** and recognise the old patterns. Revising the old patterns and trying something different follows. The exit point allows us time for space and self-reflection. This is also the beginning of taking space needed to nourish our healthy self.

If you wish to make a diagram about separate and shifting self states, go back to Chapter 9 and look at the diagram made for Graham. Find a coloured card and write on it 'healthy island' at the top and 'observing in relation to observed' underneath. Then get some more bits of coloured paper or cards and write one description on each one of your own recognised states with reciprocal role. You might like to keep some blank cards for when you become aware of a previously unrecognised state so that it always has a place. Assemble them together on one piece of paper and see if you can see which ones lead to the next state, then make an arrow between the states. Whenever you find yourself in a particular state, tracing the arrow back will help you to see how you got there. Whenever you are uncertain or confused, practise imagining you are standing on the healthy island and see if you can concentrate on the image of an observing self. Over time you will be able to make other exits to the states.

FOURTEEN Techniques for working through the process of change and holding on to change

So far, we have described how to write our life story, how to make a chart of problems with aims for change, and how to make a diagram with exits for change. Also, we have talked about looking at these charts or diagrams each day and monitoring problem areas. Change is best consolidated if achieved slowly and thoroughly. A major change is already happening, that of self-reflection and self-observation. This change will already be bearing fruit.

Now, how do we go about making change when some of our habits are lifelong? Please be encouraged by three things:

1. The human mind is more expansive than is generally understood. Once we develop and consolidate a practice of self-awareness we may travel further than we ever imagined.
2. The ripple effect – throw one small stone into a pond and the ripples are far reaching. Once we begin to change the smaller things – often the traps or dilemmas – other changes follow naturally.

3. Philosophical thinking such as ancient Taoism and modern psychology both share an understanding that nature abhors a vacuum and that the principle of homeostasis – meaning movement and balance – operates to prevent rigidity or lopsidedness. Life tends to offer us wake-up calls for us to have the opportunity to find balance, to embrace both dark and light.

Perhaps you have had a 'wake up' and this is why you are reading this book now. It may confirm what you already 'knew' but hadn't put into words. Many of us fear change and the unknown; we allow ourselves to be limited by what others will think. Buddhist philosophy tells us that we already have all that we need, it's just that we don't see it. Clearing the mirror in which we look at ourselves is a good start to getting to know ourselves, freer of conditions.

There are many different ways of bringing about changes and shifts in consciousness, and there are many therapeutic styles that can assist in this. In this chapter we will look at a number of these, and you may be drawn more to one than another. **There is no one way of working, the best way is the one that works for you**.

Self-monitoring

Self-monitoring helps us develop awareness of our different patterns. It is best to choose something specific to monitor, like depressed or negative thinking, traps or dilemmas. Or, unwanted thoughts, difficult feelings, physical symptoms. Use a small notebook to note the time of day, place, who you are with, what else is happening and **what you are thinking and feeling**. Keep this notebook for a week before looking at your entries. Sometimes we have to keep up the monitoring for three or four weeks before we can see any kind of pattern emerging.

When you are ready, read through and select one or more words or phrases that you use frequently, and identify a repeated theme, person, time or place. For example, through self-monitoring one man learned that his tinnitus grew worse whenever he was unable to be assertive. It became a reminder to express himself and not be passive or placatory.

With increased awareness we see how one thing leads to another in terms of our own and others' reactions. This observation allows us to halt the process when it leads to things going wrong.

Journal-keeping

Use a larger notebook in which to make a record of your inner life, feelings, associations, hopes and dreams, as you journey to know yourself more fully. You may like to keep your journal each day, or just for when you feel things strongly or make a connection about something.

At times of personal investigation or assessments, and particularly in times of crisis and despair, we often find ourselves drawn to symbolic language such as drawings, images, poems or prose. Just go with the flow and your own language will find form inside your journal. You may not understand it fully at first, but as time goes on, and certainly when you look back on it, it will give you a vital link with your inner world and to whatever meaning you might be seeking.

Mindfulness

The contribution of Mindfulness in everyday Western life is growing. We choose what is to be the object of our mindfulness and we focus on it, just as it is, without trying to change or control it. The object of mindfulness may be a sound, an image, a feeling, the body or breath. The intention within mindfulness is to slow down the busy mind and hurry sickness that clouds our concentration. We allow thoughts to come and go, not following them but recognising them as 'just thoughts' and return to the object of our mindfulness. We release ourselves from being slaves to our thoughts. The results of mindfulness may not appear significant, but over time we may find calm and clarity. Whilst mindfulness is a reflective rather than active process, not designed to go anywhere or achieve anything, it can offer, as Amanda (p. 134–136) found during her depression, 'somewhere to go and something to do that was not depression'.

If you are attracted to learn more about mindfulness look for opportunities in your area to join a mindfulness meditation group or course and a teacher who suits you. This may take time. Once we are open to looking for an appropriate teacher, one often does appear, often unexpectedly. The important thing is just to start practising exactly where you are, right now, in the present moment.

Vietnamese Zen Buddhist teacher Thich Nhat Hanh writes about the nourishment offered by mindfulness practice. He speaks of going back to the island within. When we nourish our healthy island through practice we are less likely to be swept away in times of crisis by our thoughts and feelings. This does not mean we are not affected by crises or that we do not feel. Mindfulness offers us a vehicle through which our experiences may be felt, processed and expressed. It can bring a quality of peace and relaxation into our lives, although this is not an aim in itself.

You will have read how Amanda and Susannah both used mindfulness as a way to help their more difficult feeling states.

In Appendix 2 and on the companion website to this book there are mindfulness exercises for you to practise.

Imaging, visualisation, active imagination and body drama

There is no situation to which the creative use of your imagination cannot be applied usefully and safely. We all have this capacity, even though many people say 'I've got no imagination'. To test yourself, close your eyes for a few minutes and lean back in your chair. Imagine yourself picking up a lemon from your fruit bowl. Place the lemon on a board and take a sharp knife out of your drawer. With the knife cut the lemon in half. Pick up one of the halves and put it in your mouth. Notice what is happening. Is your mouth watering, are your eyes tightening or squinting, is your tongue curling? If it is, then you have just imagined yourself eating a lemon with a full body reaction. There is no lemon in sight, so where did that reaction come from? Imagination!

Negative thoughts and damaging internal views are perpetuated by the combination of our repeated thoughts and the power of the imagination to make them more concrete and dramatic. In phobic disturbance and anxiety the most infectious negative thought is that 'It will happen again'. Many people who are fearful and seek to avoid their fears carry images of what might happen 'if'. The range of our imaginings can be from childhood fears, to the pathologically jealous wife or husband who sees the imprint of the non-existent lover wherever there is a space.

Imagination, except in the world of the arts and music, is often dismissed or trivialised, its power feared and, because it's non-scientific, it has had only a shadowy place in medicine or psychology. Memory is always selective, and it has a mercurial quality. Images and sensations have meaning unique to each individual. We need to make sure we do not over-identify with the products of our imagination and harden down or take literally those images and sensations that emerge. They need a light touch as stepping stones to information.

If you discover through the exercises in this book that you have difficult painful memories or flashbacks, particularly of violence and abuse, please go very slowly and find someone safe, respectful of your needs and well qualified to work with you.

Imagination has the power to bring forward hidden images from years ago that return when something triggers them. We have seen how imagining a lemon can make us salivate, we have seen that imagination can recapture the original fear of agoraphobia or the terror of a panic attack. If imagination can do all these things it can also be used as a resource and work for us positively.

Take your notebook and look at the number of images and descriptive words you have used, the number of times you have written, 'I feel like a ...' or 'It's like a ...'. You have created images and are already in the world of the imagination. When you are out walking, let yourself look at the shapes of the landscape rather than seeking to name trees and plants or count the number of bird species. When people are talking to you, whether on the television or in your life, see if you can find an image for them – something they remind you of, or a shape or colour. When you listen to music, lie on the floor and let the music conjure up images. When you are reading, read fiction, romance, poetry, fairy tales, children's stories, texts that are fun and full of simple wonder, that make you laugh. Getting into the realm of the imagination means getting out of the rational, logical, way of thinking. When you go to sleep at night, ask yourself for a dream.

Using the powers of the imagination positively and safely

Reframing problems through visualisation

Choose one of your problem areas. If you have identified with the 'doing what others want' trap, imagine yourself with someone you have always felt you had to please, and imagine yourself saying 'no' to them. Set the scene for yourself – a room – and decorate it in your mind, giving it colour and shape. Choose where and how you will stand or sit, what you will wear. Watch what you do with your hands and feet. Place the other person where you can see their eyes. Make sure your eye level is equal so you are not placing yourself in an inferior position. Have an easy conversation with this person, speak to them as if you were in charge: say the things you would really like to say, rather than waiting to respond to their needs or questions. Then visualise that they ask you to do something you do not want to do. Smile and say, 'I'd love to be able to help but I really can't at the moment.' Practise it out loud. Say it several times. There may be other versions of things you would like to say. Watch the other person's face. Notice what kind of look or gesture would normally trigger off your placatory response. Say 'no' to this gesture and look. Say it again. Practise it with a real person.

TRACEY

Tracey identified 'bottling-up feeling or making a mess' with 'having to give in to others', and with 'having to do what others want', and found that her main dilemma in terms of relating to other people was that she felt she was either a *battering ram* or *modelling clay*. She felt that she had been modelling clay all her life, giving in to others, doing what they wanted. But if she expressed some of her feelings or was assertive in any way, she felt as if she were a battering ram. One week she spontaneously reached a middle position that married the positive value of each pole of her dilemma. Her image and her new position and aim was to be 'like springy steel'.

Painting and drawing

Images may be anchored by painting or drawing. Keep these as spontaneous and natural as possible. Make the paintings or drawings as soon as possible whilst the image is still fresh, with all its detail. Interpretation or meaning can come later. Sometimes we don't understand the exact nature of an image until later, when something happens and the impact of the image becomes clear. Once we become accustomed to using our images creatively, as part of our lives, we are rewarded by other insights into their potential use and meaning, We may realise that we have inside us a rich resource for future assistance with struggles and difficulties.

Drawing and painting are best done on the floor, as if we were playing, using colours freely without constraints. As well as painting or drawing we may like to model something in clay, play-dough, papier mâché. One woman made masks for the different parts of her and used them to help her be aware of their impact. We may find magazine or newspaper pictures that describe our images or feelings, and paste them into a collage. It's a good idea to keep important images somewhere near – in your wallet, diary, over the cooker, by the bathroom mirror, etc. Look at the images every day without judgement.

Exploring traps or dilemmas through the body

This is where we allow our body to show us how it feels to be in a trap or dilemma, or to express the image we have discovered. Stand, sit, lie or get your body into a position that describes your image or your feeling. Stay with the posture and let your body tell you something of the nature of this posture as you hold it.

Lila used this technique to get in touch with the tremendous tension she felt. In response to the request 'allow your body to get into the position of tension' she found herself literally trying to climb the wall. She was shocked to find how extreme this was and how evocatively her body behaved when asked to express itself.

Martha described her dilemma as 'either I'm a doormat or one of the Furies'. When she invited her body into the position of a doormat she experienced the sensation of everyone walking over her. When asked to describe the doormat she said, 'It's soft and brown and it's got WELCOME written on it.' In contrast, her body position for the Furies involved spinning, spitting, kicking, hissing. Her experience of the 'Furies' frightened her; she could then see how her 'doormat' position was a way of avoiding such intense feelings. When she moved between the two positions, spending a few minutes in each, a third position appeared. Her body spontaneously placed itself straight upright, looking ahead, arms swinging to and fro freely, shoulders back, knees supple. 'I'm ready for action,' she said. 'I can move fast or be still as I wish.' In this third position she felt in control, and in charge of her choices. No longer limited by her dilemma.

Being aware of how we use our body, either when we are on our own or with others, can help us notice unexpressed feelings. Sometimes we tell two stories; we may say: 'I'm fine thank you' whilst our eyes are looking dead and sad, and our body is as tight, telling a different story. Sometimes the smallest body change, from arms tightly folded when talking about the narrowness of our life, for example, to those same arms opening out widely to embrace something new, can begin an actual change. Martha was never quite such a welcoming doormat again, nor was she hurled about inside by the Furies. Something memorable always happens when we work directly with the body.

Sometimes, when we work with the body we contact a part that feels very little. The roots of many unhelpful beliefs live in the child consciousness within us. If we are able to connect with the energy and simple language of the child in us we may wish to help him or her become freer of unhelpful old beliefs. If you are co-counselling you might like to offer 'I don't know why they said that to you but what I do know is that you did your best.'

Exploring traps, dilemmas and other problems through objects

Make a box of small objects, some you like, some you don't like, some to which you feel indifferent – shells, stones, toys, sticks, glass, bits and pieces you have around your house. Clear a space on the floor and place a rug or cloth in the space. This will be the boundary for your 'drama' enactment. Now get down on the floor, either on your own or with your co-counsellor. (This exercise can be fun to do, either alone or helping someone else.)

Decide which trap, dilemma, family scene or relationship struggle you wish to depict. Choose first an object for yourself, to represent you. Don't think too hard, just go for something you really like that will stand for you as you are now (or perhaps as you were in the past, if you are exploring a past situation). Hold your own object for a while and get the feel of it; get to know it well. When you are ready, place it in the centre of your space on the floor. Next take an object to represent one of the people in your current drama.

That could be father, mother, uncle, aunt, sister, brother, friend, colleague, lover, neighbour, animal – anyone you wish. After you have chosen the object, look at it and see why you have chosen it for this person. What qualities does the person have? If this is not immediately clear, the reason may emerge as you go on with the drama.

Go on choosing objects until you have one for everyone you intend to include. Place each one on the floor in relation to how they are currently in your life, or were in the scene you are recapturing. Notice the spaces between each one, whether they are close, or if some appear to block, or seem far apart. If it's a scene from when you and your siblings were together, get the feel of what happened when the scene changed, as when someone left home or went into hospital, or when someone new entered. When you do this, allow the objects themselves to take on the drama and illustrate the impact of what happens.

It is quite fantastic what strong feelings this exercise can evoke when the objects are allowed to unfold their story. For example:

objects may be all of similar size or material and then suddenly something quite different is introduced and everything changes. You may notice that, in order to communicate with certain members/objects, you have to make huge leaps across the floor.

Everything that happens in terms of the objects is useful in portraying family structures: pairs and triangles; sizes and shapes; who is easy to approach and who isn't; what is needed in terms of change or movement; what needs to happen for one object to reach another; how it feels for the rock that is your father to approach the tiny shell that is your sister or the piece of string that is wrapped around your uncle.

You might like to focus on a particular event and then ask the question: 'How would I have liked it to be?' And let the objects show you.

Writing letters you never send

This is useful when there are many things left unsaid to people who are perhaps dead or unapproachable. Start the letter, 'Dear Mum ...' or whoever you wish to write to. Then begin with something of what you feel. For example, 'I am writing to you because I could never find the words to say what you meant to me', or 'All my life I feel you have put me down'. Write as if this were your last chance fully to express what that person has meant to you, however difficult. Do not let guilt get in the way, or any moralising about blame or fairness or pride. You will never send this letter, but you need to write from yourself for yourself. It may be gratitude and love you want to express, that you regret not passing on in the person's lifetime; or, it may be more painful and negative feelings, as in the following unsent letter, written by Stephanie from Chapter 11. Here is the letter she wrote to her father:

> Dear Dad,
>
> I tried to feel what life would have been without you; it was unimaginable except for the feeling of an immense weight lifting from me. Life without that burden. When I tried to imagine life without my mum, I could imagine some other good woman looking after me well enough.
>
> I tried to think of an image to describe how it felt to be your daughter. What came to mind was that when I was small, over a period of time you slit me open, placed a box of maggots between my heart and my stomach and slowly and deliberately sewed the scar away. Your living legacy was that I could never again feel peace, goodness, satisfactions – just

rottenness at the core. That shocks me. It is like hating and blaming my own limb to hate and criticise you. You seem old and often very pathetic, and nothing at all to do with the person who came and planted the maggots. I feel very sorry for you, but it becomes confused with feeling sorry for myself.

I do feel like I have been tortured enough, and I would like you to let me go now, please. You and Mum tut-tut about the relationships with men that I form, but each is modelled on the way things were with you. I had to learn to trust and love somebody who hated parts of me, loathed others, merely criticised most and demanded that I thrive and flourish and serve their every need.

I was at Uncle Jack's house lately. He thinks you have been a pretty dreadful father to me. He wanted to do something nice for me. He offered me a drink and brought me a cup of coffee – no strings. It made him feel good because he had done a nice thing. It made me cry, because in twenty-seven years my own father has never done such a simple act of kindness for me.

Guilt and mixed feelings apart, I think that I have to tell you that you have been a complete bastard. It fills me with an anger which I transfer to many people, and in particular all of the men I meet. Every skill you gave me you used against me; you tutored my brain, then devoted yourself to undermining my intelligence; if someone is treating me badly I can't call you in to protect me because you would agree with them, etc.

Such a small and pathetic man, not content with losing his own chance of happiness and satisfaction, you had to have mine too. I would like to destroy you. I would like to spit all that hatred back at you. Strange that I should think you smaller and more pathetic than your own child. Strange that I should believe that even a fraction of the hatred you gave to me could destroy you. And you had my mum completely devoted to salving your every need from the moment you met aged fifteen. She has become quite a contortionist to be able to constantly feed your every need and still remember to keep herself alive.

I wish I had had a different father. I hope I can trust enough to allow the manly half of the human race to make some positive contribution to me and my life.

Dreams

Dreams are the language of the unconscious, a rich symphony of undiscovered material reaching the daylight of consciousness through imagery, motif, story and feeling. We all dream every night, but not all dreams are remembered. When an important dream occurs the feeling evoked can stay with us throughout the day and beyond. Dreams can contain insights that are useful. They offer a balancing influence upon consciousness by making us aware of our unconscious longings, symbols and unfinished business.

How to work with our dreams

Keep a dream notebook to record your dreams. Write them down as soon as you wake, even if it is the middle of the night. If a dream wakes you, it is important. If you go back to sleep thinking you will record it in the morning, it will slip back into the unconscious. If the dream message is important it will come again. Learning to listen to the language of dreams can help us release what is blocked and help to restore balance, as well as offer us exits and third positions for traps and dilemmas.

When you have written your dream down, ponder on its general shape, on its images and motifs. Note the feeling of the dream, the time and place – current time or past time, your age if you are represented in the dream. Note the time of day and consider its meaning. Morning or afternoon, evening or night.

The most important question when pondering on your dream is: **what does this mean to me?** If you appear as age seventeen in your dream and you are in fact thirty-five, what aspect of your seventeen-year-old self are you being shown? Does the figure seventeen hold any other significance? What does the memory or meaning of being seventeen mean for your life as it is now?

It is helpful in the amplification of your dream if this approach is followed for all other aspects, symbols or images. If there is a house in your dream, what kind of house is it – colour, shape, size? Is it familiar? What country or place does it remind you of? Where are you, the dreamer, in relation to the house?

Another important aspect of amplifying your dream is to consider the order of events in the dream. There seems to be no ordinary linear time in dreaming, and death in dreams does not necessarily mean mortal death. Death in a dream is symbolic and may be interpreted on many different levels – as an ending, a transformation, a dying off, a falling away of a particular aspect of your life.

Look closely at the order of the events in your dream and see if you can understand some of the links between sequences, events or images. For example: 'In the dream an old lady rides a bicycle down a steep hill. At the bottom of the hill she is stopped abruptly by a small girl bearing a bunch of flowers. She wants to keep going, to use her downward speed to help her gain impetus to ride up the hill, but has to accept the flowers from the child first. She then begins her difficult ascent up the hill, but as she is going more slowly she sees the view of the fields more closely.' The order of the dream indicates that the old woman (an aspect of the dreamer) has to curb her irritation to stay with the child. The dream suggests that, in slowing down in order to accept a gift from a younger self, the dreamer is offered another more spacious view of her effort in the climb up the hill – possibly a symbolic representation of growing old!

Sometimes dreams come in series, and the series may occur all in one night, around a main theme, as if there is an important process to which our unconscious seeks to alert us.

Dreams may produce images that are frightening, startling or powerful and which bear no resemblance to anything we know rationally. When this occurs, what is hidden in the image that is of importance to us wants very much to be noticed and understood. Draw your dream figure, and share it with another person if you feel the dream content to be too disturbing or worrying. Although the figure in the dream may represent something you don't like, once explored and made conscious the figure and what it represents is never so frightening or overwhelming.

AMANDA

Amanda (see p. 134) had two significant dreams during her depression that drew attention to her suicidal impulses. In one dream she is swallowing pills with people around her encouraging her to continue. There is a feeling of ease in the dreams of just continuing taking the pills and quietly fading away into oblivion. The dream had such a powerful feeling that, on waking, Amanda felt terrified that it would be easy to go along with the dream. She remembers speaking to her therapist on the telephone, who indicated she was in fact in control of whether she took her own life or not and the important thing was that she could be in charge of the choice. She was not being told what she should or should not do, although she writes that she remembers the therapist suggesting that she took all the pills she had stored in her cupboard into a pharmacy for disposal!

The other dream was of someone trying to smother her and was recurrent. She explored it through role-play in her therapeutic session with the therapist approaching her with a pillow and Amanda working at stimulating the muscles of her arm to push the pillow away. She was being encouraged to develop her own assertive resources and to say 'no' to destructive forces. For a while the dreams left her. Then, about a year later, the dream returned; she still could not resist or shout out except in her head and she realised that she was not frightened but very, very angry.

She also knew that she was stronger, that the dream in itself couldn't harm her. Amanda had been able, through her therapy and its work with her dreams, to acknowledge her angry feelings that were so deeply buried. In doing so she gained a sense of freedom from the destructive anger that was turned against herself, that could have led to her killing herself.

If you become interested in your dreams and in knowing more about how to work with them in your life, you may be helped by reading any of the selected books listed in the Further Reading section on the companion website to this book.

Assertion and aggression

As we continue to process change we may need to be more assertive about our thoughts, needs and desires. It's easy to confuse assertion with aggression and thus hold back, and this confusion can get in our way. You may find that it is difficult for you to be assertive, and express your needs directly. In the 'fear of hurting others trap', we believe that just saying what we feel will be hurtful; or we may fear being seen as aggressive, as too 'pushy'. Keep on noticing the old beliefs. Keep trying to refine the way you express yourself with others so that you *are* clear and straightforward in what you ask for or how you express feeling. If we avoid being assertive out of unrevised beliefs, others may well ignore or take us for granted, because *they* actually do not know what we think or feel.

Being assertive is perfectly acceptable. People who do not respect us must either be stood up to or left out of our life.

If the art of assertion is a skill you lack and need to learn, there are many places where this can be practised. Joining a group or class can really help to consolidate the changes you may wish to make. Being able to practise saying 'no', or saying what we really think with others as witness, and being able to test out newfound ideas or strengths, is a potent and lasting way of keeping hold of change.

Creative ways of practising with and holding on to change

Hold your troubled mind in the cradle of loving kindness.

Pema Chodron, Omega New York, June 2014

Throughout this book we have been challenging old beliefs, having seen the way they can influence what we think and believe about ourselves and other people. It is this empowerment of our orchestrating, reflexive and assertive sense of self that brings us more dialogically into both inner and outer world, and this increases our sense of spaciousness and individual narrative. From experiencing our enacted patterns as the person I am, as laid down by the power of early caregivers, we shift into experiencing these patterns as something I have learned to do habitually. Self-monitoring and writing help to move hidden ideas from the obscurity of our minds into the daylight and allow us to look at them afresh. Some of us might be amazed at the influence of an apparently simple but mistaken belief. This awakening may be sufficient to bring about change. Many problems, however, result from strongly built-up defences against early woundings, and the difficulty in changing these defences appropriately comes about because the fear involved is very great. Change takes courage. It takes courage to risk feeling into our fears rather than avoiding them. It takes courage to go with anxiety rather than letting it limit us. But finding ways to be more present with the reality of difficult feelings, and trying new responses, empowers us. Staying with and feeling into, are not the same as giving into or being passive.

Anything freshly learned needs time and practice to become established. Old patterns of thinking have been around for most of our lifetime; it is not too much to ask that we give a proportion of time to practising the revision; and not to give up! **If you fall down, the most important thing is to get up again, not to lament the falling down**. The quality of Maitri, of unconditional friendliness, will be your companion to help develop the dance of *kindly accepting unconditionally* in relation to *supported/encouraged*, assisting you during the process of change.

There is usually relief, but there can also be loss, when we change how we think and what we presume. If we have built relationships largely upon our 'survival' self then these relationships will be challenged. Someone who has been used to us pleasing them, giving in to them, caring for them, may be disgruntled at first when they see us operating differently, and they may even be actively discouraging or threatening. Change does challenge all levels of our life and in particular those we are closest to. Living with what may feel like the opposition of our partner or closest friend or colleague is hard, but it is important that this opposition does not put us off. If it does we risk colluding with the original fear that kept our old beliefs unrevised, and things will go back to being just as they were, with our healthy self still compromised.

What I have found is that when friends and colleagues realise the importance of change to the person trying to change, and how much relief there is when old redundant patterns are eradicated, they too are pleased. Only when relationships have become fixed and one-sided do things tend to get more heated. Then each of us has to make a choice. And the choice is frequently 'him (or her) or me?' If we risk losing others because they want us to stay the same we must ask whether we really want or need those others in our lives. Sometimes we have to step into an open space and believe that we will make new friends and acquaintances.

The first priority for holding on to change is therefore courage and the determination to stick with it. Pick out four or five ideas from the following checklist that are helpful to you and write them out. Look at this checklist every day to encourage you to stay with the changes you have chosen.

- Keep saying 'courage' to help you continue with the changes you have decided upon, even when others seem to discourage you or disapprove. Internal changes that need to be made to release more of the healthy island will not harm other people; rather they will tend to enhance your exchanges with others.
- Believe in what you are doing and allow others to see your quiet conviction.
- Recognise yourself for what you are. Stop trying to be like other people or as other people demand you to be.
- Changing is not easy, and many fears are being challenged. Accept that sometimes it will be hard and that it is important to stick with your goals and aims.
- Celebrate your feelings and your needs. Don't let them isolate you.
- Know your fears and anxieties, take them with you into situations and bring your mindfulness practice to be alongside them.
- Don't judge yourself with thinking: 'I shouldn't be like this, I'm silly.'
- Learn the art of listening. Listen to yourself, speak and note the tone you use. Listen to what your body is telling you, notice your body language.
- Be aware of the destructive power of negative thinking. Recognise, notice and replace with 'I'm doing the best I can'.
- Be aware of the power of positive thinking and the healing that arises from this.
- C.S. Lewis (1961) believed that only a real risk can test the reality of a belief. Take risks and check out your own beliefs.
- Make sure that you laugh every day. Be with people who make you laugh or with whom you have fun.

- Allow the symbols or images that have emerged during your reading be useful to you, helpers along the way.
- If you get stuck at times or feel faint-hearted, say to yourself, 'this too will change'; 'this isn't all there is'.
- Every day give yourself permission to change and to hold on to change.
- Give space for your healthy island and the experience of yourself you have in this space. Let it have a proper life and the careful nurturing you would give to the ground in which you would plant a precious seedling entrusted to your care.

Developing compassion

Genuine compassion arises when we are touched inside by the suffering of another. There is often a softening in the area of belly and chest. This requires a mindful foundation, a firm base of body, feeling and mind. We cannot offer compassion through thinking about it or over-identifying with another's suffering. When we offer genuine compassion we soften and join rather than harden and separate, letting go of fear and resistance.

Karen Armstrong writes, in *Twelve Steps to a Compassionate Life* (2011), that whilst compassion is a natural aspect of our humanity it has become alien to our modern world, with its individualistic and competitive economic systems of capitalism, its many global and tribal wars and conflicts. And yet most of us understand, particularly when we see it in action through wise people such as Desmond Tutu, the Dalai Lama and Thich Nhat Hanh, that the practice of true compassion is inspiring, often helpful and sometimes transforming.

The foundation of compassion is to first develop it for ourselves, and this can be hard for Westerners, who can easily mistake compassion for indulgence. We do this by imagining ourselves surrounded by all those people and teachers who have offered us kindness and love. We receive their kindness and love in gratitude. We then go on to offer compassion or loving kindness to family and friends; then to people we meet as part of our everyday lives; to people we have difficulty with; and finally to all living beings. The important understanding here is that we need to nourish our own well of compassion and connect with the wider well formed by all who practise compassion, in order to offer it genuinely to others. This helps our well to grow deep and to weed out any self-centredness or 'holier than thou' attitudes. (See Appendix 2 and the companion website to this book for mindfulness meditations and exercises.)

If we are able to practise and develop self-compassion, the practice itself can become a CAT exit when we meet core pain or procedures. When Alex found herself in the cage of her deepest depression she practised saying 'May I be well; May I be free from suffering; May I be free from danger'. Leonie practised with an exit she made using the phrase 'May I accept myself just as I am'. It is possible to develop some short sentences for ourselves based upon what we need.

In *The Mindful Path to Self-Compassion* (2009), Harvard psychologist Christopher Germer suggests practical ways that we may develop self-compassion, such as softening into the body; noticing and containing thoughts; befriending feelings and savouring our potential for spirituality. You can see that the basis for these practices is acceptance and unconditional friendliness, qualities I have been mentioning throughout this book. In this country the Compassionate Mind Foundation developed by evolutionary psychologist Professor Paul Gilbert takes a biopsychosocial approach, offering us an understanding that when the brain is in the mode of 'self-protection' its other potentials, including compassion, are less accessible (Gilbert, 2009). Sometimes the most compassionate thing we can offer is a real understanding of our 'fight/flight or freeze' response (see p. 21 and p. 50) and know what it needs.

PART EIGHT

Changing within a Relationship

One of the secrets of equable marriage is to accept one's partner for the person he or she is. Each can have only what the other has to offer. Expecting more leads to frustration and disappointment.

Susan Needham, Chairman, London Marriage
Guidance Council, 1990–1995

FIFTEEN   Love is not enough

Relationships *always* challenge our learned dance of relating! Whether they are relationships with people at work, in groups, within our families or with friends. Intimate relationships press us on our core pain: on our fears associated with getting close, feeling dependent or needy, our fear of rejection or abandonment, of feeling jealous and envious. It's possible, through revision of our individual procedures and the way these interact with those of our partners, to elicit changes that free us to enjoy relating.

Idealisation and reality in relationships

In his book *Love Is Never Enough*, Aaron Beck (1988) writes about how marriage or intimate relationships differ from other relationships. He describes how the intensity of living with someone fuels dormant longings for unconditional love, loyalty and support, and sets up expectations and desires. These are often based on an idealised image of love and acceptance. Idealisation is present in every hope and is useful for initiation, but it can set up impossible and unrealistic standards that cannot be met by another person. People with a history of early losses or poor bonding sometimes develop an over-idealised image of how relationships should be as compensation. While dreaming about this imaginative, 'happy ever after' world might help us cope with unhappiness, it cannot serve as a basis for relationships with others. When there is an over-idealised idea of how relationships 'should' be, whatever a partner does or does not do tends to be judged against these expectations, with each individual blaming the other for their disappointment and sense of failure. Relationships can become blocked when each person carries only one end of the reciprocal role and there is no room for flexible dancing or dialogue. The relationship remains at a superficial level and the deeper layers of potential within the couple cannot be reached.

Falling in love and sexual attraction are only the initial (but important!) triggers that draw two people together. *How* two people live together and sustain differences and difficulties is a test of maturity, generosity, endurance and humour. If we remain individually limited in our thinking and movement, we lack the flexibility required to dance in time with another, perhaps very different, person. Revising individual beliefs and the way they continue, can be the beginning of allowing a relationship to flourish.

It's easy to understand how we may choose partners from our internalised child self who confirm the old beliefs and maintain the core pain. Even when there is goodness between two people it can be undermined by outdated procedures. Someone with an over-idealised view of how relationships should be who was neglected as a child will long for fusion and closeness, and at the same time fear being abandoned. They may set up impossible demands which force their partner to flee, so confirming their belief that it is not worth getting close because everyone always neglects or leaves you in the end. What needs revision is the procedure for dealing with deprivation, which needs to be recognised and cared for first, so that we do not expect this hunger to be met totally by another.

We have seen many other patterns of relating throughout this book. We have seen someone who, when close to another person, becomes 'mother' or 'father', taking care and control of the other and denying their own needs, only to feel used and lonely. We have seen how the fear of loss of control can lead someone to seek to take charge of every interaction, creating a suffocating atmosphere where sooner or later one person will either explode or hit out, so establishing the very chaos the control pattern was designed to avoid.

Suggestions for couples

This section is for couples who are concerned about their interaction with each other and wish to make changes. Work individually first to establish your own individual pattern of procedure.

Read through Chapter 3, 'Problems and dilemmas within relationships'. Then make your own individual diagram for reciprocal roles, as guided in Chapter 13. It might help to notice how you feel with your partner at times when things seem to go wrong. Are you feeling like a crushed child or a furious parent? A critical carer who can only be martyred or a rebellious infant who wants to stamp its feet and run away?

Keep a journal individually (without reference to the other), for one week, of the times in which you have been pressed on a core pain place, or pushed into that bottom-line 'as if' core pain statement. Try not to make assumptions or judgements, but simply keep a record. Write down which traps, dilemmas, snags or unstable states apply to you, and which procedures for coping with core pain are most dominant in your life.

See if you can predict which problem areas your partner would identify with. Then look together at how each of you sees the other.

As part of gathering information, you might also like to go back in time and make a note of the qualities that attracted you to your partner when you met. What were you hoping for from these qualities? Having made this note, make another column to record how you feel about these qualities now. If they seem to have changed, ponder on this. Sometimes when we are drawn to certain qualities in a person it is both because we like and respond to those qualities, and also because we want to develop them in ourselves.

Drawn to opposites: FRANCES and MIKE

Frances, an only child, grew up in a very serious household. When she met Mike, who came from a large, noisy, fun-loving family, she was immediately attracted to what she had not experienced. For Frances, living with Mike was both a rebellion against her serious parents, who thought Mike a renegade and drop-out, and a challenge to her own learned seriousness. She hoped that Mike would help to heal her loneliness and allow her to expand her spontaneity. While this was ultimately a healthy option for her, in their first years she found herself being snagged by feelings of guilt for choosing such a different life from her aloof parents, as if her fun was at their expense. She had visions of their lonely existence in front of the one-ring gas fire while she was dancing the night away. This made her anxious, but she dared not confide in Mike because she did not want to spoil their enjoyment. She began to have panic attacks and to fear going out, returning instead to lying alone in bed and to the idea that she was not, after all, meant to go out and enjoy herself. A revision of her 'magical guilt', and speaking to Mike and her parents about the reality of their lives, helped her to begin to claim the life that she had chosen.

Drawn to similarities: BILL and EMILY

Bill chose Emily because she was just like his mother. Bill hated change, which he saw as rocking the boat. He wanted someone to be there for him when he came home from work, who would look after him and serve his needs. For Emily, who came from a rather cold background where she had had to placate in order to feel a sense of worth, it was heaven to be so wanted. But over time, because the glue that bound them together was based on earlier needs, they began to come unstuck. Bill found Emily boring and demanding – just like his mother in the *bad* sense. And Emily found his need of her oppressive and began to have angry outbursts and tantrums. She felt that he never listened to her but was always demanding, and she started to dream of being alone, of leaving, or of having an affair with someone she was attracted to at work.

If each set of individual procedures is locked together unhelpfully, without revision, the relationship can reach crisis point where the only solution seems to be to get out. This does not have to be so.

Hidden complementarities: FRANK and MAGGIE

Frank and Maggie find it difficult to live together without continual angry rows, when things get said which are regretted, only to be used as fuel for the next argument. They have separated several times, but found it equally difficult to live apart. Figure 15.1 is a diagram of how their relationship moved from initial closeness to anger, separation and then loneliness and reconciliation.

Frank and Maggie had actually separated when they first came to see me, and saw our meeting as a last-ditch attempt to save the relationship, although both were pessimistic, and both were deeply entrenched in their survival modes. Maggie was frightened, shaking and withdrawn; Frank aloof, controlled, calm, but his face white and muscles tense. By the time we had worked on their individual stories they had got together again and were both moved when each read out their story to the other.

In the early days they worked by doing simple self-monitorings. Frank was to monitor each occasion when he thought, 'I've had enough, this is terrible, I'm getting out'; similarly, Maggie was to monitor the times she thought, 'I want more, this isn't enough, this isn't how it *should* be'. It appeared as if these thoughts developed into a compulsion to act which, when followed through, served to keep the trap going. Both found self-monitoring very difficult. But as they gradually came to understand more of the other's history and to allow for each other's fragility, they were able to

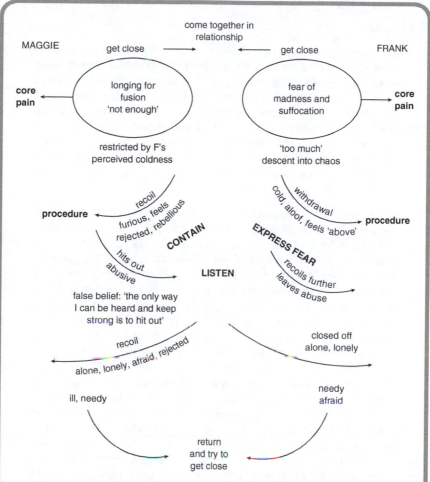

Figure 15.1   Frank and Maggie's relationship trap

hold on to the space long enough to listen, and later to have a discussion. To this end, they used their tape recorder to record conversations, later setting aside time together to listen to what had transpired between them. They were frequently shocked and moved by what they heard.

This is what I wrote and then read aloud to Frank and Maggie in therapy:

The three of us agreed to look afresh at the situation within your marriage, which operated to make it difficult to live together or apart. You had been in different therapies, both individually and together, in a quest to find answers to the dilemmas you both face as a couple. A great deal of perseverance, time and effort has gone into this

(Continued)

(Continued)

quest, perhaps indicating a desire to find a way to be together more harmoniously, and perhaps out of a yet-not-understood love for each other. The individual reformulations (life stories), gained over three sessions, reveal similarities. You are both intelligent people with damaged siblings. There is considerable self-negation and disappointment in all four parents' lives. 'Magical guilt' is strong in both of your lives. You both learned not to appear too well or happy. Magical guilt presupposes that we have received something good at another's expense, and that if we have what we want later on in life someone else will be damaged.

In Maggie's case, her unconscious involvement with self-sabotage revealed itself immediately in terms of the appointments we made, and that it took us five arranged appointments to result in three actual sessions. It was 'as if' something operated in Maggie's life to prevent her from getting help, fulfilling obligations or growing and becoming happier and more fulfilled. Maggie has recognised how she follows patterns of depriving and punishing herself in order to feel good about herself, and talked about the fact that she doesn't dress as well as she might because she feels she doesn't deserve it. All good things, because they make her feel 'bad' and guilty, have to be either denied or demolished in order to fulfil the unconscious pull of self-sabotage. Maggie's self-sabotage feels at its heaviest when it links in with the part of Frank she sees as 'Superman': superior, clever, successful, controlled and better than herself. Because her antennae are tuned to expect personal demolition and criticism, it gets set up unconsciously, again confirming the myth of magical guilt. And when this happens, and she feels criticised or punished, she falls back on survival tactics, becoming either rebellious and aggressive or passive, ill and in need of care.

Self-sabotage in Frank's life seems to operate in the way he does not feel free to express himself emotionally or with any vulnerability, and in the fact that he feels compelled to 'walk on eggshells' for fear of triggering Maggie's wrath or abuse. Early in his life, control, success and intellect were very important, and emotion and feeling were associated with chaos and madness. His professional life is successful and free of chaos. But in personal relationships there is another challenge. He was possibly drawn to Maggie because it would enable him to become more in touch and comfortable with a whole range of feelings. At difficult times he experiences emotional inertia and feels stuck, putting up with unpleasantness and appearing cold and unresponsive, or, more recently, allowing anger to surface.

Magical guilt carries with it the fury and rage at the restrictions it imposes. Each of you offers the other a vehicle for this magical guilt. Freeing yourselves individually from this would mean that it would not have to be played out in the drama of marriage.

The other area that links you together negatively at present is the struggle around closeness and intimacy. It seems as if you have opposite ideas, and idealised ideas, of what being close means. For Frank, closeness is self-contained and intellectual, and any-thing else feels suffocating and frightening, out of control. For Maggie, closeness is fusion, being constantly together, contained and safe, perhaps reflecting an inner longing to be held in a com-plete, symbiotic way. If you keep holding on to these polarised ideas your relationship will be a constant battle. Perhaps if you question the validity of these ideals and work towards making them less absolute, you could find a reasonable place from which to be close to each other. Freeing yourselves from magical guilt would mean that you could allow for, and maintain, good feelings and closeness, without having to sabotage it by all the 'as ifs' we have mentioned.

This is what Frank and Maggie wrote in return:

What we've taken home

We are learning that each of us carries substantial burdens from the past, which result in 'snags'. For example, for different rea-sons, each of us has difficulty with intimacy. Rage and frustration always get in the way of our being close. We are each well advised to make the effort to accept the reality and validity of these snags in the other, even though we may not always like the resulting behaviour. To deny and reject these personal characteristics in the other is futile. It also devalues the other person and therefore causes unhappiness.

So, we need ways to cope. We must learn to use them effectively. First, we can understand them and empathise. We can also grace-fully fall back and use and cede space. Apartness need not be rejection, and sometimes can be constructive.

On top of this, we realise that each of us has difficulty delivering on some of the other's primary needs. These were detailed by Liz in one of her reformulation documents. Just sensitising ourselves to this reality is a step forward. We must also think constructively and take more initiatives.

(Continued)

(Continued)

Finally, it should be said that our continuing resolve and application shows that we love and need one another. But it's a rocky, non-placid road that we are gradually learning to travel. The good times are worth it.

Frank and Maggie are still struggling to listen to and contain the feelings produced by their very different responses to getting close. Although their relationship is not easy, they are still together, and there are some good times which make the effort feel worthwhile.

SEAN and MARY

Sean and Mary sought help as a couple because of the painful rows which threatened their relationship. Their dreadful quarrels seemed to develop a life of their own and escalate out of control. They each began to look at their individual traps, dilemmas and snags, and kept a record of exactly what happened, what they were thinking, what was said and when they had a row.

Sean's early experience was of a critical father, before whom he felt inadequate. Mary felt that Sean constantly criticised the way she did things. Her own pattern was to take the blame for any disagreements. After one of their rows, each drew up their own diagram (see Figures 15.2a and b).

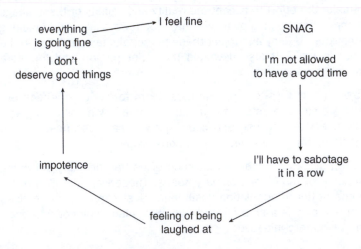

Figure 15.2(a) Sean's diagram

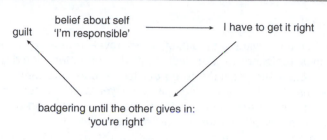

guilt

belief about self
'I'm responsible' → I have to get it right

badgering until the other gives in:
'you're right'

Figure 15.2(b) Mary's diagram

One row occurred when they were laughing and joking, and about to make love. Mary said something which she thought was very funny but which had a dramatic effect: Sean turned away, seemed to lose all interest and became very angry. Mary became upset, and very soon they were deep into a conflict from which they could not extricate themselves. When Mary had made her jokey remark Sean had experienced her as the critical and contemptuous castrating father. For Mary, Sean's withdrawal was devastating. She needed desperately to please in order not to be rejected. She took the blame for the row and badgered Sean to tell her what she had done. This only increased Sean's feeling that he was being harried and put down, and that he must give in to Mary even though he did not agree with her. Following the row, and Mary's appropriation of the high moral ground, Sean withdrew, which left Mary feeling frightened and abandoned, just as she had experienced as a child.

Sean and Mary quickly saw how their responses to each other had been affected by earlier maladaptive ways of communicating, which were now preventing them from seeing each other clearly. For Sean, Mary had become the castrating, rejecting father; and for Mary, Sean represented the rejecting father for whom she could never do anything right. It was a shock for Mary to discover that Sean's perceptions were entirely different from her own. One of the values of working together in this way is the opportunity it gives to each person to hear the other's side and to witness their learned patterns of response.

The following is an account of the focused therapy Sean and Mary had with two cognitive analytic therapists.

The previous hypotheses of Sean and Mary's traps and dilemmas were given added confirmation during the following session. Once again they had had a row which had lingered on in a desultory fashion. It was as though Mary had to keep picking at Sean in an attempt to put things right, trying at the same time to do and be what she thought he wanted of her, and in the process ignoring what she wanted. Sean, unaware of Mary's needs and feeling only a sense of being smothered

(Continued)

(Continued)

and of her underlying withholding of approval, retreated behind his newspaper resigned to the fact that the situation could not be resolved. Later they decided to go out to the park and then on to an AA meeting they had attended for some years. This, however, only intensified the tension between them, because Sean had to wait for Mary to get ready, all the time becoming more and more irritated at the delay. From this we were able to tease out the trap and dilemma that Mary was in (see Figure 15.3a).

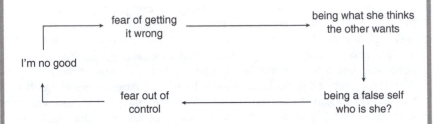

or to put it in terms of her dilemma:

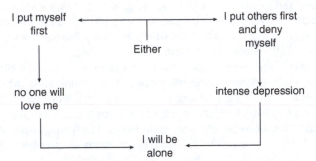

Figure 15.3(a)   Mary's trap and dilemma diagrams

What seemed to be happening for Sean was that he felt, once again, he could not win. This brought back two important memories of his father. In the first, he and his father were staying with a much-loved jovial uncle in the country. The two men had arranged to go somewhere. Sean's father, up and ready early, stood in the middle of the room, jingling his keys and almost bursting with irritation at his brother, who was taking his time putting on his boots, completely unconcerned by the other's impatience. Clearly, in the incident with Mary it was Sean who had become the irritated, impatient father, while Mary had assumed the role of the laid-back, disorganised uncle.

The second memory involved Sean's desire to become a car mechanic. His father, however, had wanted him to have a more respectable, higher-status career in management. Unable to go against his father and choose what he wanted to do, but equally reluctant to go along with his father, Sean fell between two stools and ended up in a series of jobs where he did just enough to get by. It was as though if he were to succeed, particularly at something his father disapproved of, he would incur not only his father's envy but also his anger. On the other hand, if he failed he risked his father's contempt. It seemed as though the only course was simply to get by. This was seen not only in his work but in his behaviour at home. He would start something – putting up shelves, decorating, etc. – have piles of wood all over the flat, and then leave the jobs half-done, a source of irritation to Mary and incomprehension to them both. We were able to see here how the memory of his father once again seemed to be intruding (see Figure 15.3b).

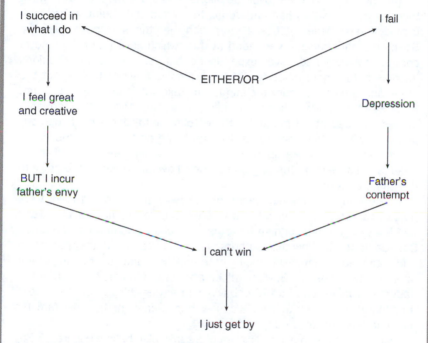

Figure 15.3(b)   Sean's trap diagram

In the fourth session we linked their responses to the relationship between them to possible past modes of behaviour. For example, in response to the first trap, avoidance, Mary felt responsible for Sean and for the possibility that they might split up, so she had to prevent this by trying to do what he wanted. This had parallels with her earlier life, when she had needed to be both in control of her siblings and responsible for their welfare, particularly after her mother died.

(Continued)

(Continued)

With Sean, his fear of standing up to his father led to a self-fulfilling prophecy that he was no good, followed by inevitable depression. What became very clear was that his fear of succeeding in his relationship with Mary stemmed from his conviction that he must pay for success, and so he has to sabotage it.

Both Sean and Mary were very afraid of something within them that seemed out of their control. Sean's other procedures were his avoidance of his feelings about partings and loss, and his destruction of his creativity, which he longed to enjoy. For Mary we highlighted her need always to take responsibility for others' feelings, and her pattern of being unable to value, and thereby destroying, her creativity.

The nub of the work over sessions 6–15 focused on analysing together any rows they had had during the week, and seeing where their individual false beliefs got tangled up with the other's in these quarrels. Sean and Mary became very good at this, which gave them a sense of control that they had never experienced before. The weekly sessions became both a safe place to defuse explosive feelings held about the other, and a place to learn techniques to take with them for the future. Both Sean and Mary liked the idea of seeing their often-repeated procedures caught on paper for them to refer to, and would regularly point out where they saw themselves as being on their diagrams. Sean put it this way: 'It's like opening a book and seeing all the stuff in my head laid out plain on the page. I can see how all my life I have got into the same patterns.'

In the early and middle weeks of our work the reported rows were fierce and felt catastrophic, but it was exciting to see how quickly Sean and Mary began to recognise patterns from childhood in their behaviour. Both came to see how their fathers' voices chimed in on them so often and stopped them from being themselves and expressing their spontaneity. In session 8, Mary talked about her struggle to confront her daughter's unjust and hurtful behaviour in saying things about her to a third party that were untrue. We saw her caught in the now familiar dilemma (see Figure 15.3a).

Mary was able to make a diagram of Sean's false beliefs (Figure 15.3c) and through doing this was able to see that the exit here was to hold on to the right to her own feelings, and to express them. Sean witnessed her struggle with this problem and was able to be protective and supportive in a helpful way. At the end of session 8 we suggested each of them compose a description of themselves, as if written by a loving friend. Mary, we found, was able to really enter into this fully and present herself as the warm, ebullient person she is, but Sean found it hard to see himself in a favourable light and could only come up with a description of how he would like to be. This brought home to Sean how hard it was for him to be appreciative of himself. His father's critical voice was pervasive.

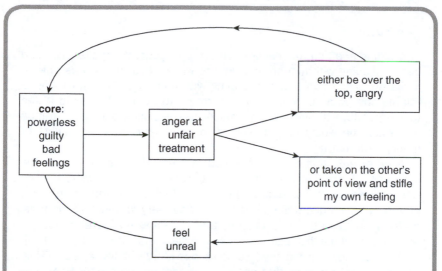

Figure 15.3(c)   Mary's diagram of Sean's false beliefs

In the middle of our work, in session 9, there was a big row that seemed to be connected with their feelings about the therapy coming to an end. Apparently they felt they were not getting enough from us as therapists, and were taking out their anger about this on each other. Mary said she had left the last session without feeling the closeness to Sean that she usually experienced at the end of a session. She felt let down, and this was transferred onto Sean. She said Sean seemed depressed, and in swung her need to jolly him out of it: if he were down, it must be her fault (as with her parents when she was a child). She then felt guilty and that Sean was critical of her (when in actual fact he did not feel that at all at the time). It was clear to see how plugged in to each other's moods Mary and Sean had become. They could see this and were able to identify the points at which they had each pinned their own feelings on the other.

A key issue for Sean came up at this time. Mary was bringing to the sessions her painful feelings at the death of a close friend, which in turn resonated a whole untouched area of feelings about the death of her father. She was able to express her rage and hurt forcefully, and explore some key issues about the rejection by her sister and mother. This was so hard for Sean to witness, as his pattern had always been to swallow feelings about loss and endings. He was surly and irritated at Mary's outpouring of feelings of grief at the death, and by the fear, anger and hurt she displayed at the thought of losing us. Sean was able to say it frightened him. We noticed at this point that his false belief charts showed that no progress had been made on changing his usual pattern

(Continued)

(Continued)

of avoiding grief, so this became an area of focus. We realised we had been colluding with him on this. As the weeks went on he was able to make two significant steps in dealing with this problem: (1) actually to tell his son, when he was leaving to return to Ireland, how hard it was to say goodbye to him and how much he loved him; and (2) to tell us how much he would miss the sessions and was afraid he might not manage without us.

Another area that Sean confronted in the middle sessions was the child part of him that needed constant reassurance from Mary that he was allowed to do something (e.g. watch football on television). This pattern worked quite well between Sean and Mary for much of the time, as Mary would be the reassuring mother to Sean's reassured child.

At this point the therapists sketched the diagrams shown in Figure 15.4.

At times, however, his need would exceed Mary's ability to keep giving, and we traced the rows that ensued. Yet another pattern for Sean was his jealous and rivalrous feelings when Mary paid attention to others. She was a sponsor for other AA members, who would often phone and she would spend considerable time talking to them, sometimes adopting what Sean called a flirtatious manner. He would then become sullen and withdrawn, which would in turn evoke Mary's need to take responsibility for his feelings and her sense of guilt – his moodiness was her fault. Both were able to recognise this pattern, as well as the way in which Mary's attention to others evoked the insecure jealous child who was afraid of rejection in Sean. These feelings also came out in a dream Sean brought to the session at this time. He dreamed he was on a coach sitting beside Mary who was making love with the man next to her. In the dream Sean went off and sat by himself away from Mary.

A breakthrough came in another session over the escalation issue. There had been a small row over a football match. Sean and Mary had both been watching the game on television. Mary left the room to do something during a break for advertisements, but Sean failed to call her when the match started again. The reason for jubilation was that Mary,

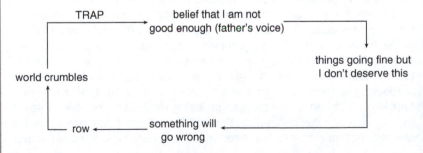

Figure 15.4(a) Therapists' diagram of Sean's false beliefs

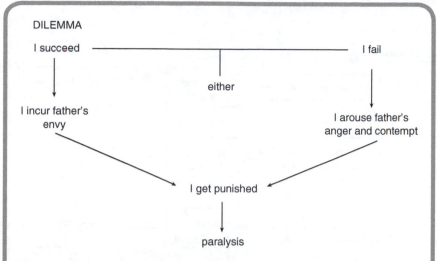

Figure 15.4(b) Therapists' diagram of Sean's dilemma

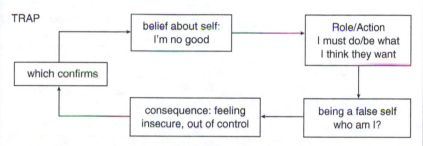

Figure 15.5(a) Therapists' diagram of Mary's trap

rather than nursing her anger and allowing it to swell inside with a kind of masochistic pleasure, was able to let go and the row did not escalate. We all four felt triumphant at this.

Another issue that surfaced at this time was that of differences. We all noticed and discussed how different were Sean's and Mary's patterns of response to situations. Mary tended to feel anxious and insecure if Sean saw things differently from her – for example, if he took an opposing view to her at an AA meeting – and could see how this was linked to the hurt she had felt as a child whenever differences arose between her parents. She and Sean were able to say, 'We are different, and it is acceptable to be different, to be ourselves.'

In sessions 12 and 13 the focus turned particularly to Sean's sense of despondency at never finishing anything creative he planned. He said he felt things would be better between himself and Mary if he could have

(Continued)

(Continued)

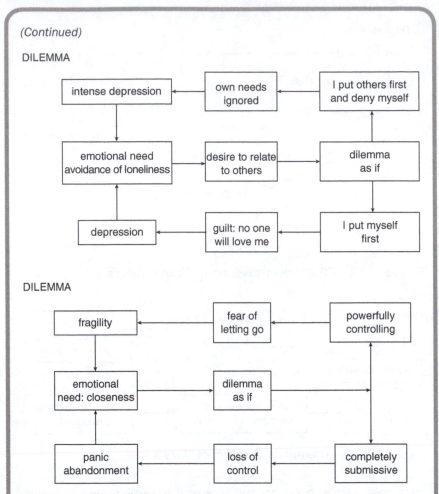

Figure 15.5(b)   Therapists' diagram of Mary's dilemmas

something purposeful to do. We laughed and joked over all the unfinished DIY jobs, the half-completed bed. He was able to hear his father's voice clearly telling him nothing was good enough. The exit from this snag was 'to have a go', he said.

The last four sessions were full of feelings about the ending and reported activities. Sean and Mary expressed their great disappointment that their respective son and daughter had let them down at the last moment by cancelling plans to visit them. This deprived Mary of her fantasy of creating a warm, happy, safe family, and she saw how her hurt over this could have been directed at Sean. This session revealed the pathological part of each of them, how the terrible, enraged, hurt, afraid child could burst in and destroy good things, especially their relationship. It was a sobering session. Mary had told Sean to leave and not come back when, or so it seemed to her, he had put his daughter ahead of her. Sean had replied, 'If I do it might be fatal,' and Mary was then able to tell Sean that she hadn't meant it and they managed to de-escalate the row. We reminded them that it is alright to get angry and have rows.

The next session focused on how hard it was to bring our sessions to an end and on their sense of not having had enough. Even Sean was able to name this. There was some anxiety that there hadn't been a row. On one occasion Sean had felt resentful of Mary's laughter over the phone to someone else and he had been able to express this and be understood by Mary. Sean said in this session, 'Nothing in my life has made a bigger impression than this work.' In the next session Mary reported that on three occasions she had succeeded in taking care of her own interests rather than putting the other person first. She was triumphant at her refusal to be domineered, and was encouraged in this by Sean.

During our last but one meeting the issue of ending came up very forcefully. Mary strongly vented all her fears and rage at losing us. Sean was more hopeful, saying he wished he had more time but that he felt they had the tools to go on by themselves. We confirmed that we would meet for a follow-up session in three months' time.

In our last session Sean arrived with a package which turned out to be a painting that had given him great pleasure to do. This was a great delight to all of us. We exchanged goodbye letters, ours being a joint letter to the two of them with separate sections for each of them. We spelled out again the patterns we saw that tripped them up, the enormous progress we had seen them make in finding exits from these snags, traps and dilemmas, and the good things we had got out of working with them. They in turn each gave us their goodbye letters. Each in their very individual way let us know what a landmark experience therapy had been for them. Sean's letter was much longer than Mary's, and once again we saw how they each felt the other must have performed better, as Mary convinced herself that Sean's letter must have been far more thorough than her own. Again we emphasised that it is alright to be different from one another. Both Sean and Mary felt they had gained a great deal of good experience and understanding to enable them to defuse their quarrels themselves, and both could see that using their creativity brought good feelings and was helpful in the relationship. They each expressed their thanks and sadness. We talked of all the changes we had witnessed, their courage, hard work and tenacity, and gave them more forms to enable them to continue the work of monitoring themselves.

Sean and Mary were able to use CAT to change their relationship. They were able to defuse their quarrels, to laugh at the tangles they got into and to confront things in the 'here and now' rather than carrying

(Continued)

(Continued)

them around like a time bomb. Overall, they had fewer devastating rows, which is what they originally set out to achieve in therapy. This change came about because they were each able to see how a lot of the anger and disruption really belonged to childhood experiences. For each, the procedure of trying to placate a powerful father loomed large and got in their way.

Sean recognised how the presence of his father's critical voice inside him created a trap, preventing him from enjoying his creative abilities and reducing his efforts, as well as ensuring that he withdrew from Mary whenever he heard his father's voice in her. He decided to 'have a go' and to enjoy himself, as well as reassuring his inner child and encouraging him to express himself.

Mary came to understand her fear of putting her own needs first for fear of others' rejection. Her difficulty with expressing her own needs remained hidden under her urge to punish when feeling rejected by being critical or withdrawing. When she began to express what she was feeling, particularly her fear at losing someone, this had a powerful effect on Sean, who was able to share and respect her feelings.

Sean and Mary write that now, five years on, they are still using the diagrams made in their therapy, and are communicating well.

Exercise

Write your individual life stories, separately, using the third person – for example, let 'I' become 'he' or 'she'. Pick a time when you can be alone together and each read your own life story aloud to the other. Put your observer hat on and just listen respectfully to the storyteller and the drama behind the story.

Try not to judge, criticise, object to, take personally, overrule or rationalise the other's story. If you do find yourself doing any of the above, make a note of it so that you can refer to it later. Listen for the tone of the person who is trying to emerge. Note the way in which your partner has observed their own procedures and how they have survived their early life.

Give some time to the effect of reading the stories together and for each other's response.

Write something together about how your individual core pain and your procedures for coping affect the other.

Make a diagram for yourselves about the ways in which you repeat the ritual of your procedures during a row or difficulty. Note:

1. the assumption or 'false belief' that leads to the behaviour ('I believe that ...')
2. how this is received by the other which triggers their assumption ('so I do this ...')
3. how this assumption results in behaviour ('he/she sees that I believe that ... so this makes me do ...').

Each keep a copy, so you can check where you are if you get into difficulties.

Spend the first week just observing and noting with each other what is happening. Don't yet try to change anything, but use your recognition not to get into the trap or dilemma to which your relationship usually falls prey. See what happens to the space, see what wants to emerge.

If you find yourselves having strong feelings, write them down, and see where or to whom they belong.

When the energy in a relationship is not taken up with fighting old procedures there is time for other things. Experiment with how you like being together, and give feedback to each other on what works and what doesn't.

Exercise

Predict which myths rule your partner's actual thoughts and beliefs, as well as their hoped-for myths.

☐ Name the myths which together you feel dominate your relationship.
☐ Write the myths as you would like them to be!

PART NINE

Resources for Students and Therapists and for Co-counsellors

SIXTEEN The theory and practice of CAT

The practice of CAT

CAT is a time-limited, active, focused therapy. Its time limit means that the importance of ending is on the agenda from the beginning. The structure of the sessions offers scaffolding for therapists to work within many different settings and modalities and to work with their own preferred methods of 'moving therapy along', such as art, drama, music, dreams, EMDR, mindfulness; individually, with children, adolescents, couples and in groups. Steve Potter writes: 'CAT is potentially a versatile therapy and the therapist is seeking a dialogic framework that allows a creative hovering between fixed points of view (such as target problem procedures) and capacity to engage at one moment in the small detail, at another at the bigger picture of language and ideas and at a third level in the personal experience of the relationship in the room' (Potter and Sutton, 2006: 5).

There are two aspects of CAT practice.

The first aspect involves the **'tasks' of CAT** where therapists take responsibility for recognising and naming links between past and present.

[1] Giving the psychotherapy file and noting the responses.
[2] Taking in the results of self-monitoring or journal-keeping at the same time as drawing out the person's history through questions such as 'when did you first notice this pattern?'

[3] Keeping an eye on the phase of the therapy and naming the number of sessions, as in 'we're half way through'.

[4] Formulating the content of the sessions into traps, dilemmas, snags and unstable states.

[5] Experimenting through dialogue with finding words or metaphors for reciprocal roles and how they are invited or enacted both inside and outside of the therapy.

[6] Intervening with a reflection on or question about a possible trap, dilemma or snag as it appears in the content of conversations in the room. This might mean interrupting a patient's dialogue – a great challenge to therapists trained in analytic or Rogerian theory – by saying something like: 'I wonder if what you're telling me right now is part of your placation trap/getting close dilemma'. This may initially invite useful irritation that can be worked with. Therapists put the spotlight on unhelpful ingrained procedures – a bit like a gardener digging in compacted soil!

[7] Past and present relationship patterns are shared and understood jointly and a written reformulation developed, often in the form of a letter with the patient collaborating in its formation. This is then read aloud by the therapist. Many therapists invite the patient to write their own letter in reply. Also constructed jointly during sessions are diagrams of learned sequences which describe both reciprocal roles and their subsequent beliefs and actions that maintain problematic procedures. These specifically CAT tools become the focus for the work. Therapists think about the patient in between sessions, reading both written and diagrammatic reformulation and referring to them in note-keeping.

Anthony Ryle, writing specifically for this section of the book, says:

> The first and central role of therapists [in CAT practice] is to acknowledge the patients' difficulties and pains. The early reformulation of patients' histories identifies damaging reciprocal role procedures [RRPs]; describing these gives patients the possibility of more control over them. These and other specific techniques support the early development of a genuine, human and non-collusive therapy relationship. Working within pre-determined time limits usually prevents the development of unhelpful dependency, accelerates therapeutic change and makes therapy available to more people. Involving patients in the joint construction of these verbal and diagrammatic descriptions of what needs to be changed establishes a cooperative relationship, sets the agenda of therapy, enlarges patients' psychological awareness and supports their

development of a greater sense of responsibility and agency. It allows therapists to anticipate unhelpful patterns which may be mobilized in the therapy relationship. The work of reformulation is itself powerfully therapeutic and many symptoms and problematic behaviours may fade without being directly addressed.

The second aspect emerges from within the subtle steps of the therapeutic relationship. The therapist's capacity to witness, meet and mirror back the verbal and non-verbal (tone, gestures, expressions) dialogues as they arise, supports the process of naming accurately the core emotional pain and procedures learned to manage it. The therapist's preparedness to put themselves fully into the relational dance and dialogue as invited involves anticipating the other's next move and maintaining fluidity. There is also the therapist's personality, tastes and experience, different therapeutic skills and techniques, and what they bring to their encounters of themselves. As with all therapies, we all need to be able to tell our own scripts from the elicited ones.

In patients with a more borderline structure, the work is akin to family therapy. Through the help of the shared diagram, the therapist learns to know and feel which of the patient's internalised figures is speaking and define this. This interaction helps the formation of a healthy, kind observer whose intention is to include all and not get drawn into one. Each intervention of this kind helps to build a new reciprocal role of observing in relation to observed, safely.

Therapeutic change, in the CAT understanding, involves *firstly* the revision, control or elimination of the dysfunctional RRPs which are the source of the patient's symptomatic and mood disturbance and of their negative attitudes and behaviours towards self and others and *secondly* increasing the integration of markedly dissociated procedures. Some such changes follow the insight and control achieved during the reformulation process and the emotional impact of the therapist's concerned and accurate attention. This rapid early change may be stable but may result in idealization of the therapist which needs to be recognised and challenged, as does the predictable subsequent disillusion. Maintaining awareness of the shifting manifestations of problem RRPs and detecting them in the patient's accounts of daily life is a subtle and often difficult task; therapists are aided by the reformulation process and tools, and in the case of more disturbed patients will need a level of supervision which attends to the shifting transference and countertransference. A full and moving account of a difficult therapy is given by Kate Freshwater, then a clinical psychologist and CAT trainee, in Ryle and Kerr (2002: 189–97). This conveys the demands of working in this way and the value of the reformulation and of supervision, and shows how, beyond ideas and techniques, therapy has an underlying ethical and existential dimension. Therapists often need to convey more faith in patients and in the possibility of a meaningful life than are within their present capacity. But the faith has to be genuine and realistic, not bland or sentimental. (Anthony Ryle, writing for this book)

Phases of the work

Assessment

At the assessment session the number of sessions will be agreed. This will vary and also be governed by resources. A traditional CAT is sixteen sessions, but CAT is such a versatile model that six, eight and twelve sessions may be appropriate, and twenty-four sessions for more complex presentations.

The beginning phase

The first four to five sessions in CAT therapy involve bringing together the results of the outer tasks and experiences in the week with all that happens in the room between therapist and patient. We gather information, weaving the fabric of what is to be the reformulation. We are also noting which reciprocal roles we are being invited into and finding language with the patient for both poles of the role.

The middle phase

This is where, with many patients, we may relax into a slower and more playful dance within the scaffolding of the reformulation and diagram, and the emergence of manageable exits. The sessions are focused on noticing, examining and trying something new.

Ending phase

At around session 11/12, when ending is in sight for a sixteen-session therapy, there is often a return of symptoms or bringing of new material.

It is unnerving for new therapists when this happens, and hard to remain with both focus and time limit. The tendency is to feel that the patient is not ready and the end date extended. The art is to hold the vessel of dance and work with the emerging feelings in relation to ending. The pain of previous endings will surface and can be accepted, shared and lived through in a new way. Difficult revelations are often left until toward the end, perhaps as a way of avoiding pain; or to speak before it is too late. This is why ending must always be on the agenda; it provides a vital edge for more difficult, often key, underlying issues to be met. Some therapists choose to offer the 'goodbye letter' at the penultimate session and some at the very last session. Patients are invited to write their own letter and these letters are read aloud. They are an important and powerful communication.

Follow-up

The follow-up session occurs traditionally after three months but earlier follow-up appointments may be made according to an assessment of the patient's needs. The written reformulation and goodbye letters supports this gap. It offers an opportunity for patients to practise the focus of the work on their own and share how it has been.

The therapeutic relationship

Therapy is based upon relationship and the maintenance of this is the therapist's responsibility, especially when working with inconsistent and destructive self states. Psychotherapy involves joint activity and the creation, use and internalisation of mediating tools. CAT aims to help patients through both relationship, and also by providing a revised appraisal of experiences, clarifying the links between experience, intentions and consequent action. These tools consist of the descriptive reformulation of dysfunctional procedures which equips patients with the means for accurate self-observation and also guides the therapist in maintaining a real but non-collusive relationship. Successful therapy results in the internalisation of relational dances, the addition of a 'new voice' to inner dialogue and the integration of any fragmented procedural system (Ryle, 2001a). As well as training and theoretical framework, therapists bring to each encounter their own internalised dialogues. These voices, with therapists, supervisors and teachers, live on, informing ways of working. Into the dance also comes the therapist as a vulnerable human being, with qualities and wounds. We learn much about ourselves with each encounter. Within this dance of relationship with another flesh and blood human being is the possibility of a two-way process; being listened to, accepted and cared for, thus inviting us to accept, listen to and care for ourselves in a new way.

We never know where a patient may take us

This is a relationship unlike any other, often intensely intimate and guarded by professional boundaries it forms a strong and safe vessel for relational work. This vessel of relationship needs to:

> withstand the struggles and fragmentations of personality and difficult transferences, be able to bear the chill winds or suffocating cloaks of the past, and fiery rages when the heat is on. The vessel also holds the potential for fantasy – how it might have been, how it could be; for illumination, change, for transformation and for the growth of love; for the ever present possibility of coming home to one's self and recognising it as such. (Wilde McCormick, 2000: 23–4)

My colleague Annalee Curran, a therapist for many years and an ACAT founder, writes of what she holds in mind for her work with patients:

> A hope to help them find a better relationship with themselves through challenging the regime of reciprocal roles under which they have been living; and to discover more life-enhancing reciprocal roles so that they can be kinder to themselves and find better ways of interacting with others and of dealing with their problems.

Working with the body

Many therapists feel that the body has been neglected, even left out, of the talking therapies. Whilst CAT is not a body psychotherapy, the dialogic model indicates an inner dialogue through sensation and image with the physical body in which we are housed. We are in dialogic relationship with our body from our time of conception, even when we experience our body as 'out there'. It is through our bodies that we experience cold, heat, touch, taste, smell, feeling and emotion, and empathy with another. These experiences are often stored as images. We attach different thoughts to these experiences later and also learn that thoughts themselves have physical charge. Working with images can help create a safe and useful bridge between hidden memory with its often overwhelming emotion, and consciousness. When the images are drawn, embodied, or shaped through objects, they become mediators of a greater awareness. Someone who has never felt embodied and pictured themselves in outer space without a body can experiment slowly with starting the journey back into their body through drawing. Someone who feels flooded with body sensations and feeling may, through use of objects, find a safe way to communicate with both feeling and body. The presence of this kind of imaginative intelligence is potentially in everyone and indicates a healthy self who has carried all that has happened in a form that is accessible.

In *Body Psychotherapy* (2002: 120), Margaret Landale writes: 'Creating a space for the body in the psychotherapeutic environment starts with an ongoing observation of a client's body language: how they hold themselves, the way they speak, the texture of their skin, the clothes they wear and mannerisms they use.' If the therapeutic relationship is established and there is attunement, when we notice a particular posture, repeated gesture or phrase, an intake or holding of the breath, we can ask 'tell me what's happening right now in your body?'; or, 'if that feeling in your arm, pain in your chest, could speak, what would it say?'

Thanks to developments in neuroscience, psychologists and therapists are more than ever aware that our physiological state governs our perception of the world and that our body response to emotional chaos – fight, flight, freeze – shuts off the prefrontal cortex that we need to think and reflect (Schore, 2003; Porges, 2005; Seigel, 2007). In recognition of this, psychological work needs a safe environment – often challenging in a hospital or clinic setting – in which patients can orientate and explore. Psychoeducation and teaching self-regulation (p. 21) helps to develop a self-to-self dialogue with arousal levels and resources, so that other dialogues may flow freely. Helping patients to discover and relate to their own resources, which may have been unrecognised, early on in the therapy process, is also part of trying to keep a 'safe enough' environment for new and often painful dialogues to flow.

In CAT we are aware right from the beginning of the invitation into reciprocal roles and therapists' countertransference feelings begin within the body. Recognition and allowing accurate descriptions to arise becomes our daily work. Becoming attuned to what is happening in our clients' bodies and in our own body continues all through the sessions.

Being aware of what is happening somatically is always important as a source of information and a guide on pacing and what next. In patients who have no words for feelings (alexithymic) this becomes even more essential. Bessel Van der Kolk writes:

> Prone to action and deficient in words, these patients can often express their internal states more accurately in physical movements or pictures than in words. Utilising drawing and psychodrama may help them develop a language that is essential for effective communication and for the symbolic transformation that can occur in psychotherapy. (Van der Kolk et al., 2007: 193)

Working with mindfulness

In *Mindfulness and Psychotherapy* Christopher Germer writes: 'mindfulness is a technology for gradually turning the patient's attention toward the fear as it is happening, exploring it in detail with increasing degrees of friendly acceptance. A mindfulness-based approach includes exposure, which is a key ingredient in the treatment of anxiety' (Germer et al., 2005: 152). He describes how a mindfulness approach gradually shifts our relationship to what we fear from fearful avoidance to friendship. He suggests that therapists use the three elements of true mindfulness – awareness, present-centredness and acceptance – as a touchstone for identifying mindfulness in therapy.

We saw in Chapter 8 that Amanda practised the 3-minute breathing exercise (see Appendix 2) each morning and evening. She was also able to bring this practice into her everyday when she felt anxiety rise. When depressed feelings in her body were particularly heavy, mindfulness of breath and the image of the lifebelt helped her create enough space for new thinking. The most profound effect was on her suicidal ideation when, in the space created by being mindful of what she was thinking – to cut herself with a broken bottle in the park – it gave her the choice to choose to walk away.

In their article in *Reformulation* entitled 'Playfulness in CAT', Sophie Rushbrook and Nicola Coulter (2010) write of working with a patient suffering from borderline personality disorder who was very depressed, with flat affect and little engagement:

> Following many attempts at therapy, she had yet to tell her story, for fear of exposure. The therapist initially started off the sessions with mindfulness; however this had limited impact as the client appeared to dissociate. So the therapist suggested that they practice mindfulness in throwing a ball to each other which seemed to allow the client to remain focussed, particularly when she was given some trickier shots. She began

to aim at the therapist's head and vice versa until both therapist and client ended up giggling. When they resumed talking, the client was much more engaged. Furthermore her dissociation markedly decreased and she started to develop her playfulness in treatment sessions and in her life. Whilst not taking away the pain of her past, it provided an opportunity to process it and alleviated the misery of the present.

This article illustrates that as well as the benefits, there is a need for caution in the use of mindfulness. In patients who tend to dissociate or blank out, mindfulness needs to be carefully tailored to areas where the object of mindfulness is within the zone of proximal development. In this case it was through the playfulness of using the ball and focusing on the throwing experience that changed affect. This also illustrates that when patients are in the hypoaroused state (see p. 21, Figure 1.3) their brain and autonomic arousal systems need activity rather than silence. In this country the research of Paul Gilbert, founder of The Compassionate Mind Foundation, stresses the importance of understanding that it is our more evolved contemplative part of the brain that needs to be free to develop and offer empathy and compassion. But when our much older tribal, reptilian brain, responsible for fight and flight, is dominant we are more likely to be on the lookout for predators and therefore not safe enough to receive either kindness or compassion (Gilbert, 2009).

It is possible to start and end therapy sessions with a few moments of mindful breathing as long as this does not evoke too much anxiety. I sometimes speak of this as 'clearing the space' so that the person might allow what is less conscious time to arise. It is also possible to use an intervention such as 'shall we sit together and follow the breath and see what arises in the silence?' Some patients value this and find feelings and sensations followed by words that help them make sense of habitual patterns. All approaches to psychotherapy and counselling that include a contemplative, mindful or compassionate intention are dependent upon the practice and skill of the therapist who nourishes his or her own mindfulness practice. These approaches come from within the therapist and cannot be learned in isolation, or as 'add-ons' to an existing approach.

CAT theory

CAT and reciprocal role relationship theory

Early CAT reciprocal role theory was drawn from a cognitive revision of object relations theory, largely from the version of Harry

Guntrip and Ronald Fairbairn. The subsequent development of the Object Relations Procedural Sequence Model involved a rejection of many psychoanalytic assumptions about the dynamic unconscious, but included an appreciation of Thomas Ogden's proposal of reciprocal leaning – that we learn how to be loving in the shared experience of being loved; we know how to be challenging in the experience of being challenged. This understanding, re-stated in the concept of the reciprocal role procedure, has become a fundamental element in CAT understanding of early development and in the transformed accounts of transference, countertransference and projective identification (Ryle, 1985). The influence of Mikael Leiman's introduction of the ideas of Vygotsky and Bakhtin (Leiman, 1994) offered an explanation of the process of internalisation and examined the interplay of biological, internal psychic and social influences on development thus establishing a dialogical perspective on the self. Our human biological evolution co-occurs in an evolving social context resulting in our extreme openness to social formation. CAT theory could be called a semiotic object relations theory, a view entirely consistent with observational studies of early development. Observational studies of early infant–caretaker interaction confirms that joint activity with caretakers based on mutual imitation, rhythmic activity and expressive communications is the basis of an evolving repertoire of relationship patterns, named in CAT as reciprocal role procedures that embody memory, perception, feeling, meaning, anticipation and action. Through the shared exploration of social and physical reality and the conveying of meanings by signs and later by language, the human infant enters culture (Carpendale and Lewis, 2004). Only through this process, sustained by adequately secure emotional attention and support, can the child realise the innate potential of the evolved human brain (Donald, 2001). We are not merely influenced by social relations and culture, we are created and maintained by them.

Role procedures have, as their aim, the responses of others; in addition, these same patterns are internalised and determine self-management, and the accompanying dialogue is also internalised and becomes the instrument of thought. Conscious thought and self-reflection depend on the semiotic tools, eventually language, acquired through the early years of life.

While these structural understandings are crucial to psychotherapists they have wider implications: for example, in clinical management and in education, where collusive responses to dysfunctional RRPs are often elicited. The CAT model of self-processes challenges the individualistic Cartesian assumptions of much contemporary psychology by emphasising the essential role of interpersonal activity and communication in the formation and maintenance of individual self-processes and the sense of self. More generally, the CAT model, by pointing to the social formation of individuals, demonstrates the way in which cultural beliefs and practices are transmitted from generation to generation and challenges the fashionable overextension of Darwinian biological evolutionary theory into areas best considered in terms of *cultural evolution*. Dr Anthony Ryle says:

> In practice as therapists, the dialogic perspective reminds us of the importance of our jointly elaborated reformulation procedures, which produce the focused signs which assist internalisation of the reparative dialogue of therapy. It reminds us that we are always in the patient's field seen as reciprocating or failing to reciprocate their role procedures or as imposing ours, not only in what we say, but in how, and in what context we say it. (Ryle, 2001b)

CAT and multiple self states[1]

The most significant patterns acquired in early life are concerned with issues of *care or neglect* in relation to *need* and *over-control or cruelty* in relation to *submission*. 'The self' is normally multiple as individuals acquire a repertoire of RRPs, different ones being mobilised in ways appropriate to the context. 'Normal' multiplicity may include the manifestation at different times of contradictory patterns, but in general, links between patterns and awareness of the range is established. However, this is not the case where adversity and predisposition result in a *structural dissociation* of the individual's repertoire of role procedures. In such cases the sense of self is fragmented and discontinuous. These emotional unstable states, sometimes referred to as borderline personality disorder, present as abrupt switches with little recollection in between. It is confusing to the patient and to all around them, including clinicians, who as a result may feel 'de-skilled' and may become rejecting.

Therapists and other clinical staff need to support integration of the dissociated reciprocal patterns. This can be aided by verbal and especially by diagrammatic descriptions of the repertoire of RRPs which demonstrate their dissociation into separate self states and trace the switches and links between them. Self State Sequential

---

[1]Much of the text in this section is extracted from A. Ryle, *CAT and Borderline Personality Disorder* (2008, ACAT Reference Library), with kind permission of Dr Anthony Ryle and ACAT.

Diagrams support the consistent, non-collusive attentive engagement of clinicians. They also have a direct therapeutic role in helping patients recognize their states and state switches and so gain more control over them. These are the essential elements of the Multiple Self States Model (MSSM) of borderline personality disorder as described by Ryle (1997).

Many patients with emotionally unstable states are prone to switch into states of uncontrolled anger. Rather than relying on anger management, the CAT response would be to trace the dysfunctional RRPs that *precede* the switches into anger with the aim of establishing more adaptive modes. These prior dysfunctional modes usually represent long-term strategies evolved in response to deprivation, and are attempts to avoid anger. They typically involve patterns of resentful compliance, emotional distancing or the avoidance of vulnerable need, all of which maintain a sense of deprivation and pain from which switches to rage states may be triggered. These states, whether expressed in hurting self or others, are liable to provoke rejection and hence perpetuate deprivation. CAT would seek to modify these preceding patterns as well as developing recognition and control of the switches.

Borderline personality disorder (BPD) is characterised by the narrow and predominantly negative range of RRPs, the repertoire including patterns of abuse and neglect in relation to deprived victimhood in all cases. While BPD patients commonly inflict abuse on, or accept abuse from, both self and others, they may also enact avoidant, compliant and idealising roles. The CAT written reformulation offers an outline of the patient's story in a way that can transform the often chaotic account of events in which the person feels subsumed. This also clarifies responsibility and challenges irrational guilt and acknowledges what harm has been done. To the narrative reconstruction is added a Self States Sequential Diagram (see Dave's case study on the companion website to this book) illustrating the process currently maintaining the person's problems and difficulties. These, tested out within the relationship, serve to understand ongoing patterns and to anticipate how dysfunctional RRPs are likely to affect the therapy relationship. Variations in the underlying patterns are concerned with core dimensions – care–dependency; control–submission; abuse–victimisation – and are features of common borderline states demonstrated by research (Ryle and Golynkina, 2000). Diagrams describe the different states and trace switches between them. Patients are often moved by this pulling together of their chaotic inner and outer worlds, and become actively involved. But before long the dysfunctional procedures of commonly idealising, passively resisting, destructive or emotionally distancing, are likely to manifest. The active use of the understandings and tools to challenge generates intensely emotional interchanges and can initiate change in a very short time, but phases of inertia may still occur. Stable change can be achieved and, given the suicide risk, is a basic aim. Untreated borderline patients often learn to maintain emotional distance from others so as to avoid mobilising their more dangerous procedures and therapy may at times do little more than encourage voluntary control of this sort. In many cases, however, learning to modify or replace the dysfunctional procedures that have elicited negative reactions from others can open the way to the more effective use of support and treatment, and to more satisfying modes of relating to others and hence to continuing change. Such changes can be achieved in a twenty-four-session CAT intervention with follow-up meetings at one, two, three and six months.

CAT and research

Evidence for Psychological Therapies is evaluated in the UK by the National Institute for Health and Care Excellence (NICE) and CAT does not fit neatly into their criteria. Dr Jason Hepple, Chair of the Association for Cognitive Analytic Therapy, writes:

> CAT does not have a starting point for diagnostic categories. Instead it sees symptoms such as anxiety, depression and behavioural disturbance as manifestations of developmental and relational patterns that can be unravelled with the help of its dialogic and collaborative model and method. This is not in opposition to a neurobiological model, but rather it seeks to complement other paradigms of treatment while being true to its relational heart (much as CBT for depression is not against the use of antidepressants). However, diagnostic systems have grown up around biological and cognitive developments in psychiatry in a way that is self-perpetuating and exclusive. If a case of 'panic disorder' doesn't respond to the cognitive model of treatment for panic, is it 'panic disorder' at all, or is it something else? It is the 'something else' that CAT uses as a starting point, treating each person, their symptoms and their clusters of symptoms as unique occurrences explored in a unique setting – the relationship between *that* client CAT and *that* therapist.

As a general approach to working relationally in mental health and psychotherapy the concepts and tools of the cognitive analytic approach have validity for practitioners from different professions. As a specific treatment intervention it will continue to be researched within the limits of evaluating a relatively high-level intervention to human distress where the abiding aim is to step back from the symptoms and to work with the person as a whole in their social context.

There are a large number of studies into the effectiveness of CAT and details of these are available from the ACAT website: www.acat.me/org. They include:

- A study in Melbourne, Australia by Paul Chanen et al. (2008) using CAT with adolescents at risk of developing borderline personality disorder
- A comparison between CAT and diabetes specialist nurse education for adults with poorly controlled type 1 diabetes (Fosbury et al.,1997)
- Comparison of CAT with person-centred therapy for adults with anxiety and mood disorders (Marriott and Kellet, 2009).

Current ongoing studies include:

- Comparison of treatment of anorexia in adults with CBT and CAT
- A study by Dr Peter Taylor, University of Liverpool, into CAT and psychosis
- A study by Caroline Dower integrating embodied awareness into CAT as a supplement to mapping using biofeedback
- An ongoing study of EMDR and CAT with Dr Alison Jenaway at Addenbrooke's Hospital
- Ongoing studies into the impact of the CAT prose and diagrammatic reformulation and goodbye letters; working with patients with learning difficulties; a dialogic approach to using CAT in groups.

Map and talk is a way of developing relational understanding and reflective practice in multidisciplinary teams and has been developed by Steve Potter and used with multidisciplinary teams, probation and social work, artists and in conflict resolution. It is currently being evaluated in a number of centres.

APPENDIX 1

The Psychotherapy File: an aid to understanding ourselves better

Sometimes our familiar ways of understanding and acting can be the source of our problems. In order to solve our difficulties we may need to learn to recognise how what we do makes things worse. We can then work out new ways of thinking and acting to change things for the better.

This questionnaire is designed to help us recognise our own particular patterns.

Keeping a diary of moods and behaviour

Symptoms, bad moods, unwanted thoughts or behaviours that come and go can be understood and controlled by learning to notice when they happen and what starts them off.

Start keeping a diary each day focused on a particular mood, symptom or behaviour. Try to record this sequence:

1. How you were feeling about yourself and others and the world before the problem came on.
2. Any external event, or any thought or image in your mind that was going on when the trouble started, or what seemed to start it off.
3. The thoughts, images or feelings you experienced once the trouble started.

Noticing and writing down what you do and think at these times helps recognition of learned habits. Often, feelings like resentment, depression or physical symptoms are the result of ways of thinking and acting that are unhelpful.

Keep a daily record for 1–2 weeks, then discuss your recordings with your therapist or co-counsellor.

Working with the Psychotherapy File

Look through the descriptions of traps, dilemmas, snags and difficult states and mark how far they apply to the way you feel. Some will be familiar, others will not. If a description feels familiar but is not quite right cross out the words that do not apply and write in how things are for you in your life. **There is no 'right' way; your own descriptions are essential.** Together with your therapist or co-counsellor you can name your unhelpful patterns and get the descriptions as accurate as possible. This is the first step towards making helpful changes.

Traps

Certain kinds of thinking and acting result in a 'vicious circle' when, trying to deal with feeling bad about ourselves, we think and act in ways that tend to confirm our badness. For each one, rate your answers against 'Applies' like this:

Applies strongly ++   Applies +   Does not apply 0

1 Fear of hurting others trap

Feeling that it is wrong to be angry or aggressive we can be afraid of hurting other people's feelings so we don't express our feelings or needs with the result that we are ignored or abused, which makes us feel angry; this confirms the feeling that it is wrong to be angry.
  Applies:

2 Depressed thinking trap

Feeling that we will mess up tasks, relationships or social situations we can believe that if we try we will do it badly, so when we do try

we are ineffective and things go wrong; we often feel that things went disastrously, which confirms the feeling that we will always mess things up.
Applies:

3 Trying to please and can't say 'no' trap

Feeling uncertain about ourselves and wanting to be liked we try to please others by doing what they seem to want; we may also find it impossible to say 'no'. This results in our feeling out of control and being taken advantage of; we can feel angry and used but also as if we have failed to please, which confirms our uncertainty about ourselves and of our right to say 'no'.
Applies:

4 Social isolation trap

Feeling that others may find us stupid or boring we lack confidence in social situations and feel anxious, so we don't approach others or respond when others approach us; as a result others may see us as unfriendly and go away, which confirms our feeling that we are stupid or boring.
Applies:

5 Worthlessness trap

Feeling that we can't ever get what we want or have what we need, it can feel that if we try to get needs met we will be punished, rejected or abandoned; sometimes it feels as if we have been born cursed. We give up trying and feel hopeless and helpless, and can even feel suicidal, as if everything is impossible.
Applies:

6 Self-punishment trap

Feeling bad, weak or guilty, we can feel agitated or upset and feel as if we must punish ourselves. We can hurt or harm ourselves in different ways that can make the feelings of badness or guilt go away briefly but only confirms that we are bad and should be punished.
Applies:

Dilemmas (false choices and narrow options)

We often act as we do because the only other ways we can imagine seem as bad or even worse. Sometimes we assume connections, as in 'If I do *x* then *y* will follow'. These false choices can be described as *either/or if/then* dilemmas. We often don't realise that we see things like this, but we act as if these were the only possible choices. Do you act as if any of the following false choices rule your life?

Applies strongly ++   Applies +   Does not apply 0

1. Either I keep things bottled up or I fear a terrible mess.
2. Either I spoil myself and feel greedy or I deny myself things and punish myself and feel miserable.
3. Either I keep feelings bottled up or I risk being rejected, hurting others, making a mess.
4. If I must, then I won't; it's as if when faced with a task I must either (1) gloomily submit or (2) passively resist. Other people's wishes, or even my own, feel too demanding, so I put things off or avoid them.
5. If I must not, then I will; it's as if the only proof of my existence is my resistance. Other people's rules, even my own, feel too restricting, so I break rules and do things that are harmful to me.
6. If other people aren't expecting me to do things for them or look after them, then I feel anxious, lonely and out of control.
7. If I get what I want I feel childish and guilty; if I don't get what I want I feel frustrated, angry and depressed.

Dilemmas about how we relate to others

Do you behave as if any of the following apply in your life?

Applies strongly ++   Applies +   Does not apply 0

1. Either I'm involved with others and feel engulfed, or I stay safe but feel lonely.
2. Either I'm involved with someone and likely to get hurt or I don't get involved, feel in charge, but lonely.
3. Either I'm a brute or a martyr.
4. Either I'm safely wrapped in bliss or I'm in combat; if in combat then I'm either a bully or a victim.
5. Either I look down on people or feel they look down on me.
6. Either I stick up for myself and no one likes me; or I give in and get put on and feel cross and hurt.

Snags

Snags are what is happening when we say 'I want to have a better life but ...'. Sometimes the snags come from the important people in our lives not wanting us to change, or not able to cope with what our changing means to them. Often the resistance is more indirect, as when a parent, husband or wife becomes ill or depressed when we begin to get better.

In other cases we seem to 'arrange' to avoid pleasure or success, or if they come, we have to pay in some way, by depression, or by spoiling things. Often this is because, as children, we felt guilty if things went well for us, or felt that we were envied for good luck or success. Sometimes we feel responsible, unreasonably, for things that went wrong in the family.

It is helpful to learn to recognise how this pattern is stopping you getting on with your life, for only then can you learn to accept your right to your own gifts.

Indicate by circling the number if you recognise that you feel limited in your life:

[1] By fear of the response of others: for example, I must sabotage success

  [(a)] as if it deprives others
  [(b)] as if others may envy me or
  [(c)] as if there are not enough good things to go around.

[2] By something inside yourself: for example, I must sabotage good things as if I don't deserve them.

Difficult and unstable states of mind

Some people find it difficult to keep control over their behaviour and experience because things feel very difficult and different at times. Indicate by circling the number which, if any, of the following apply to you:

[1] How I feel about myself and others can be unstable; I can switch from one state of mind to a completely different one.
[2] Some states may be accompanied by intense, extreme and uncontrollable emotions.
[3] Some states may be accompanied by emotional blankness, feeling unreal or feeling muddled.
[4] Some states may be accompanied by feeling intensely guilty or angry with myself, wanting to hurt myself.

[5] Some states may be accompanied by feeling that others can't be trusted, are going to let me down, or hurt me.

[6] Some states may be accompanied by being unreasonably angry or hurtful to others.

[7] Sometimes the only way to cope with some confusing feelings is to blank them off and feel emotionally distant from others.

Different states

Everybody experiences changes in how they feel about themselves and the world. But for some people these changes are extreme, sometimes sudden and confusing. In such cases there are often a number of states that recur, and learning to recognise them and shifts between them can be very helpful. Figure A1.1 sets out a number of descriptions of such states. Identify those that you experience by ringing round them. You can delete or add words to the descriptions and there is space to add any not listed. If one state that you have ringed round leads on to another, join them with a line.

zombie – cut off from feelings or from others, disconnected	feeling bad but soldiering on, coping	raging and out of control	extra special – looking down on others, unrecognised genius	control freak – in control of self, of life, of other people	cheated by life, by others, untrusting	hiding secret shame
provoking, teasing, seducing, winding-up others	clinging, frantic, fearing abandonment	frenetically active, too busy to think or feel	agitated, confused, anxious, panicking, desperate	feeling perfectly cared for, blissfully close to another	misunderstood, rejected, abandoned, desolate	hurt, humiliated, defeated, always in the wrong
contemptuously dismissive of myself, worthless	vulnerable, needy, passively helpless, waiting for rescue	envious, wanting to harm others, put them down, knock them down	protective, respecting myself, respecting others	hurting myself, hurting others, causing harm or damage	resentfully submitting to demands, a slave, under the thumb	frightened of angry others
secure in myself, able to be close to others	intensely critical of myself, and of others	cheating others, cheating the system, lying, hiding the truth	feeling hopeless, no one can help, life is pointless, suicidal	spaced out – distanced from others, as if acting a part, double-glazed	flying away, running away, escaping	overwhelmed by grief and loss
seeking revenge, stalking, harassing, murderous	knight in shining armour rescuing others, righting wrongs	as if poisoned or contaminated	like an unexploded bomb	watchful, suspicious, jealous, paranoid		

Figure A1.1 Different states

APPENDIX 2

Mindfulness exercises and meditations

The Body and Chair exercise

This exercise was given as part of a Continuing Professional Development training day in CAT in Norwich, led by integrative psychotherapist and trainer Margaret Landale, in October 2007.

Take your seat on a chair. With eyes closed or just half-closed, allow your attention to rest on your experience of your body in the chair.

Notice the areas of contact between your body and the chair. Notice the support the chair is offering to you right now. Become aware that the chair is supporting your body right now by carrying most of your physical weight. Allow this to happen, allow a comfortable sense of heaviness to spread through your body, supported and carried by the chair.

Notice the rise and fall of the breath. Notice any tension you are holding within your body, the neck, shoulders, down the arms, the weight of the head. Notice any tension in your back down the spine, into your buttocks, legs, ankles and feet. Notice any tension in your belly or chest. Each time you notice any tightness or difficulty in these different parts of your body allow it to drain into your chair, be absorbed by your chair.

Just rest in this experience of being supported by the chair for a few minutes.

Whenever you are feeling anxious, unsupported or lonely, return to this practice which helps to build a nourishing reciprocal role such as caring or supporting in relation to being cared for or supported.

3-Minute breathing exercise

Here is my own version of a 3-minute breathing exercise based upon a meditation from Thich Nhat Hanh.

Place a clock where you can register the minutes.

Take a seat in a comfortable position, feet on the ground, back straight.

Eyes may be open, half-closed or closed.

Relax the body as much as possible.

1st minute: Place your attention on your in-breath and out-breath, just as it is, saying silently:

Breathing in, 'I know I am breathing in'

Breathing out, 'I know I am breathing out'

2nd minute: Continue to focus your awareness on in-breath and out-breath, this time saying silently:

Breathing in, 'I breathe deeply'

Breathing out, 'I breathe slowly'

3rd minute: Continue your attention on in-breath and out-breath, saying silently:

Breathing in, 'I know I am in the present moment'

Breathing out, 'I know it is a wonderful moment'

If at any time you are distracted, just notice this kindly, and return your attention to in-breath and out-breath. If you wish to continue for longer than 3 minutes, this is fine!

Befriending fear exercise

This next exercise uses the mindfulness of breathing exercise and incorporates promises on the in-breaths and out-breaths. When we are aware that what we are feeling is fear, we say to our fear:

'Breathing in, I know you are there my fear'

'Breathing out, I will take care of you'

We simply practise this over and over. We may also practise with our anger, or loneliness.

Unconditional friendliness or loving kindness meditation

Find a place to sit comfortably with your body and shoulders relaxed.

Take a few minutes to connect with rhythm of in-breath and out-breath, allowing this rhythm to help relaxation in the body.

Then, allow some memories or images of being given kindness, however small, to arise.

Notice the sensations in your body – tingling, opening, softening.

Let the in-breath touch these sensations to expand until they fill your whole being.

Allow yourself to be cradled by these sensations and feelings connected to kindness. Become aware that you are being filled with loving kindness.

Let yourself bask in this energy of loving kindness, breathing it in, breathing it out, as if it were a lifeline, offering the nourishment you were longing for.

Invite feelings of peacefulness and acceptance to be present in you.

Some people find it valuable to say to themselves: 'May I be well', 'May I be free from danger', 'May I be happy'.

Once you have established for yourself a centre of loving kindness you can take refuge here, drinking at this renewing and nourishing well.

You can then take the practice further. Having established the well of loving kindness within your own being you can let loving kindness radiate out and direct it wherever you like.

You might like to direct it first to members of your family or friends, visualising them and sending them loving kindness.

You can direct loving kindness toward anyone – those you know and those you do not.

You can also direct loving kindness to those you are having difficulty with.

And finally, you can direct loving kindness energy to all sentient beings, animals, plants and the universe itself.

APPENDIX 3

Finding a therapist

Having read this book you may feel that you would like to consult a therapist. The subject of 'what is a good therapist' is still hotly debated in both professional and lay circles. You may find someone with excellent qualifications with whom you have no rapport; you may be seduced by someone's kindness and friendliness, only to find they have no stamina when the going gets tough. Finding a therapist with recognised qualifications is important, because it means that they have had to meet both personal (all good therapists have to have their own therapy or analysis for a required period of time) and professional standards and commitments.

If you are attracted by the ideas in this book, which come from Cognitive Analytic Therapy (CAT), you may want to consult the Association for Cognitive Analytic Therapy at www.acat.me.uk. Or write to: ACAT, PO Box 6793, Dorchester, DT1 9DL. The telephone number is: 0844 800 9496. Emails should be sent to: admin@acat.me.uk. Office hours are 9 a.m.–5 p.m. Monday to Thursday. Through the website or by email to the office you may find a CAT-trained therapist in your area. There are CAT-trained therapists in England, Scotland, Ireland, Finland, Spain, Italy, Greece, Australia, New Zealand and South America.

There are now a growing number of CAT-trained therapists working within different settings – doctors, psychiatrists, psychiatric social workers, community nurses and psychiatric nurses, occupational therapists, social workers, GPs, counsellors and psychotherapists – who are working in short-term therapy within their specialty using the methods outlined in this book. Accredited therapists have to meet a wide range of standards and requirements and be in regular supervision.

What is a 'good enough' therapist?

A 'good enough' therapy will allow you to explore your needs safely and within manageable boundaries, at the same time as encouraging you to develop the healthy island already present within yourself. A good therapist should receive you as a client with equality, acceptance and an open mind. Every therapist will have his or her own individual style, just as you do. The chemistry in the working therapeutic partnership is crucial. Having read this book you will know more about your relational dances and be aware of how they might be activated with another person. Many reciprocal roles will be enacted and this is good because it gives you an opportunity to see them in action in an almost laboratory setting. You can scrutinise them, express the unexpressed feeling in a safe place and also begin to develop new, more helpful reciprocal roles.

Do not feel duty-bound to put up with a therapist who:

- doesn't speak to you properly, or at all, during the first session
- abuses their position by trying to be over-interpretative, or who does not adhere appropriately to boundaries (for example, the therapeutic hour is yours: a therapist who is continually late, takes phone calls, leaves early or who is frequently distracted is not adhering to the boundaries of the therapy, for which you may well be paying fees)
- who is judgemental or disparaging about your feelings and your life
- seems overly interested in some aspect of you for his or her own personal purposes

It is not helpful if a therapist talks too much about themselves or their own life. Whereas there may be times when personal disclosure is appropriate and a real gift to you as client or patient, too much destroys the freedom and sanctity of the professional hour. The same can be said for physical contact. Some body-orientated therapies use touch within their clinical work. Therapies that are unclear about touching and physical contact can create confusion, and as a patient we can feel invaded. A therapist who hugs you when you arrive and when you leave, may feel cosy and accepting at first, but this can create difficulties, confusion and misinterpretation of motives, as well as lack of freedom later on. Again, there may be times when one hug or hold is exactly right for the moment, and is mutually anticipated, but these genuine moments are rare, and a lot of woolly mistakes in the name of 'warmth' occur when physical boundaries are not adhered to with integrity and honesty.

Transference

There may be times during a therapy when you have very negative feelings for your therapist: anger, fury, fear, hate, despising, contempt. These feelings are usually part of what is generally known as 'transference' (i.e. they are 'transferred' from some other person who has affected you, and who may have originally produced such feelings, or from part of yourself). They form a useful part of the therapy, because these feelings can be discussed, interpreted and understood, and although painful, can be liberating.

CAT is a particularly useful therapeutic model for anticipating and naming the sort of transference that might well be invited in the therapeutic relationship because of the description of reciprocal roles. Together you can look at where you and the therapist might be on the diagram and what sequential loops you might be encountering.

If you have any negative or difficult feelings, like being attracted to your therapist, talk about it and allow it to be part of the work. If your therapist does not allow such feelings to be part of the work, or judges you for them, you may need to challenge, or leave the therapy if the issue does not reach a satisfactory conclusion.

Practicalities

Most therapeutic 'hours' are fifty, fifty-five or sixty minutes. Reliable timekeeping is important. Many areas within the NHS now offer psychotherapy or counselling. In the private sector there are many more therapists and a wide range of training. The higher range of fees tend to be charged by therapists with a medical background. Most good therapists work on a sliding scale of fees if they possibly can. The value of a short-term therapy is that the cost is known in advance and limited. If you have any reservations about your therapy after reading the above, talk about it to your therapist. As a 'consumer' looking for a therapist you are allowed, indeed entitled, to feel valued, respected and to be given help by the therapist.

Having decided upon your choice of therapist, take along your notebook of findings, drawings or personal recollections and realisations that you have gleaned from this book, and share them, as part of your therapy.

Bibliography

Armstrong, K. (2011) *Twelve Steps to a Compassionate Life*. London: Bodley Head.

Bakhtin, M. (1986) *Speech Genres and Other Late Essays*. Austin, TX: University of Texas Press.

Beck, Aaron (1988) *Love Is Never Enough*. London: Harper & Row.

Carpendale, J.E.M. and Lewis, C. (2004) 'Constructing an understanding of mind: the development of children's understanding of mind within social interaction', *Behavioral and Brain Sciences*, 27, 79–150.

Donald, M. (1991) *Origins of the Modern Mind: Three Stages in the Evolution of Culture and Cognition*. Cambridge, MA and London: Harvard University Press.

Donald, M. (2001) *A Mind So Rare: The Evolution of Human Consciousness*. New York: WW Norton.

Eichenbaum, L. and Orbach, S. (1985) *Understanding Women*. Harmondsworth: Penguin Books.

Eisenberg, L. and Belfer, M. (2009) 'Prerequisites for global child and adolescent mental health', *Journal of Child Psychology and Psychiatry*, 50 (1–2), 26–35.

Epstein, M. (1998) *Going to Pieces without Falling Apart: A Buddhist Perspective on Wholeness*. New York: Broadway Books.

Fox, J. (1995) *Finding What You Didn't Lose: Expressing Your Truth and Creativity through Poem-Making*. New York: Tarcher Putnam.

Fraser, S. (1989) *My Father's House*. London: Virago.

Friedman, M. and Ulmer, D. (1984) *Treating Type A Behavior and Your Heart*. New York: Knopf.

Gendlin, E. (1996) *Focusing-Oriented Psychotherapy*. New York: Guilford Press.

Gerhardt, S. (2004) *Why Love Matters: How Affection Shapes a Baby's Brain*. London: Routledge.

Germer, C. (2009) *The Mindful Path to Self-Compassion*. New York: Guilford Press.

Germer, C., Siegel, R. and Fulton, P. (2005) *Mindfulness and Psychotherapy*. New York: Guilford Press.

Gilbert, P. (2009) *The Compassionate Mind*. London: Constable.

Hamill, M. and Mahony, K. (2011) 'The long goodbye: Cognitive Analytic Therapy with carers of people with dementia', *British Journal of Psychotherapy*, 27, 292–304.

Jenaway, A. (2016) 'Incorporating Eye Movement Desensitisation and Reprocessing (EMDR) into Cognitive Analytic Therapy – reaching reciprocal roles that other therapies cannot reach', *Reformulation*, Winter (Issue 47), pp. 21–8.

Jon Kabat-Zinn (1990) *Full Catastrophe Living.* New York: Delta.

Jon Kabat-Zinn (1994) *Wherever You Go There You Are.* New York: Hyperion.

Kornfield, J. (1993) *A Path with Heart.* New York: Bantam Books.

Landale, M. (2002) 'The use of imagery in body-oriented psychotherapy', in Tree Staunton (ed.), *Body Psychotherapy.* Hove: Brunner–Routledge, pp. 116–32.

Leiman, M. (1994) 'Projective identification as early joint sequences: a Vygotskian addendum to the Procedural Sequence Object Relations Model', *British Journal of Medical Psychology*, 67, 97–106.

Lewis, C.S. (1961) *A Grief Observed.* London: Faber & Faber.

Minton, K., Ogden, P. and Pain, C. (2008) *Trauma and the Body.* New York, WW Norton.

Porges, S.W. (2005) 'Social engagement in attachment: a phylogenetic perspective', *Annals of the New York Academy of Sciences*, 1008, 31–47.

Potter, S. (2004) 'Untying the knots: relational states of mind in Cognitive Analytic Therapy', *Reformulation*, Spring (Issue 21), 14–21.

Potter, S. and Sutton, L. (2006) 'Making the dialogic clearer in the practice of cognitive analytic therapy'. ACAT Reference Library.

Rushbrook, S. and Coulter, N. (2010) 'Playfulness in CAT', *Reformulation*, Winter (Issue 35), pp. 24–7.

Ryle, A. (1985) 'Cognitive theory, object relations and the self', *British Journal of Medical Psychology*, 58, 1–7.

Ryle, A. (1997) *Cognitive Analytic Therapy and Borderline Personality Disorder: The Model and the Method.* Chichester: Wiley.

Ryle, A. (2001a) 'Cognitive Analytic Therapy', *Constructivism in the Human Sciences*, 1&2, 51–8.

Ryle, A. (2001b) 'CAT's dialogic perspective on the self', *Reformulation*, ACAT News (Autumn), p. x.

Ryle, A. and Golynkina, K. (2000) 'Effectiveness of time limited cognitive analytic therapy for borderline personality disorder: factors associated with outcome', *British Journal of Medical Psychology*, 118, 323–7.

Ryle, A. and Kerr, I.B. (2002) *Introducing Cognitive Analytic Therapy: Principles and Practice.* Chichester: Wiley.

Schore, A. (2003) *Affect Regulation and the Repair of the Self.* New York: WW Norton.

Segal, Z., Williams, M. and Teasdale, J. (2002) *Mindfulness Based Cognitive Therapy for Depression.* New York: Guilford Press.

Seigel, D. (2007) *The Mindful Brain*. New York: WW Norton.

Seigel, D. (2010a) *Mindsight: The New Science of Transformation*. New York: Random House

Seigel, D. (2010b) *The Mindful Therapist*. New York: WW Norton.

Smith, S. (1983) 'Anger's freeing power', in *The Collected Poems of Stevie Smith* (arranged by James MacGibbon). New York: New Directions.

Thomas, C.A. (2006) *At Hell's Gate*. Boston, MA: Shambhala.

Thoreau, H.D. ([1854] 1988) *Walden*. Princeton, NJ: Princeton University Press.

Trevarthen, C. (1993) 'Playing into reality: conversations with the infant communicator', *Journal of the Squiggle Foundation*, 7, 67–84.

Trevarthen, C. (2001) 'Intrinsic motives for companionship in understanding', *Infant Mental Health Journal*, 22, 95–131.

Tutu, D. (1999) *No Future Without Forgiveness*. New York: Random House.

Van der Kolk, B., McFarlane, A. and Weisaeth, L. (2007) *Traumatic Stress: The Effect of Overwhelming Experience on Mind, Body and Society*. New York: Guilford Press.

Wellings, N. and Wilde McCormick, E. (2005) *Nothing to Lose*. London: Continuum.

Wilde McCormick, E. (2000) 'The therapeutic relationship', in E. Wilde McCormick and N. Wellings, *Transpersonal Psychotherapy*. London: Sage.

Wilde McCormick, E. (2002) *Living On the Edge*. London: Continuum/ Sage.

Wilde McCormick, E. and Wellings, N. (2000) *Transpersonal Psychotherapy*. London: Sage.

Winnicott, D.W. (1979) *The Maturational Process and Facilitating Environment*. London: Hogarth Press.

Index